Praise for Larry Chase's
Essential Business Tactics for the Net

Chase gets that the Internet is more than a marketing channel. It's a whole new paradigm shift in the way we conduct business.

Mary Lou Floyd
General Manager, Electronic Publishing
Network Commerce Services Division, AT&T

Read this book. You'll learn a heck of a lot and have a great time in the process.

Marianne Cohn
Director, Internet Marketing, 3COM

ESSENTIAL BUSINESS TACTICS FOR THE NET

ESSENTIAL BUSINESS TACTICS FOR THE NET

Larry Chase
with
Nancy C. Hanger

WILLEY COMPUTER PUBLISHING

John Wiley & Sons, Inc.
New York • Chichester • Weinheim • Brisbane • Singapore • Toronto

Publisher: Robert Ipsen
Editor: Cary Sullivan
Assistant Editor: Pam Sobotka
Managing Editor: Erin Singletary
Electronic Products, Associate Editor: Mike Sosa
Text Design & Composition: Benchmark Productions, Inc.

Designations used by companies to distinguish their products are often claimed as trademarks. In all instances where John Wiley & Sons, Inc., is aware of a claim, the product names appear in initial capital or ALL CAPITAL LETTERS. Readers, however, should contact the appropriate companies for more complete information regarding trademarks and registration.

This book is printed on acid-free paper. ∞

This publication is designed to provide accurate and authoritative information in regard to the subject matter covered. It is sold with the understanding that the publisher is not engaged in professional services. If professional advice or other expert assistance is required, the services of a competent professional person should be sought.

Internet World, Web Week, Web Developer, Internet Shopper, and Mecklermedia are the exclusive trademarks of Mecklermedia Corporation and are used with permission.

Library of Congress Cataloging-in-Publication Data:

Chase, Larry, 1953–
    Essential business tactics for the Net / Larry Chase.
        p.   cm.
    "Wiley Computer Publishing."
    Includes index.
    ISBN 0–471–25722–2
    1. Business enterprises--Computer networks. 2. Internet marketing--Cost effectiveness. 3. Electronic commerce. 4. World Wide Web (Information retrieval system) I. Title.
    HD30.37.C37   1998
    658.8'00285'4678--dc21   98–13040
                                                    CIP

Printed in the United States of America.
10 9 8 7 6 5 4 3

I dedicate this book to Becky Rich, who so dedicated herself to this project. I also dedicate this work to Jan Gennet, who was there with me when I was a lone voice in the wilderness.

CONTENTS

Chapter 3 Mining the Internet for All it's Worth   57

Chapter 4 http://007 Spying on Your Competitors and Yourself   91

ACKNOWLEDGMENTS

The truth is, I wrote the book just so I could write this page. I thank Internet author and journalist Daniel P. Dern, who is that man behind the curtain with his hands on the steamship levers. He introduced me to Marjorie Spencer, at John Wiley & Sons. In turn, Marjorie introduced me to my delightful Acquisitions Editor, Cary Sullivan. Daniel also introduced me to Nancy C. Hanger, who worked with me on this book.

Much gratitude also goes to Wiley's Pam Sobotka for her deft editorial touch. The editors of my *Web Digest For Marketers*, Eileen Shulock and Dianna Husum, helped with research and always added value to this project. Deep appreciation also goes to Matt Lederman for lending his support via his well-timed and laconic sense of humor.

So many others have contributed to my Internet experience over the years. An incomplete list is made up of Silvia (with an "i" not a "y") Rich, Dane Atkinson, Steve Glusband, Don Abrahams, Chris Graham, Bob Tinkelman, Sean Allen, Chris Knight, Dan Janal, Mac and Marji Ross, Bernard Zick, Dick Rich, Carol Miles, Mike Sloser, Stephen Fink, Richard Seltzer, John Verity, Karen Egolf, David (Ad Age) Klein, and the New York Studios of RFB&D—especially Myra Shein, Rosemary Darmstadt, Reva Fox, Robbie Capp, and Lisa Douglis. Finally, I offer gratitude to Dr. Ralph Wilson, Bill Russo, Neil Raphan, Marty Freimer, Howard Greenstein, Joost Steins Bisschop, and Kim Hill.

But wait! There's more. . . Nina Rich, Mark Stacks, John Rice, Don Vainonen, Jay Abraham, *Chicken Soup* co-author Mark Victor Hansen, Rick Frishman, David Thalberg, Karen Bierman, Carmela DellaRipa, Larry Fox, Gus Johnson, Deborah Lilly, Tony D'Amelio, Jerrold Jenkins, Tony Alessandra, Helmut Krone, Joe Karbo, Richard G. Nixon, Rush Limbaugh, and finally, Mary Ann Packo, President of Media Metrix.

ABOUT THE AUTHOR

Larry Chase is an international Internet consultant, author, and speaker. He has consulted with Fortune 500 companies such as Con Edison, New York Life, 3Com, and EDS, as well as some of the Internet marketing pioneers themselves, like Hotel Discounts, Auto-By-Tel, and 1-800FLOWERS. Since Chase saw the potential of the Net early on, he was prominently featured in the pivotal *Business Week* cover story, "How the Internet Will Change the Way You Do Business," way back in November of 1994. The *New York Times*, *USA Today*, *Inc. Magazine*, CNNfn, CNBC, plus scores of trade magazines and newsletters regularly seek him out for his insights. Reviews from *Larry Chase's Web Digest For Marketers* newsletter (http://wdfm.com) are syndicated to *Advertising Age* and *Business Marketing* magazines. "Ironically, more people read my reviews in print than online." Additionally, his columns and seminars are seen worldwide.

Chase started one of the first two commercial Web sites in New York City. Prior to that, he worked for New York's most celebrated ad agencies as an award-winning strategic copywriter. After working on consumer brands such as Heinz, Volkswagen, Polaroid, CBS, and Avis, he chose to focus on hi-tech products and services, "since there are always new and unique selling propositions worth writing about." Chase worked for technology clients such as AT&T, Compaq, IBM, Digital, GTE, Xerox, NYNEX, and "just about anything that had an 'x' in it." He specialized in technology 10 years before it was fashionable to do so: "Now, it's chic to be geek."

Mr. Chase lives and works in New York City and can be reached via email at larry@chaseonline.com. For more information on Mr. Chase and his services, visit his firm's Web site at http://chaseonline.com. If you have questions thereafter, call (212) 876-1096.

INTRODUCTION

Integrating the Internet into your business is what you will find in this book. Whether you're a two-man startup in 800 square feet of space, or a product manager in a multinational corporation, you'll find practical options and opportunities you need to know about.

This book is rooted in reality, giving you examples and anecdotes from my experiences and those of my clients. If you want frank assessments of what works and what doesn't, keep reading. If you're already online, you'll undoubtedly pick up some practical tips you've seen nowhere else. If you're new to the Internet, this book will answer the question of, "Why bother being intimidated by the Internet?" You see, this is more than a "How To" book. It's a "Why Bother" book as well.

Practical. If I were to describe the Net in a single word, that would be it. For that reason, this book takes the exact same approach. I want you to know what practical things you can do right now, after you close this book. I also want you to see what is realistically possible in the near term. I will share with you rules of measure that I use to determine whether something new on the Net is worth paying attention to, or whether it's a fleeting fad. Knowing the difference isn't always easy. In Figure I.1, you see a letter written from Thomas Alva Edison to my great-grandfather, Edmond Gerson, who was a showman and promoter in the mid-nineteenth century. In that letter, Edison referred to the "musical telephone," which we might think of today as a type of cable radio. You see, the wizard of Menlo Park himself couldn't always predict just how a technology would ultimately be used, once put into motion.

This book is divided into two basic sections:

1. Knowing how to use the Net for your company's "internal affairs"; that is, how you can run faster, cheaper, and smarter.

2. Employing the Internet for your company's "external affairs," whereby you use the Net as an effective communications tool for reaching those outside your firm.

Figure I.1 Thomas Edison's letter to Larry Chase's great-grandfather shows not even Edison always knew how new technology would ultimately be employed.

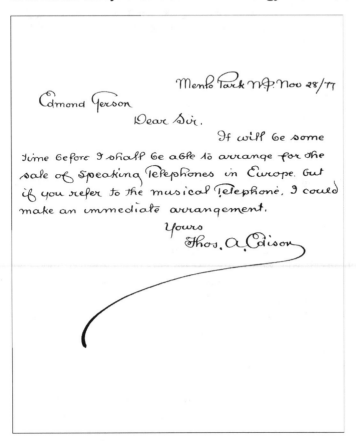

Part I: Integrating the Internet Inside Your Company

Chapter 1, "Cutting Costs Across Your Enterprise," shows you how the Net can do just that: bring down your faxing, phone, mailing, and other day-to-day costs to which you may hardly give a second thought. The resulting new-found savings pour directly into profit margins, which are already being squeezed from every direction.

Chapter 2, "Using the Net as a Resource for Human Resources," points out ways you can tap into distant labor markets. Distance training and learning can also help you run a tighter ship and reduce costs.

Chapter 3, "Mining the Internet for All It's Worth," shows how you can have a field day digging up valuable information for free. Other information that used to be way beyond the budgets of many companies is now offered at bargain basement prices as well. I'll give you a road map to both.

Chapter 4, "http://007 Spying on Your Competitors and Yourself," shows you how to spy on your competition, as well as yourself. You'll be able to get so close to what your competitors are thinking, you'll quite possibly be able to predict what their next move will be. Take advantage of your competition by learning from them. Let them show you what they're doing right and what they're doing wrong. Learn from their mistakes.

Part II: Integrating the Internet into Your Marketing

Chapter 5, "Your Brand Image and the Internet," gives you proven guidelines, case histories, and never before shared success stories of how to represent yourself online, both as a person and as a company.

Chapter 6, "Retail: Setting Up Shop on the Net," walks you through the different options you have to open up your online doors for business. Written in plain English with whimsical asides, you'll see what to look for when figuring out the best approach for your given situation.

Chapter 7, "Online Events, Promotions, and Attractions: How to Make a "Scene" and Draw Them In," shows you how to breathe life into your Web site, setting up a calendar of happenings that circulate key prospects through your online space on an ongoing basis.

Chapter 8, "Direct Marketing and Sales Support," shows you how the Internet employs similar tactics and practices to the disciplines of traditional Direct Marketing. It's also important to understand where these two disciplines diverge. This chapter not only shows you the differences, but demonstrates how you can develop instant, inbound leads on the Internet as well.

Chapter 9, "Public Relations, the Internet Way," shows you exactly why the Internet is proving to be the golden age of public relations. Learn some of the most closely guarded secrets of how to practice new media public relations that will serve you right now and in the future.

A Road Map for Readers

Should you read this book from front to back, or on an as-needed, "á la carte" basis? The answer is "yes" to both options. I wrote it both ways. I want you to benefit from the best practices and experiences used by the Internet cognoscente. If you're going to read

Section Two primarily, I urge you to glean creative ideas from the first section. If you plan on primarily using Section One, consider looking at the second half for a well-rounded look at the importance of marketing. After all, as Figure I.1 further underscores, Edison himself was keenly aware of how important marketing was to his business.

No matter which way you read this book, don't miss the special offer in Chapter 3. There you will find the password that gives you one year of free access to the archives of my *Web Digest For Marketers* publication (http://wdfm.com). This is, in itself, a $25 value (see Figure I.2). Furthermore, most chapters in this book have an online resource center at http://www.wiley.com/compbooks/chase containing hyperlinked site reviews. These are the sites that I consider worthy of your valuable time.

Finally, it is necessary to point out that any book written about the Internet is like taking a picture of a horse race, since the Internet is a dynamic and rapidly changing medium. Web addresses that are valid today may not be tomorrow. Things that are true this year may not be so next year. I want you, the reader, to know that I have put my best efforts forth in putting together that which I think will benefit you most. I also urge you to do additional and continuous research in those specific areas that are germane to your pursuit.

Figure I.2 Home Page of Larry Chase's *Web Digest For Marketers*, where owners of this book can access the extensive archives free for one year. The password is in Chapter 3.

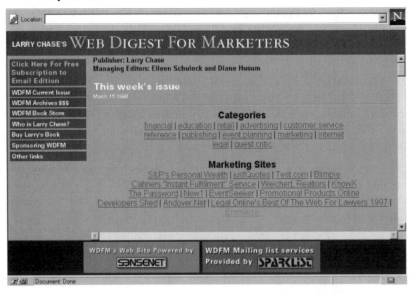

ESSENTIAL BUSINESS TACTICS FOR THE NET

PART ONE

INTEGRATING THE INTERNET

Inside Your Company

CUTTING COSTS ACROSS YOUR ENTERPRISE
How to Run a Tighter, More Competitive Ship

Skeptics of the Internet's influence on businesses often ask the question: "How much money have you made on the Internet today?" For most companies, that's the wrong question to ask at this time. A better question to ask companies right now would be: "How has the Internet made your operation run faster, smarter, and cheaper?" Whether you're a purchasing manager in a global enterprise, or a two-man startup in a basement, you will both have certain practices in common. Both companies buy office equipment, utilize communications networks and instruments, travel, employ personnel, and need to further exploit the Net to their respective ends in order to keep a competitive edge. This chapter will help you do this for your own company. You'll learn the basics about the following:

- Optimizing your purchasing power
- Buying the tools of your trade
- Customer service savings
- Data mining
- Strengthening sales support via the Internet
- Distributed printing

Optimizing Your Purchasing Power

In "geek-speak," the Internet is known as an open-computing environment. This openness has a monumental impact on the marketplace as well. Putting scores of competitors within one click of each other makes for a truly open, and often brutal, marketplace. Purchasing professionals are starting to take advantage of this open marketplace. The American Management Association (AMA) queried 3500 of its members on a wide range of their Internet usage patterns as of 1997 and what they're anticipating by 1999. The AMA found that 6 percent of purchasing professionals are using the Internet for purchasing in the first half of 1997, while 46 percent plan to use the Net for such activities by 1999. The cited statistic refers to a sample of 3500, which included purchasing professionals, who operate as purchasers. That's a dramatic increase for what is usually considered a conservative group of professionals. What are they seeing out there that is causing them to move in such numbers? Let's take a look.

There are two ways to look at buying on the Net. First, you can look at things that all businesses have in common, such as office supplies, travel, and communications. Then there are indigenous purchases for the particular trade you're in. If you're in dairy, you may be in need of a 400-gallon vat with a rapid-pour spigot, while a guy in reprographics might get excited about a Heidleberg Press at half price. Let's start with those things that everyone has in common.

Using the Internet to Clip Communication Costs: Sending Faxes over the Net

Whether your company is large or small, you send faxes. You send them from point to point and very often, from one point to many. Using the Net to transmit faxes in any number seems like a no-brainer, given the cost savings in long-distance bills alone. Why make a toll call for a traditional fax if you can make a local call by connecting to the Net? Unlike sending voice over the Internet, there's little or no qualitative difference when sending faxes this way. There are several basic kinds of fax services currently offered via the Net, and we'll look at each in detail.

Sending a Fax Point to Point

FaxStorm is a product offered to local Internet Service Providers (ISPs) by NetCentric (http://www.netcentric.com) that enables you to send faxes over the Internet (see Figure 1.1). How long does it take to send a fax? Well, it depends on how much information is on it. If it's a cover sheet, with basic information such as how many pages the fax is, the date, and so forth, it doesn't take long at all, maybe 30 seconds. If a fax page is intensive with graphics, detail, and wall-to-wall text, it will take longer. If you're sending a lot of faxes, try to keep the graphics to a minimum. In fact, many people use low-resolution graphics on their faxes for exactly this reason.

At the time of this writing, you can often get the same rate of 15 cents per minute using traditional methods of faxing using the telephone. Those rates, however, are often off-peak (i.e., after business hours). Many people find this perfectly acceptable,

Figure 1.1 Your ISP may offer you inexpensive online faxing with software from NetCentric.

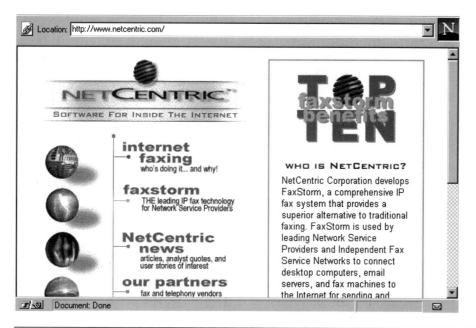

as fax machines are often overloaded during the day. In fact, many companies prefer to transmit their faxes at night precisely for the cheaper rates and easier access to the receiving fax machines. Nevertheless, many business phone plans can and do charge considerably more, up to and exceeding 55 cents per minute, especially when faxing overseas. By the time you read this, I strongly suspect that the prices will have dropped considerably, as online faxing takes off and competition heats up as a result.

ITSG (http://www.itsg.com) offers some interesting options in this area as well. For example, in addition to sending to someone's fax machine from your computer, you can send to that same machine from your email account or from your fax machine. ITSG's rates are comparable to NetCentric's. A minimum usage of $10 per month is required.

You can even set up an 800 number with HTNET (http://www.twsp.com). With this service, clients don't incur long-distance charges when faxing you. Of course, you might find it infuriating if you have to pay high amounts each month for unsolicited faxes. This package will end up costing you $29.95 per month, plus

$19.95 for a one-time setup fee. Additionally, any fax to the 800 number costs 15 cents per page.

Send Faxes for Free . . . Sometimes!

There is a host of free faxing services out on the Net, too. Typically, you fill in a form that includes the message you want to send, along with the fax number you're sending to. You then click on Submit and these services will send it for free, often in exchange for an ad of theirs on the faxed page. I wouldn't advise sending faxes like these to your clients because it looks cheap and is confusing. Additionally, these services have a very high turnover rate, so you'll probably find yourself switching from a service that no longer works to a new one that is just starting out. If the churn is worth your time and effort, then check it out. But I find it very tedious searching "free fax," coming up with way too many search results, and having the first handful not work because the service has gone out of business since the search engine last updated its page results.

Broadcast Faxing

Broadcast faxing over the Net works pretty much the same way as over traditional channels. If you send broadcast faxes often, your savings will be more substantial since the more you use, the more you save. Of course, the same can be said for broadcast faxing through the telephone networks. Since the quality is basically the same between the two media, I suggest you compare prices and play one off against the other. Look for the Internet to apply downward pressure on the cost of communication, both on and offline. In other words, traditional fax services and telephone services have a whole new bevy of competitors. Because of this intense competition, a good number of these services will not survive. Therefore, make sure that whomever you go with, online or off, has a good track record and is apt to stay around. The last thing you need is to wake up one day, only to find that your fax provider no longer exists. For this reason, it's wise not just to shop on price alone but on constancy, credibility, and continuity as well.

Fax Mailbox on Your Computer

Using the services of a firm such as JFAX, you can have not only faxes show up on your computer, but voicemail as well. Here's how it works: For $12.50 a month at the time of this writing, you get a phone number from JFAX (see Figure 1.2). When people call, they're prompted to either leave a voicemail message or start sending a fax. You can pick up your faxes and messages from your laptop computer even while you're on the road. If you see that you have three faxes waiting, you can look at them and respond accordingly. You can then play the voicemail messages and do likewise.

Figure 1.2 When on the road, pick up your voicemail and faxes on your laptop with JFAX.

This ingenious system was created by a German rock-and-roll musician who was frustrated by missing his faxes while on tour. He also accrued large expenses by picking up his voicemail, since many of his calls to receive his voicemail were international. Through JFAX, he was able to stay in the loop and cut costs simultaneously. If you travel to Europe and your client wants to fax you something, you're also saving the client money. He or she doesn't have to send your fax overseas, where the tariffs are high. Clients have to love you for this.

According to a survey conducted by Pitney Bowes and published in *tele.com* (http://www.tele.com), a publication worthy of your review on these matters, 40 percent of a large company's telephony budget is dedicated to faxing. If you can save even a fraction, it's well worth your time to investigate this area. In addition to the online fax providers cited, you may wish to check out ISPs that are offering similar services at similar prices. Well-known providers, such as NetCom and PSINet, are currently offering online fax services to their customers. They need to, since Internet connections have quickly become loss-leaders for service provider companies—simply providing "on-ramp services" no longer pays all the bills for most ISPs. These ISPs must strive to keep the customers they have and attract new ones by offering such services as online faxing, as well as transmitting voice calls.

Sending Your Voice over the Net: Internet Telephony

Many skeptics out there say that widespread use of the Internet as a phone network is a fad. Whether it manifests itself as a medium for voice, fax, or document sharing, there is a place for Internet telephony. It's in your best interest to see if this place is in your company.

Let's start with using the Internet to transmit and receive voice. There are three ways you can do this:

1. Computer to computer (where your computer is the telephone)

2. Computer to telephone (where you call someone from your computer and he or she answers on the phone)

3. Phone to phone (where you use the Internet as the network between two telephones, rather than traditional long-distance companies such as AT&T or MCI)

Computer-to-Computer Telephony

Computer-to-computer telephony on the Net is fun; how productive it can really be is something else. However, you must be aware of the following: While ongoing service is free, there are some one-time costs that you initially incur when buying the software and a soundcard. You may even want to buy a *duplexed* soundcard for optimal results, so you can both speak at the same time. I remember buying early software that allowed me to talk to my colleague in California. Our phone bills were out of control. Our conversation was pretty comical. We were both shouting at our computer microphones, with a substantial time delay. The conversation went like this:

"… ear you!"

"… 'm fine. _ow about _ou?"

"_ot bad"

"_ear the delay?"

"_es!"

We went back to using the telephone. To its credit, the telephony software has gotten better over the years. A company called VocalTec offers NetPhone, a package for your computer with a one-time cost of $49.95. There are software packages that are free, but you will not get a great deal of technical support. In addition, the other person has to have the same package in order for it to work.

Another downside to this option concerns your IP address, which is the actual address of your computer when you are on the Net. Typically, when you dial in to your local ISP, you are assigned a random number as your *address*. This means that every time you log on, your address is different. Just think what life would be like if everybody's phone number changed every day! To sensibly succeed at using Internet telephony, you need to have a *static IP address*, which most Internet service providers do not offer anymore, due to the proliferation of Internet users. If they do offer it, you usually have to pay a premium. For example, at the time of writing, Panix (an ISP in New York City) offers Internet access with a static IP address for $35 per month. Other services that offer similar technical support and few busy signals charge you $20–25 per month, but you do not get a static IP address for that price. For all these reasons, I doubt you'll find your investment of time well spent pursuing this particular avenue for telephony. However, keep an eye on this segment; the software is improving, and PCs are becoming more powerful, which means voice processing will become faster and more effective.

Computer-to-Phone Telephony

Computer-to-phone telephony allows you to call someone's regular phone from your computer. This can be handy while you're using a laptop and connected to the Net, where you're online and talking to someone simultaneously. The cost per minute for such services at the time of writing is around 8 to 11 cents. IDT, another ISP, offers such a service. It's called Net-to-Phone. The quality is better than the computer-to-computer transmission, and there seems to be less delay. Call me old-fashioned, but I like my telephone to be a telephone and my computer to be a computer. Similar to computer-to-computer calling, you'll also need a soundcard or a duplex soundcard to enjoy fluid and normal conversation. Otherwise, you'll be communicating CB-radio style, by saying "Over" when you want the other side to speak.

As I write this, IDT, in addition to other companies, is starting to roll out phone-to-phone long distance (see Figure 1.3). This works by first dialing an 800 number in order to get into the IDT network. The network then routes the call over the Net, instead of MCI or Sprint. The current cost is around 8 cents per minute, but I'm sure that will come down shortly. For my trial run, I called Karen Egolf in Chicago, editor of *Business Magazine* and *Net Marketing*. Karen was also the editor of *Telephony Magazine*. The two of us had an interesting time analyzing the quality of the call, and we came to the conclusion that it wasn't all that bad. It reminded me of a cellular call on the rim of its primary coverage area. The delay was substantially shorter than the other methods previously examined.

Figure 1.3 IDT was one of the first to offer its users phone-to-phone service using the Internet as a conduit.

Phone-to-Phone Telephony

The reason that the phone-to-phone calls sound better is simple: When your voice travels over the Internet, it gets broken up into thousands of packets that all have to be reassembled at the other end. That requires a great deal of computing power. The phone-to-phone system uses more powerful computers than the ones on a typical desktop. The software needed to send and receive these packets that make up your voice are Web servers that are using a good deal more bandwidth than someone with a 28.8K modem. So, the overall quality is improved, while the delay is shortened.

As the prices come down for phone-to-phone connections, you may find yourself using this type of system for talking to your field offices and reserving your primary long-distance carriers for client calls, which require a clearer signal.

Also, keep in mind that as these voice services flourish and compete for your business, they will provide you with additional services, such as call waiting, three-way calling, voicemail, and so on, in addition to reducing the per-minute cost. Calling Europe will cost a small fraction of what it costs now using traditional long distance circuits. It will be interesting to see if the existing phone companies move to impede the use of this type of telephony, which bypasses their networks altogether.

Companies with wide area networks (WANs) are looking at this phone-to-phone system closely. If they're only using 50 percent of that network at a given time, why not fill it up with some phone calls, or faxes, for that matter?

> **TIP**
> Before you make an investment in the hardware, try it on a short contract with an outside provider. You might want to test the medium before plunging in. Simply farm out those functions that you're considering and test them during short-term contracts that you negotiate with a provider of such services. If it works, replicate the scheme in house. If it doesn't, you've just bypassed beaucoup headaches and investments.

In any of these scenarios, it seems likely that you'll maintain a primary long distance telephone provider and siphon off some of the traffic to a secondary voice network where you can save some money. Here again, look to the ISPs such as IDT, NetCom, PSI, and the like to aggressively market voice on the Internet the same way they do with faxing. The more bundled services they can offer you, the more apt you are to stay or join up with them in the first place.

Sharing Documents on the Net in Real Time

In October 1997, MCI rolled out a service called NetConferencing, which allows you to share a document in real time with other people on the Net. Here's how it works: Your document is posted to a Web site at an arranged time. You invite other people to come and see that document, while you are presumably on the phone with them at the same time. Only the people you specify can manipulate or change this document that everyone is seeing. This application can be very handy for investor relations, press conferences, or distributed workgroups. It takes advantage of NetMeeting, which is part of the Internet Explorer 4.0 application that sits on a user's PC. NetMeeting allows one PC to share a document with another PC. Whereas NetConference is one-to-many, NetMeeting is one-to-one, or point-to-point, communication. At the time of launch, NetConference costs $180 an hour for 10 users and uses 15-minute billing increments. Watch the clock closely. Both graphics and text can be manipulated in these sessions. If you're using Netscape 4.0 or Microsoft Internet Explorer 4.0 or greater, the software needed is already baked into these programs. If you're not, you'll need to download an application from MCI or from Microsoft's homesite. You will need a true TCP/IP Net connection for this program to work. If you are connected through AOL or CompuServe, you will need to dial in, then start up the NetMeeting software separately.

ICQ from Mirabilis, Inc. (http://www.mirabilis.com) offers direct conversation with another party using point-to-point chat (with unlimited users joining the chat session), instant messages, offline messaging (if your party isn't on the ICQ network when you want to call, you can leave a message for later), file transfer, mail message checking, and interconnectivity with almost all major Internet telephony and voice programs, including the aforementioned NetMeeting. If someone doesn't have ICQ, he or she can even "page" you and leave you an ICQ message through regular email. It's a pretty small program and allows for privacy. Be aware that your instant messages do go through their servers; however, if you open a direct point-to-point chat with another user, you are connected directly, for security's sake. More and more small businesses appear to be using this method for communication with customers and remote employees.

Video on the Internet

For a small business user, I don't think it's practical to use videoconferencing on the Internet yet—maybe someday. It does, however, deserve mention here. With a 28.8k modem or better, it's rare that you're going to get more than four or five frames through per second. You can buy a black-and-white Connectix camera (which looks like a disembodied eyeball with a cord on it) for under $100; color costs about $150, at the time of writing. Many PCs will require an additional videocard and possibly video RAM as well. The more sophisticated Macintosh models have this built in; however, I found the audio quality to be extremely choppy with these systems.

One of the most popular videoconferencing schemes on the Internet is CUSeeMe. Developed at Cornell University, it has spread worldwide quickly (see Figure 1.4). When you visit a CUSeeMe reflector site, you see two, four, six, or more frames of people who are participating in a choppy discussion. Since the audio is problematic, there is also a text box in which people can write their messages to everyone else participating. The conferencing is free and random. I've known people who occasionally use CUSeeMe with the audio turned off (thus allowing more video frames per second). Then, for the audio, they simply call the other party on the telephone. Even optimizing for video quality produces a funny-looking product. Everyone looks very pixelated and stilted.

If you think you can use CUSeeMe as a conferencing vehicle, keep in mind that these reflector sites are public and, therefore, are viewable by perfect strangers who may saunter in and offer their unsolicited input to your business meeting. If you want privacy, you have to set up a reflector site of your own.

Since CUSeeMe's introduction, there has been a whole gaggle of videoconferencing schemes, some of which claim to offer up to 15 frames per second (fps). I

Figure 1.4 CuSeeMe was one of the original online video conferencing solutions designed by Cornell University. It's fun, but not very private.

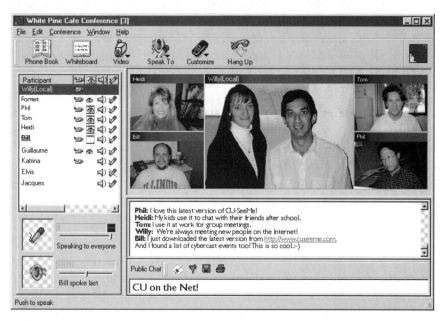

remain skeptical for the small business user, because the bandwidth that a typical modem provides and the processing power needed to process all the video images do not usually meet up with the task at hand. If you have ISDN or better, it may be worth your time to investigate. Keep in mind that whatever system you find that is optimal for your circumstances will have to be duplicated at the other end. Also remember that the actual size of the picture is approximately that of a 35mm slide. If you increase the size of that picture, the imagery becomes more stilted. If you have a video accelerator board in your computer, this becomes less of an issue. Since there is no ubiquitous standard, you'll need to coordinate with the people with whom you plan on conferencing, be they employees, suppliers, or clients. A whole book can be written on this topic and be outdated by the time you read it. Therefore, I point you to http://www.yahoo.com/Business_and_Economy/Companies/Telecommunications/Conferencing/Videoconferencing, or http://www.freenet.msp.mn.us/people/drwool/webconf.html as resources that will be more specific to your circumstances and the time frame in which you need the technology.

In addition to using the Net as an alternative network to buying long-distance services and the like, you can also use it to purchase and compare rates of traditional carriers like AT&T and MCI. At http://www.callcost.com/usform.html, you can compare U.S. and overseas rates between the well-known carriers and lesser-known players who offer substantial discounts. This calculator seems to be very honest in that it shows who has stronger pricing at various times in different parts of the world. Even though your current long-distance provider may be providing you with an overall good deal, your calling patterns may warrant a service more finely tuned to your needs.

Cutting the cost of communications can save you substantial amounts of money, but be forewarned. Very often, what happens when you cut the cost of communication is that you simply wind up using it more. Additionally, there are times where it will be a necessity to travel in order to have a face-to-face (f-2-f) meeting. Speaking of travel, let's now take a look at how to use the Net to transport yourself from point A to point B less expensively.

Using the Net to Trim Travel Costs

Travel is one of the fastest-growing industries on the Internet. Airline seats and hotel rooms are known as "vanishing commodities." It is considered sinful to let an airline seat fly empty; it would be better to have someone in that seat at 30 percent on the dollar rather than at nothing on the dollar. An airline never recoups the cost of transporting an empty seat, and there is always a potential customer who would be delighted to have an airplane seat for a discount. Travelocity, at http://www.Travelocity.com, brings the carrier and such customers together (see Figure 1.5).

This site allows a traveler to map out where and when he or she is going. The service will then show the traveler what is currently available, as well as email updates of alternatives. I've known executives at Fortune 100 companies who note that online prices are often considerably less than their inhouse travel desks, who are supposed to have good prices due to their purchasing volume. Microsoft's Expedia at http://www.expedia.com offers similar services. Both sites offer good and in-depth information on destinations, as well as helpful travel hints, which is to be expected these days. With more and more of these sites arising, each one must differentiate itself in a visitor's mind by providing a unique service or an out-standing deal. This is the result of that highly competitive marketplace referred to earlier. As the Internet expands, the unexpected can, and often does, happen. Keep this in mind from both a selling and a consumer point of view. Exploit this to your own benefit.

In addition to paying close attention to Travelocity, Expedia, TravelWeb, and other travel center sites that will undoubtedly come online by the time you read

Figure 1.5 Travelocity is a major hub where travelers can find discounts on air-fares and hotel rooms.

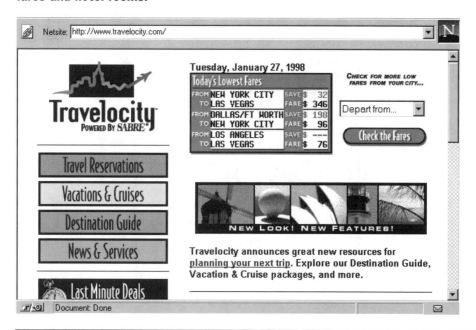

this, keep tabs on the airlines that fly in and out of your airport as well. Many of them offer their own discount programs, such as American Airlines' NetSaver, which emails you every Wednesday with the latest bargains. USAir, Continental, and other carriers offer similar update services. At this point, it almost goes without saying that these sites also offer ETA (estimated time of arrival) and departure times online, for tracking flights.

While we're on the subject of airlines, let's make sure you get the best frequent-flyer deal possible at WebFlyer (http://www.insideflyer.com). This site will keep you posted on which airlines are offering the best deals on fly miles. There's a calendar that charts who's doing what and when. Be sure to sign up for the email updater when you visit (see Figure 1.6).

As you might expect, there is also a flurry of constant, ever-changing hotel deals. Many of these deals will be found on the Travelocity-type sites mentioned earlier, while others will run standalone promotions on their own sites. I also noticed that hotels and car rental companies will do package deals with airlines. Just like the rest of the Internet, there is no one source that has a comprehensive

Figure 1.6 Keep tabs on which airline is running what frequent-flyer programs and when with WebFlyer.

listing of all deals that are happening at all times. You may get a great deal on an airline seat with one carrier and not realize that there's a package deal offering you more savings through another airline, hotel, and car rental company. If you're a frequent traveler, it is especially important to sign up for email update services offered by each site. Let's face it, unless your core business is only travel, you're not going to spend most of your time constantly surfing all these sites. If you did, you wouldn't have much time to travel!

Since you're buying airline reservations and hotel rooms online, you might as well consider buying your next company car on the Internet. Whether you're buying a single company car or leasing an entire fleet, the chances are good that you'll only pay a little bit above wholesale on a vehicle. Lots of people are already doing their research online for their next vehicle, so why not you? It makes perfect sense, since a car is a *considered purchase* item. In other words, once you're spending a great deal of money, you will want to do your homework in order to make an educated buying decision. As you know, the Internet is excellent at providing this in-depth information.

Internet Auctions

Nowhere else is the open market principle more apparent than in the scores of auction sites that now populate the Web. Some are real-time auctions, in which the price goes up with each competing bid (http://www.onsale.com), while others are Dutch auctions (http://klickklock.com), in which the price keeps dropping until someone buys the merchandise. Still others are silent auctions; you put a bid in and return now and again to see if someone else has countered your offer. Rather than going to every single site to see if they're hawking what you're in the market for, you should check out http://www.usaweb.com, where you'll find a search engine that keeps track of what many auction sites are selling (see Figure 1.7). Enter the word *printer* in the BidFind search field and it will present you with those sites auctioning off printers. This site also points to over 100 auction sites on the Web, and even many auctions offline as well.

If you're looking for the state-of-the-art computer that just came out yesterday, you may not find it on these auction sites. More often than not, the merchandise auctioned off is close-out products. Very often, there are odd lots bought up that aren't worth putting in the manufacturer's catalog again because there aren't enough left. The computers may be last year's model, without the various bells and

Figure 1.7 Find out which auction sites are selling what you need at USAWeb.

whistles, but you may not want or need these extra features anyway. I recommend that you check brand names very carefully, along with the warranties and return policies. In many cases, sales are final.

 TIP Put your bids in early. When there's a tie, which often happens, the person who put his or her bid in first gets the merchandise.

The first auction site I knew of was wehkamp.nl in Holland. It used its Web site to "blow out" old inventory. An enterprising student tracked how much each item typically sold for and charted it on his own Web pages. Much to the chagrin of Wehkamp, bidders could visit the student's site to see the highest and lowest prices a product would sell for. It won't be any surprise to me if such information also becomes available for the U.S. auction sites. It enables the potential buyers to make smarter bids. Perhaps by the time you read this, these sites will spring up state-side. Look around for them!

Be careful. These auction sites can be addictive to the point of distraction! People get caught up in the bidding excitement and sometimes pay more for things than they might have elsewhere. I also know people who buy things for which they have no need, just because the costs are low.

Buying the Tools of Your Trade

Chances are there's something significant already happening on the Internet in your niche in the purchasing area. Most industries now have their early starters grabbing the first, second, and third slots.

The fact that computers are the biggest category doesn't surprise anyone. Since it's the most mature thus far, it's worth looking at how merchandise in this category is being traded on the Net. One of the first commerce centers in the high-tech/telecommunications arena was MarketPlace 2000 (http://www.themarketplace .com). You can learn a great deal about how your industry's commerce center might look in the future by visiting this site (see Figure 1.8). You will find auctions for fully configured computers or components, such as motherboards, monitors, hard drives, and so forth. Very often, you can buy these components one at a time, or save a bundle of money by buying in volume. You can bid on a mainframe computer in an auction room if you like, or meet other people in the sales chain with whom you can forge a buy/sell relationship on or offline and read news updates about the industry. Simple classified listings are now a staple of just about all industry commerce centers.

Figure 1.8 MarketPlace 2000 is a major hub for buyers and sellers of everything from computer components to mainframes.

News, in this case, has become just one commodity to be had at this trading post. Is the MarketPlace 2000 a publication? Yes, but it is also a type of commodity pit. It's two mints in one! Is it redefining how we think of a trade publication? Well, weren't there always classified ads in the back of trade publications where people sought buyers and sellers for their brand of arcania? Of course. The Net has simply made this traditional practice more interactive.

"Big deal," you say. You expect computers and travel (because they're merely packages of information that the Net can easily promote and sell), but what about an industry that doesn't cater to such a wide group of people? Perhaps I can interest you in a refrigerated shipping container that can be transported from ship to flatbed truck and then to railroad. If you're interested, take a look at TransAmerica Leasing. This site can match up your needs with a seller. At the time of this writing, the transaction happens offline, but so what? The commodity of serving as a conduit between buyer and seller is the Internet's first point of value. This site does more than match up goods with a customer, though. We'll return to TransAmerica later in this chapter to see how it serves an overlapping community of interest: its existing customers.

Intermodal refrigerated containers don't really turn you on? How about a cappuccino machine that will make 200 cups of coffee for your closest friends? Or perhaps you'd like to buy a diner booth for your living room? Check out the food service site that serves as a crossroads for such restaurateur supplies at http://www.supplysite.com. It's quite conceivable that indigenous products for a given industry might have an outside market. I don't think that people will be putting 4-ton steel fittings on their front lawn, but I could see where they may want their own milkshake machine, or an industrial-rated stove or refrigerator.

A Business-to-Business Buying Standard in the Works

Many business-to-business purchases involve large dollar volume. When that sort of volume is changing hands, the seller wants to be very sure that you are who you say you are. Rather than each seller developing his or her own standards to authenticate and run a credit check on you, in order to process payments in real time or near real time, a single system is being devised to make it easier for both buyer and seller to transact large purchases online. This is similar to the SET standards that are being developed for online retail customer buying, which is covered in Chapter 6, "Retail: Setting Up Shop on the Net."

The Secure Electronic Transaction (SET) standard is undergoing development at the time of writing. Its purpose is to provide a widespread standard for the average consumer to make credit/payment card transactions online, with even more security precautions than are currently in place.

This business-to-business system is called Open Buying on the Internet (OBI). American Express, wanting to play a pivotal role in this process, was heavily involved in the initiation of OBI. Big players on both the buying and selling sides, such as Ford, Microsoft, Oracle, GE, and Office Depot, are participating. This process is particularly helpful when dealing with a vendor or supplier from whom you may buy various services or products over the course of a month on an ongoing basis. Among other things, OBI is designed to have purchases that take place in different buying sessions consolidated and reconciled. The amount of bookkeeping is reduced substantially on both sides of the transaction, and the single payment at month's end can be transferred quickly.

Customer Service Savings

Okay, I won't drag out the Federal Express example and tell you how it saves $3.00 or more each time someone uses the Web to track a package instead of calling its

800 number and having a human do it. Nor will I roll out Amazon's searchable database of over two million books, or the U.S. Post Office's ZIP code locator, or Visa's ATM finder. "Been there, done all that," you say. While these are very good examples, there are others coming online now that can show us new things to learn from. It's well worth your while to dig deeper into using the Net as a tool for customer support. In the survey of the American Marketing Association referred to earlier, 19 percent of respondents said they are currently using the Net for such purposes, while 53 percent plan on having some component of customer service on their Web site by the end of 1999. You may not be planning on utilizing your site for such activities; however, the chances are good that your competitors are.

Very often, there's friction between the manufacturer of a product and the existing sales channels when that manufacturer opens up a Web site that speaks directly to the end user. 3Com has gone in the other direction. It uses its site to support its sales channels, even for complex network configurations. The Network Designer (which I had the pleasure of critiquing while in beta) lets end users put together their own network with all the different options and variations. The site then directs customers, using their newly customized network, to a nearby reseller.

3M is a very good example of a company that has designed a customer-focused Web site. With the use of a search engine that accesses relational databases, visitors can easily find their way to over 50,000 products that 3M offers in nearly every industry imaginable. 3M had the good sense to look at itself from the outside in, rather than the inside out, which is a discipline any company needs to consider when designing its Web site. We will discuss this further in Chapter 5, "Your Brand Image and the Internet."

As we know, answering customer service questions that can be answered on a Web site instead of by an actual person saves significant amounts of money. But simply slapping up a bunch of help files and product offerings will not induce the customer to use your Web site rather than the telephone. The challenge here is to make your site not *as* effective as the alternative phone call, but *more* effective. One solution that I respect a great deal in this category is the *step-search* feature offered by Saqqara. Step-search asks you only a few questions at a time (see Figure 1.9). Based on your answers, step-search will come back and present you with an appropriate array of options. This solution goes a long way toward avoiding the user frustration found at many customer service sites on the Internet. Here's why: Very often, customers are asked to fill out lengthy forms on a site and then submit them. Imagine if you take 20 minutes to fill out one of these long forms only to find at the very end that "You cannot get the red Chevrolet Lumina with manual transmission and air conditioning. Please start over!" Step-search avoids both wasted time and frustration.

Figure 1.9 Saqqara's step-search feature helps users navigate a labyrinth of questions they must answer in order to make a purchase.

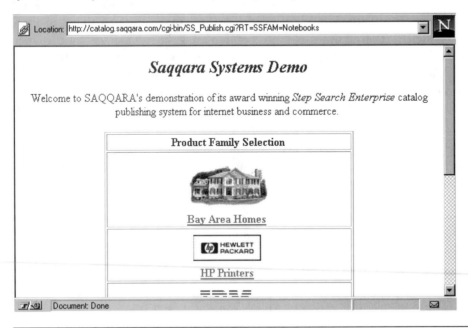

Another way to keep customers hitting your Web site instead of your 800 customer support phone lines is to have a discussion group in the customer service area of your site. This discussion group can have many "threads," or discussion topics. It looks something like a Usenet group or a bulletin board. Each thread may represent a particular product of yours. Thereunder, you might find subthreads, where customers can discuss various aspects of that product. You'll most definitely want to moderate these discussions and interact with them often. There are many free and reasonably cheap software programs that your Webmaster can put up on your site that run very easily managed discussion lists/bulletin boards. Take a look around, and discuss your needs with your site designer. Make sure you use a program that either you or an assigned employee can learn quickly and easily, since you'll want to update it regularly to provide fast customer support.

This solution has an upside and a downside. The upside, as previously mentioned, is that it can save you money. You'll also be delighted when customers answer questions to problems other customers pose. Some of these answers are ones that you might not have even thought of. You can simultaneously collect more solutions about your own products from your customers, while not having to answer those questions yourself: additional input with less output—a powerful combination. The downside is that you might find irate customers trashing your product on your own Web site. To your horror, you may indeed be sponsoring a revolt aimed at yourself! If the complaints are legitimate, then you're going to have to face the music sooner or later. Isn't it better for you to see this happen on your own site rather than in an open Usenet newsgroup? Most definitely. At your "home," you can handle the "spin control" much faster and more effectively.

If your public relations people start squawking, tell them this is a policy of containment. If you deal with the problems in a forthright manner, it will be seen as such, more often than not. If you try to squelch the complaints in a heavy-handed manner by editing them or replying in an arrogant manner, you're opening up an online can of worms that is best avoided. If the complaints are not warranted, and they're posed by a few persistent cranks out there, the rest of the discussion group will typically see this and appreciate it for what it is. There is something to be said about dealing with your vulnerabilities in an open and upright manner. It can add luster to your credibility and that of your products.

I'll Have My Database Call Your Database

As you know, data mining is becoming a hot topic. Companies are often frustrated by not being able to easily access their inhouse information. For example, you may know that you have a product shot somewhere in your organization, but don't know where it is. Since you can't find it, you have to schedule a photo shoot to capture a new picture of something you already have . . . somewhere. Both you and your customer will benefit greatly if you can have your databases all relating to each other and participating in a search name-relational database configuration.

Query Tone

One of the early entrants to this arena was Micro Strategies Inc. Michael Sailor, CEO, speaks of a "query tone," as in *dial tone*, whereby someone can easily ask an involved question and receive a response that draws on numerous databases. He wants customers to be able to ask questions that aren't easily answered right now: "Which airline that flies between New York and San Diego has the highest customer approval rating?" The information is currently known; it's just extremely hard or tedious to find it. Having Sailor's "query tone" will make accessing such information much easier. Researchers, marketers, customers, and others will have a field day as this capability comes online in the foreseeable future. How can you take advantage of the concept in the meantime? Start itemizing the information you currently have isolated in different places within your organization. Think of what system you can put in place that will make that information more accessible for you, other parts of your company, and customers. Note that more and more information that used to be uniquely internal is now being shared with clients across many industries.

Distributed Databases

Distributed databases are another way to provide data for both customers and inhouse employees. APL StackTrain (http://www.apl.com) does much more than simply give departure and arrival dates of cargo ships at various ports around the world. At its Web site, you can fill out a form that can immediately be transferred into a bill of lading. It also updates you on the availability of cargo space on ships. You can pull up maps that show its shipping lanes. This is an extraordinary example of pulling information from a very diffused array of sources. The ships, the ports, and all the links within that chain feed into this database presented to you on the Web. It's a labyrinth of satellite feeds and land lines. This is cutting-edge use of networked customer support technology at the time of writing, but as the velocity of commerce increases, it will become commonplace and we'll wonder how we ever lived without it. Look for the sourcing of numerous distributed databases to start gaining attention.

Strengthening Sales Support via the Internet

As noted earlier, the potential for the Net to create friction between manufacturers and sales and distribution channels is very real. But when done correctly, utilization of the Internet can actually enhance those all-important relationships with your channels of sales and distribution. 3Com wisely spent money on developing and marketing its Network Designer (Figure 1.10). Turning well-qualified leads over to its resellers can only enhance those existing sales channel relationships and quite probably attract more due to the extra sales support offered. Helping your vendors locate what products are where is another tactic that can be employed.

The Lee Product Locator allows partners, or anyone else for that matter, to search for a distributor that has specific product line in the colors, quantities, and sizes needed (http://www.rsvpcomm.com/scripts/foxweb.exe/findlee). Once the specific item is located, users can then find out how many miles that distributor is from them.

BuildSoft (http://www.buildsoft.com) sells construction management software, including tools for CPM Scheduling, Historical and Take-Off Estimating, Purchase Orders/Work Orders, Job Costing, and Accounting. The BuildSoft site also acts as a clearinghouse for building and construction information on the Web and as a gateway to BuildNet, the BuildSoft online services network.

Figure 1.10 3Com Network Designer helps you configure a customized network and then refers you to an appropriate reseller.

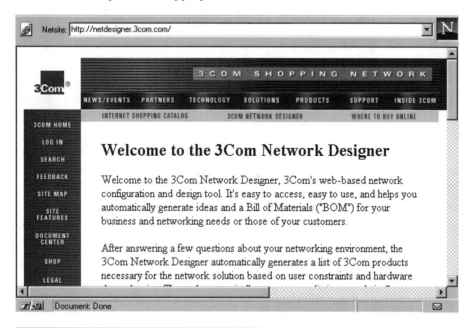

Exide makes it just a little bit easier for its value-added resellers and sales partners to promote their products with the Exide Electronics VAR Guide (http://www.exide.com/varguide.htm). The VAR kit enables resellers to "snap in" Exide Electronic product Web pages. The kit provides product pages, including photos, a UPS buyers' checklist, and educational information on power protection. Also included is coding for online sales and more. The kit is distributed via CD-ROM or from the Exide site. This is smart thinking: In addition to solidifying relationships with existing sales channels, it extends the company's message that much further.

One of the most effective sales support case histories I've come across has more to do with the powers of observation than with technology. Jim Roth works for Document Services Sales Support. The Web site he administers is behind a firewall, so we can't look at it from the open Internet. The site is devoted to supporting the salespeople out in the field. He checks the logs on the search engine to see what people are keen on. If he sees that a particular product is searched for often, he's apt to put up more information on that product. Remember, though, that what people *don't* find can be just as important as what they *do* find. When he sees salespeople searching for things they aren't finding, he moves to put that information on the site.

In a very real way, Jim is using the extensive tracking information as a type of barometer. What's hot? What's not? Since these sites support the people in the field, they get a real pulse for what the marketplace is asking for through the queries submitted by their sales and field analysts. This Web site now handles 75 percent of the traffic, while the phones handle 25 percent. The Web site is actually faster because it finds the information in real time, whereas the telephone support team would first have to assign the search and then have someone physically go and get the information and send it to the person who asked for it. Depending on the depth of the request, a physical search can take hours or even days.

"We're a cost center," Roth explains. "This means we're supported and funded by our product divisions. They always ask, 'What have you done for us lately?' The unit of measure we use to answer that question is the amount of returned hours to the field." He points out: "Since the Web site gets them the information faster, they can return to sell more in the field, or simply get back faster to the prospective or existing client with answers. On average, we return about two days to the field using this method. The old way would have that person out of action because she was either doing the research herself, or waiting for someone internally to complete the task. That's all time out of the field not selling." On the telephone, that person's case would be put in a queue, where it would stay until that queue was looked at twice a day, then assigned to a researcher. The phone system isn't a simple help desk. The questions are more profound than that. Much of the information requested is dynamic. A salesperson might want to locate a particular machine in order to train someone on it, but it's been moved out of his locale. "Where is that machine now?" is such a question that might be asked. While many people do ask the appropriate question of "How much money has the Net saved you?" this case study points out how much time the Internet can save your firm. Many people will rightfully argue that time and money are in fact one and the same.

Distributed Printing

By pushing the production of printed information out to the end user, small and large companies can save enormous amounts of money, time, real estate, and labor. This can apply to running high-resolution, four-color brochures closer to their distribution points, or printing a single coupon by a grocery shopper. Let's start small and expand out to larger applications from there.

Supermarkets.com was created by a division of Catalina Marketing Network, the folks who currently deliver purchase-based electronic coupons in more than 10,800 U.S. supermarkets. A shopper goes to this Web site and fills out his or her standard shopping list, which is then saved as a profile for later use. Each week, the customer returns to the site to see what items on his or her shopping list are being discounted with coupons. She then prints the coupons on her own printer and takes them to the store the next time she goes. In turn, the store scans and redeems those coupons, just like any others, at the register. The customer saves time and money, as does the manufacturer, and often the participating supermarket as well. Every coupon distributed online is one less that they had to print, handle, and distribute themselves. This is distributed printing in its most diffuse form, right down to the customer level. Keep in mind that not every coupon the manufacturer prints and distributes gets used. For the sake of argument, there may be 50 coupons distributed for every one redeemed. In reality, that manufacturer is saving not only on the printing and distribution of a single coupon, but that of 50 coupons.

Let's go now from the end user of Sunny Delight to the end user of Sun Sparc computers. Sun (http://docs.sun.com) puts all its documentation—manuals, guides, and answer books—on a Web site. The user can then use a Web browser interface to view and print a variety of technical information for Sun products that may reside in the docs.sun database. Over the next few months, docs.sun will include all product documentation from Sun Microsystems, including new books as well as existing books, and in multiple languages. The docs.sun online documentation system provides a robust search engine integrated with a powerful browse functionality that enables users to find information throughout all Sun document collections quickly and efficiently. You can dynamically customize your view of a very large document database, choosing only the subjects you are interested in and the types of documents you want to view.

Pushing the printing of documents down to the end user for everything from cookies to computers is only one form of the distributed printing model. What we'll look at next is a more sophisticated printing model that includes higher-volume runs and higher resolutions. While a collateral piece for a trade show in California might be created in New York, it might as well be produced in Los Angeles, rather than paying for it to be shipped across the country. The Worldwide Electronic Publishing Network (WEPN) at http://www.wepn.com offers you this capability. By using its QuickQuote calculator, you can estimate how much it will cost you to print your document in over 55 cities around the world. By the way, the actual documents are sent via private network to the local printing facilities, not the

Internet. But who cares? The point is, the Internet puts you in touch with the capability and the company that offers it.

There is a convergence of the fields of distributed printing, publishing on demand, or what some call just-in-time publishing. Xerox plays a major role in these arenas. I helped roll out a product for Xerox a few years ago called DocuTech; in fact, I was part of the crew that helped name it. DocuTech lets someone produce a limited print run of manuals, or even compilations of bits and pieces of editorial, from different sources. It takes electronic files on disk, or transmitted through the Internet or an intranet, and prints them as if they were coming from an offset press, but using Xerox's print technology instead. A binder unit can turn the product into neatly bound books. For short print runs, it is an excellent solution. A number of efforts have been under way to put a Web interface up that would feed DocuTech materials to be printed widely. So anyone, from anywhere, could conceivably print to a remote location where a DocuTech machine resides; perhaps within your own company or at a local print shop.

While people have been talking the talk, I haven't yet seen one walk the walk. The idea will happen; it's just a question of time. Perhaps it will turn the corner into reality by the time you read this. One of the hurdles is keeping track of royalties. Let's say you want to buy only Chapters 3, 7, and 8 of this book. What would you owe me? Maybe you only want certain subchapters of those selected chapters? What then? If information does get parsed down to smaller pieces, you might see new types of promotions, like a two-for-one special on a chapter. Buy one chapter of my book, get one free. Let's see if it happens.

Distributed printing of documents is in a type of metamorphic stage where it's still being defined and redefined. Another interpretation of this concept comes again from Xerox, which calls itself "The Document Company." DocuWeb, at http://199.98.32.14, allows creators and users of documents to access collections they share in common. For example, a company may have an ever-changing personnel phone book for all its employees around the world. Each local office can simply print the latest rendition of that manual on an as-needed basis. Unlike Microsoft's NetMeeting, where documents are shared live and all or some can manipulate them, these documents are tightly controlled by the creators. The recipient can change a few things on the job ticket attached to the document. He's apt to change the amount of documents to be printed, but not the contents of the document. This is similar to the way Adobe's Acrobat (http://www.adobe.com) files function: you can distribute them, but once they are created, they cannot be altered by the recipients.

Another application of DocuWeb could be as a service manual for BMW dealers. Sales promotional literature with changing specifications, 4-color visuals, on a 12-panel brochure can be sent to a local commercial printer on an as-needed basis, rather than having boxes of them collect dust in each sales office, only to have them go out of date.

These sorts of applications help companies work smarter. There's a difference between working smarter and working faster. It's fine to work faster as long as you're not simply running in place at twice the speed. Working smarter makes better use of all your resources, money, materials, and the most valuable of commodities, your time.

The larger projects described toward the end of this chapter are geared for larger operations; however, the Internet is typically utilized for smarter operations by small companies. Large firms would be wise to think small and act accordingly. See how small businesses apply the Internet to make them work smarter, faster, cheaper, and then apply those lessons on a larger scale.

Resource Center

Web Price Index   **http://netb2b.com/wpi**

This helpful tool from NetMarketing puts Web site development costs into perspective. Web Price Index is a monthly survey that looks at three hypothetical companies and their ongoing Web needs. Charts offer comparisons of site development and specific upgrades in six major U.S. cities. Each chart gives the national medians, highs and lows, for small-, medium-, and large-sized projects.

Expedia   **http://www.expedia.com**

Whether you travel virtually via mousepad or hold out for the real thing, this Microsoft site is the cherry on top of the traveler's ice cream sundae. Part online magazine and part ticketing service, the site features a travel agent, a hotel directory (with more than 25,000 choices), a flight fare tracker (get quotes via email), a slew of forums with places to trade stories with fellow travelers, image galleries, weather reports, and multimedia tours of international destinations. It gives Microsoft's motto "Where do you want to go today?" a whole new meaning.

Net2Phone   **http://www.net2phone.com**

Net2Phone enables any Internet user with a sound-equipped PC to initiate calls from a computer and transmit them over the Internet (via IDT) to a telephone. The benefits? Lower rates, as calls are carried over the Internet until they reach U.S.-based phone switches; in effect, all calls originate in the United States. This seems to be a good deal for people outside the States calling in. Sales jargon on the site promises that callers can save up to 95 percent. Only the caller needs to be online and multimedia equipped. Sound quality is still dependent on the Internet. Test it for yourself by downloading the software and calling toll-free numbers before you set up a user account.

American Airlines   http://www.americanair.com

This site is a prime example of how classic direct marketing practices can be migrated and employed on the Net. AA lures you in (call this an acquisition program) with its Net Saver discount program, which emails you every Wednesday with last-minute cheap seats. The incentive for you to buy tickets online is the offer of an additional 1000 frequent flyer miles. You can also find out how many fly-miles you've accrued by giving a PIN that lets you see your account information. Cross-merchandising tie-ins with Avis are featured, just like they are in the monthly hardcopy statements received by snail mail. The more you drill into this site, the more you learn about how to market smartly on the Net.

Auto-By-Tel   http://www.autobytel.com

Auto-By-Tel is a free service that lets you buy or lease vehicles wholesale. Are you tired of those icky slicky car sales sleuths giving you "the deal of your lifetime"? Auto-By-Tel provides you with a convenient, easy, and more affordable way to buy your next car or truck. Be sure you know all the details of the vehicle you plan to lease or buy, such as make, model, series, extras, and so forth. Submit the online request form and a subscribing dealer in your geographical area will contact you. The good part is that you have the option of choosing whether you want to buy immediately, in a couple of months, or later. You can still get the information you seek without worrying about being bugged by a salesperson. Great use of the World Wide Web for customer sales and support.

BidFind   http://www.vsn.net/af

BidFind is a search engine that's linked to about 30 online auction houses, including AuctionWeb, OnSale, and eAuction. Type in the product you're looking for, and BidFind provides a list of items and the auction houses where they're up for bid. Click on the item and jump into the action.

RealBid   http://www.realbid.com

Those in the market for commercial real estate can access information about properties for sale, conduct preliminary underwriting, and make certain offers via the Internet at the RealBid site. Buyers can keep their fingers on the market by filling out a profile that is then matched with new properties entered into the RealBid database. When properties matching the buyer profile are entered, the buyer will get an email notification. Seller listings cost between $5,000 and $25,000. Buyer participation is free.

MarketPlace   http://www.manufacturing.net

Everything you need to stay up to date on trends, events, and news in the manufacturing arena. This is a prime example of a trade magazine publisher, Cahner, converting content and contacts into an Internet community of interest. The interface is clean, attractive, and functional. Features such as the buyers' guide, industry forums, news and features, trade show listings, a jobs database, and more make this the consummate location for manufacturing resources.

Holiday Inn   http://www.holiday-inn.com

This hotel site offers the standard information about services, promotions, and locations, but also adds the powerful capability to search for a hotel by multiple criteria, check availability, and book rooms with secure transactions (in Netscape and MSIE browsers).

DocuWeb   http://199.98.32.14

As you can see from the descriptive name, this site is a bit short on creative marketing voodoo. However, DocuWeb's XDOD (Xerox Document On Demand) technology is a savvy solution for online document management. Participating members utilize a dedicated Web server for network access to document libraries. Documents (such as sales and promotion materials) can be viewed online and then easily channeled to a high-quality printer via a Java applet XDOD job ticket interface. The document library features split-screen viewing, customizable searching capabilities, and print request and document access reports for the use of the document manager.

SupplyWorks   http://www.supplyworks.com

It all started with a paper clip. The OBI Consortium, spearheaded by American Express, is attempting to create an efficient, secure, online purchasing system that meets the needs of big-budget buyers and sellers who service them. As a general framework for business-to-business transactions, Open Buying on the Internet (OBI) offers multiple payoffs: It discourages software vendors from populating the Web with proprietary systems that can't interact; it encourages participation from multiple vendors (rather than the dominant few); and heavy-hitters such as Office Depot, Microsoft, General Electric, and Oracle have already jumped on the bandwagon. AmEx is betting that OBI will foster more online transactions, and that many will be authorized, invoiced, and paid through its purchasing card programs. Interested? The OBI Consortium offers a variety of membership options to meet your needs.

Business Tools from ADP   http://www.adp.com/emergingbiz/tool/index.html

Small business owners and managers have a new place to turn for sound advice on day-to-day management issues such as finding funding, payroll obligations, and human resource management. The Business Tools section of Automatic Data Processing, Inc.'s (ADP) Web site has plenty of advice and articles about small business management. Can't find the form to apply for a federal identification number? ADP has it, and several others, available for free downloading.

Trafford Publishing   http://www.trafford.com

On-demand publishing removes the printing, marketing, retailing, and distribution hassles that small software companies, self-publishing authors, and government agencies routinely face. For approximately $1,000 and a manuscript, Trafford will partner in your creation by providing an online bookstore, marketing services (including an individual homepage and search engine registration), and on-demand printing and shipping. Trafford hopes to appeal to micromarkets that are vitally interested in their offerings to generate slow but steady sales around the world. The author sets the retail price and earns 75 percent of the retail markup. All in all, it's an interesting alternative to the competitive world of traditional publishing.

USING THE NET AS A RESOURCE
for Human Resources

2

Y ou know that one of your company's most valued assets is your employees. The manner in which you utilize this critical asset will make or break your firm, whether it's large or small. In short, you're managing brain power, or what some call "wetware." The Net is causing tectonic shifts underneath the way all companies find and manage their brain power.

With all the hyperbole out there about the Internet, you're well justified to be skeptical, but don't take my word for it. Notice the movements of Human Resources (HR) managers in large firms as we take a look at a survey from the American Management Association. Out of the 3500 members surveyed, 10.6 percent of them were in HR positions. That sample spent an average of 3.1 hours per week in 1997 on the Net in order to conduct some job-related function. By 1998, this survey reveals they will spend an average of 6.2 hours online per week for work-related activities. By 1999, those people will find themselves online an average of 7.9 hours per week. While 56 percent of those firms used the Net for some HR tasks in 1997, 73 percent will be doing so by 1999. What is making those people alter their work habits so dramatically? Read on about the following topics and you'll see why and how companies and candidates are finding each other on the Internet.

- How jobs and candidates find each other on the Net
- Getting to know all about you
- Distributed employment
- Outsourcing on the Internet
- Relocating people
- Distance training/learning

How Jobs and Candidates Find Each Other on the Net

Imagine there is a candidate looking for a company, and a company looking for a candidate. It's like two different needles in two different haystacks. When done correctly, the Net can merge the two haystacks and get the two needles to match up.

From a company's perspective, you can try to act as a magnet to your talent pool. Many corporate Web sites feature an "employment opportunities" section. If you're looking for a job at Allstate, for example, you can go to its site and see what jobs are currently offered in your area. To see a particularly good example of how jobs and candidates can be matched up on an employer's site, take a look at the "profiler" in the employment section of the Hewlett-Packard site (http://www .hewletpackard.com). A candidate is able to drill down to the right job, in the right location, and in the right salary range. This filtering process saves both the employer and the candidate time. It's a win/win proposition (see Figure 2.1).

Figure 2.1 Hewlett-Packard's employment search function is a prime example of a customized job search.

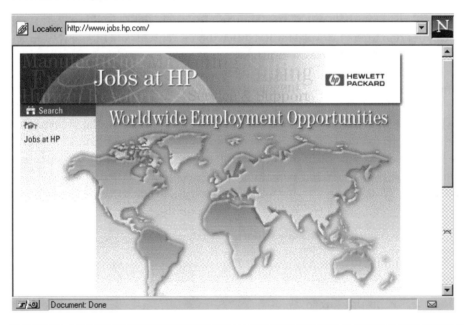

Copyright 1998 Hewlett-Packard Company. Reproduced with permission.

Another site that operates from the company's perspective is CareerMosaic. This site is the product of Bernard Hodes' Advertising and reflects the firm's vantage point. It provides a listing for firms and the jobs they offer. For additional examples of firms employing their Web sites as part of a recruitment campaign, go to http://www.interbiznet.com and look for the Top 100 Recruiting Sites.

Many candidates, however, do not look for jobs on a company-by-company basis. They're apt to look by profession, region, and salary. This is why firms often take a more aggressive approach and advertise in venues where talent pools already congregate. The Monster Board (Figure 2.2) is one such venue (http://www.monster.com). Online Career Center (OCC) at http://www.occ.com assumes a similar stance.

Another venue for job postings is local chambers of commerce and other such geographically located organizations. For example, at http://www.aimlink.org, either residents or someone thinking of moving to Omaha, Nebraska, can see what kinds of jobs and internships companies indigenous to that area are providing.

> **TIP** Don't post your résumé too publicly. It's quite conceivable that you could put your résumé on the Net and have it seen by someone in your company, perhaps even your boss. Many job boards allow only the skill sets to be viewable by the companies, until it can be ascertained that the firm is indeed not your current employer. The other side of this coin is that you may find your company advertising your job. This is what you might call, "the handwriting on the wall."

Using the Net as a pool to "fish" for talent will save your firm time, energy, and money. If the people in your firm are familiar with the Net, they can troll the Usenet groups for local talent. No one really knows the exact number of Usenet groups, since there are so many sublevels to each group. In New York City, you're apt to have many subdivisions of nyc.everything.topic. If you need someone in New York City, you may want to search the nyc.jobs section, which has a number of subdivisions in itself, such as nyc.jobs.offered and nyc.jobs.wanted. You can access Usenet groups by configuring your Netscape or Internet Explorer browser accordingly. Both of these browsers can "read" the Usenet groups, as well as the Web. The simple fact that someone is able to read and respond to a posting in Usenet says a number of things about the candidate: he or she obviously has computer skills and is able to surf the now lesser-known parts of the Internet.

Figure 2.2 The Monster Board is one of the most comprehensive job boards on the Internet.

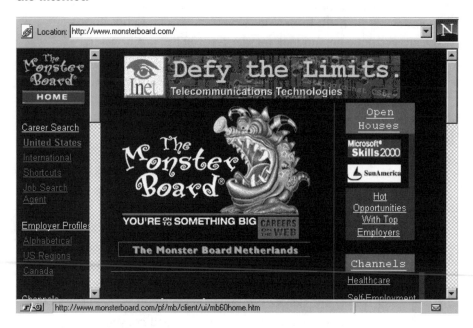

Vertical Recruiting

Vertical recruiting means industry-specific recruiting. In this many-to-many environment, birds of a feather really do flock together and create highly specific beehives of activity that are otherwise known as Web sites. To anyone outside of that specific industry, much of the information and want ads would be more than you would ever want to know about that given industry. But for those within that highly targeted niche, such a site is a gold mine.

If you visit *Advertising Age* at http://www.adage.com, you'll find a job center area there. This is a search engine for jobs that will look for the type of marketing position you're looking for, in the region of the United States you want, along with some other predilections as well. However, the search you conduct at the *Advertising Age* site is actually drawing on the marketing section of the Monster Board database. You could go directly to Monster Board, but you're more apt to be surfing *Advertising Age* if you're in the advertising business. So, in this case, the mountain comes to Mohammed, as it often does on the Net. Additionally, Ziff-Davis has a searchable database using the ISearch service as the provider of the database of jobs. The point is, these search windows pop up anywhere the candidate is likely to be. It makes the possibility of enticement that much more spontaneous.

College Recruitment

A vast majority of young people today consider using the Internet second nature, the way Baby Boomers are familiar with television. Therefore, many large firms go to great lengths to woo college students with campus recruitment efforts on the Internet.

JOBTRAK (http://jobtrak.com) is a central feeding source for many schools that accepts students' résumés, while also keeping track of companies' available jobs. From a student's perspective, he or she can simply go to the site, submit a password, and access the available jobs from the hundreds of companies that participate in the program. A student can select an industry, a date of availability, part- or full-time employment status, as well as a location. The filtering process is well-designed and sophisticated. You may even want to look at it as a benchmark for your Web site recruitment area. In order for you to access this area, go to http://jobtrak.com and click on the Student and Alumni button. You'll then see a selection entitled, "A Sample JOBTRAK University." Click on that and then enter "test" in the text field and watch what unfolds. It's one of the best recruitment interfaces I've seen on the Net to date.

Students are also able to access different listings or more specified recruitment through their colleges' intranets. Becky Rich, who currently works for me, recently graduated from Cornell University. Prior to graduating, she used the Cornell Career Services site to locate Cornell alumni within fields she found interesting. For one of her internships, she worked at a children's publishing company, Lodestar Books, after getting the contact information through a database only Cornell students can use.

Many schools also have *private Usenet groups* that are seen only by the students of that school. More often than not, there are a few groups devoted to jobs. Schools that have a Computer Science department may have a dozen or more internal bulletin boards devoted entirely to different kinds of technical jobs, such as Unix, PERL, and Java programmers. However, many of these groups are devoted to nontechnical jobs as well. If your company is seeking graduating or part-time students, you may want to figure out how to gain access to these boards. Since you don't have access to a school's network, chances are you won't physically be able to get them on your screen. You can contact the recruiting office and request that a job be posted to the appropriate group. I myself did this when I tapped into New York University's Usenet groups. As a result, I had the pleasure of employing Eftal

Sogukoglu on a part-time basis for over a year. Eftal does indeed attend the Computer Sciences school at NYU. If I ever needed someone with a skill set that he didn't possess, he always knew of someone who had such a knowledge base. Once I started with the internal NYU Usenet groups, I then continued expanding my work force by tapping into Eftal's network of college buddies.

> **Private Usenet Groups.** Any server that is serving Usenet groups to its users can set up "private" Usenet newsgroups that are only available to those who dial in to, or point their software to, their particular news server. For instance, if you wanted to set up an Elvis newsgroup server, devoted to private groups discussing the King, you could call your news server news.elvis.king.worship. Those whom you informed about the news service could then point their news readers or browsers to that news service and read all the newsgroups you created there. Usually the only news server you see is the one located at your local Internet Service Provider (ISP), which carries the more public and local newsgroups.

A current example of college recruitment from a corporation is KPMG Peat Marwick, a top-five accounting and consulting firm. The KPMG campus site targets college graduates who will be participating in on-campus interviews. It's an excellent example of using the Internet to prepare and get acquainted with candidates before meeting them face to face. The candidate gets a taste of how KPMG presents itself, while KPMG gets an early-bird insight into whom they will meet when on campus. Basically, on its site, KPMG walks job-seeking students through the entire placement process, from how to submit a résumé to likely questions asked in the interview, to follow-up procedures, all in a question-and-answer format. Other information presented includes KPMG background information and a "day in the life" piece, detailing what KPMG employees do.

At the time of writing, KPMG was running a well-conceived email trivia contest called "The KPMG In-Site Challenge." In order to participate, the candidate would have to garner pieces of information found in different places on the KPMG Web site. The winner of this challenge received a $4,000 mystery package of software.

There's only one thing worse than getting no leads off a recruitment campaign, and that's getting far too many. If your recruitment message is well-targeted and explicit enough, you may end up spinning your wheels trying to process all of the inappropriate inquires. It isn't a good idea to simply ignore these inquiries, as you might need them for other job positions down the road. Furthermore, you don't want to damage your company's image in the talent pool you'll most likely return to another day.

Getting to Know You . . . Getting to Know All About You

At this point, you could be thinking that the Net is only good for attracting high-tech talent. Well, that's definitely one of the assets of recruiting on the Internet, especially in this day and age, where good high-tech talent is a much sought-after commodity. However, the Monster Board recently put out a release saying that 49 percent of the jobs searched from its database were not high tech. HotJobs, another large job board, noticed similar findings. According to Demetre Boylan (VP of Sales and Marketing from HotJobs), the hot categories following high tech are sales and marketing, financial, and manufacturing. He points out that manu-facturing may overtake the financial category, due to its immense size. Demetre also feels that engineers and product designers will turn into hot recruitment niches on the Net. He notes that it is important to identify and then cater to a niche. Seventy percent of the people visiting HotJobs are really just "passive look-ers," who are content with their jobs but curious about what else is out there. Therefore, you really have to appeal to the lookers and not only want to hit them where they hang out on the Net, but offer some service or content that establishes the possibility for dialogue later on as well as customer loyalty.

This Is the Beginning of a Beautiful Relationship

No matter which industry you're in, people always like to know they are valued in their respective marketplaces. It's a guaranteed draw, assuming you commit enough resources to updating and promoting the site to both companies and can-didates alike. Having a good trade site that really gives a comprehensive snapshot of a given industry is a worthwhile endeavor for a firm to pursue, if for no other reason than as a tool with which to open up a dialogue with potential candidates.

The Tenagra Group (a Web development and marketing company) created a hub of activity around http://www.o-a.com. The site houses the archives of the Online-Ads Discussion List. Tenagra also keeps a high profile with its annual awards program, as well as industry news digests that are distributed periodically. These efforts by Tenagra afford them the opportunity to get close to many of the practitioners of their trade. Indeed, these venues sometimes act as the equivalent of Budapest for spies of a bygone era. Just like these undercover agents in the Cold

War would get to co-mingle with each other up close and personal, here, too, competitors can eyeball each other pretty closely. Industry intrigue awaits you at your vertical online watering hole!

Survey the information niches already out there that cater to the talent pool you are thinking of addressing. If there is a Web site or Webzine that exists, approach those publications about the cost of advertising. You may want to place an overt recruitment ad, or simply announce your own niche publication that is of unique interest to the audience you wish to address. You should have a site that is set up to accept the traffic from such a well-targeted advertising campaign. The readers of your advertisement can then click on over to your site, where they can either retrieve something of immediate value, read and respond to that job placement information, or sign up for a list that will give them periodic updates about industry-specific news.

 When guiding subscribers to your emailzine, assure them the subscription information will not be used by or sold to any external source. When I put this guarantee in my newsletter, the fulfillment rate increased 10 percent.

You should proceed with caution, however. The information you provide *must* be of significantly higher value than that which is generally available on the Internet in your niche. The reason for this is that most surfers are used to giving up only their email addresses to be part of a mailing list and no further information. Even with my disclaimer, 5 percent of the people who enter the subscription process back out when they see that I ask for their title, company, and how they heard about *Web Digest For Marketers*. It's a trade-off I can live with, since it has paid for itself many times over. The higher the quality and the focus of the content, the more license you have to ask your constituents for more detailed information.

To see what's out there, I suggest you check the three mailing list databases and 'zine directories given in the resource center on the companion Web site for Chapter 8, "Direct Marketing and Sales Support." Remember, nothing on the Internet is complete; there are new sites added every day, as well as sites disappearing. Lists change too quickly to be accurate. After checking these sources, you will want to conduct an extensive search using different search engines in order to see what other sites are out there serving the niche audience you wish to attract.

In Defense of Executive Recruiters

I was an executive recruiter for two years and remember finding that any given candidate I met on one job search would probably not be the person to land that particular job; rather, it would be another job down the road that would become the right match. It was a matter of building a relationship with a candidate until the stars were in alignment and everything clicked.

In this book and many others about the Net, the concept of *disintermediation* is often used to describe cutting out the middleman between two parties, whether they're buying and selling computers or looking for systems analysts. It should also be noted that the Net causes other intermediaries to emerge, as noted in Chapter 5, "Your Brand Image and the Internet."

In many cases, a company will farm out the job search to a Net-savvy recruiter. This concept shouldn't come as a surprise, since the exact same thing happens when trying to filter information. Human filters are becoming a new job classification; while software agents can do some filtering of information, they can never take the place of human judgment. The same holds true in human resources recruitment.

If you happen to be a job recruiter, check out Recruiters Online Network (RON) (http://www.recruitersonline.com). Membership is open only to professional recruiters. For an annual membership fee, you can get help in conducting online searches, while also having access to a resource center. Additionally, members have the option of setting up their own Web sites with RON. Interestingly enough, RON also offers some affinity marketing services. Recruiters can buy insurance through RON, as well as get attractive rates on things they need in their line of business, such as discounted per-minute rates on toll-free numbers (see Figure 2.3).

Another approach to recruitment advertising comes from the newspapers. Since the Internet is good for looking things up, classified ads will and do play a significant role in the fields that make heavy use of them already, such as real estate and—you guessed it—job recruitment. Therefore, many newspapers are migrating their classified ads to the Net, using one business model or another. Some offer you, the advertiser, an online avail by itself, while others will sell it to you for a small premium when you buy a classified ad in their hardcopy version. For a view of this approach, visit http://www.careerpath.com, where you'll see a combined listing from major newspapers, including the *New York Times*, the *Boston Globe*, the *Washington Post*, the *Chicago Tribune*, the *LA Times*, and many, many more. When I last visited this site, it boasted that it could search over 214,460 help wanted ads from across the country. Talk about merging haystacks!

There are going to be numerous ways to find both jobs and candidates online. HotJobs, at http://www.hotjobs.com, aggressively pursues the candidate, and as many recruiters will tell you, this is necessary to get the best talent. Those hot jobs listed are put there by the clients of HotJobs, such as AT&T, Pepsi, and Oracle. Once HotJobs has drawn in a candidate, he or she is asked to fill out a

Figure 2.3 Recruiters Online Network is a membership organization open only to recruiters.

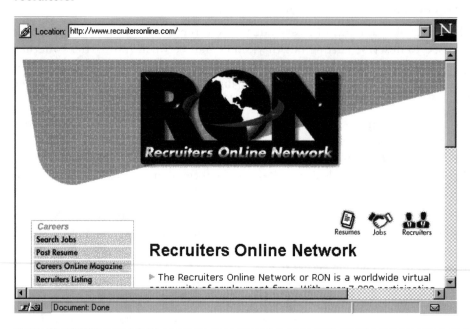

fairly simple form, which is then forwarded to the recruiter for a client. If the ad placement was done correctly, the candidate should be well qualified. A HotJobs client has literally dozens of inhouse recruiters working on dozens of different searches for many different kinds of candidates. The client pays HotJobs $6,000 for each and every recruiter and their respective searches. If you do the math, a single company with a couple of dozen recruiters times $6,000 can quickly become quite lucrative to HotJobs.

Richard Johnson of WorkHere (http://www.workhere.com), a site promoting a face-to-face job fair, feels that some online venues are less efficient than offline traditional print advertising. He feels this is primarily due to the difficulty of matching specific jobs with specific candidates found on the Web; however, he does feel the Net is a good way to promote his agenda. He advertises his site with animated banners that say, "Technical Positions Available." They are strategically placed in technically specific sites and on search engines. WorkHere gives candidates a chance to submit their résumés to companies that will be attending job fairs. Past companies in attendance have been MetLife, the New York Metropolitan Museum of Art, and Arthur Andersen. This practice allows the company to preview the candidate prior to meeting in person. If they like a person's résumé, they can then follow up on the relationship. After up to a month following a job fair, a candidate can still upload his or her résumé for a company's perusal, thus making the window of exposure considerably longer than the physical event itself.

Bonnie Halper, a new media recruiter in New York City, agrees with the idea that management style and chemistry can really only be judged in person. She says, "Neither company nor candidate would take me very seriously if I didn't have a good 'function' site. My site is simple and to the point. I regularly post tips on finding new media jobs and preparing new media résumés (see Figure 2.4). Another truism about new media and many other categories is that for the most part, résumés are emailed back and forth, instead of using a fax or snail mail. If the candidate is a

Figure 2.4 A Web site doesn't necessarily have to be complex in order to be effective.

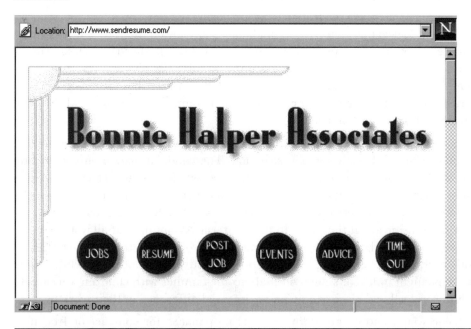

Writer: Bonnie Halper
Producer/Designer: Paul Errey
Production: Lorraine Kennedy

good fit with the firm we are working with, we can then send them a nice-looking package on the candidate."

She continues, "Regardless of the Net's impact on recruiting, finding the best candidates is still a face-to-face business. Even if someone is perfectly qualified for a position, he won't be placed if there is no chemistry. You can't gauge this until you are actually in his presence and can see whether his management style is compatible with that of the company seeking the talent."

Whether you're a recruiter planning on delving deeply into the Net or not, you would do well to make yourself acquainted with online recruitment practices and have inhouse recruiters or freelancers tap this vast resource. If your clients don't expect this of you already, they will. It's just a question of time. You might as well embrace it sooner than later and claim it as a competitive edge.

Distributed Employment: Telecommuting to Work on the Net

Once your firm has made the leap to recruiting using the Net, you'll find yourself asking the next logical question: "If the candidate is already on the Net, is it really necessary to import that person into the office every day, whether that person comes from across the city, the country, or even the world?" Veriphone, previously mentioned in Chapter 1, "Cutting Costs Across Your Enterprise," has no corporate headquarters. It is perhaps the first large-scale major company to be unshackled by the restraints of bricks and mortar.

If a person's brain power can be harnessed from her home, then both company and employee can have a win/win situation. The candidate saves on commuting time, clothes, gasoline, and so on. The firm saves on office space, electricity, and a host of other "built-in" HR costs. The more cynical employer can also calculate the increased worker productivity, since that person won't be hanging around the water cooler or grousing about the coffee in the cafeteria. Assuming that all workers don't have to work together at the exact same time, you'll find that time-shifting is another advantage. Some people work most efficiently in the morning, while others tend to be night owls. For single- or dual-income families with children, this ability to shift workload and place can mean an essential difference in their work lives.

Some would and do argue that this is no panacea for contract or freelance workers. Many will tell you they find themselves assuming higher overhead costs for essentially the same wage. From the company perspective, the downside is the lack of "face-time." An offsite employee can be diminished in importance if he is never seen. "Out of sight, out of mind," as the saying goes. A tendency to marginalize offsite employees is difficult to notice and sometimes even more difficult to correct. This is, after all, a brave new HR world. Maybe a person can come to the office two days a week and use a space that is shared by other telecommuters on other days. Your firm may choose to go halfway and have that employee commute to a telecommuting center located near him. At these centers, there are office support services, such as industrial-strength copiers, videoconferencing capabilities, faster access to the Internet, and so on. For a closer look at this practice, check out the Telecommuting Center Project in Northern California at http://www.angr.ucdavis .edu/~its/tcenters/tc.stm. For a *link pile* that will point you to different online resources about telecommuting, check out http://www.gilgordon.com/resources/publications2.html.

 Be aware of the differences between offsite contract (or freelance) employees and part-time telecommuters, even if they are using a specific telecommuting center contracted and paid for by your company. There are many legal benefits and compensations that must be clarified and met for each category of employee.

Another downside is that there are things that happen in a face-to-face encounter that just aren't going to happen in an online encounter, even using teleconferencing or video feed. In many cases, there needs to be a certain spontaneity for inspiration to spawn. That may often only happen when your employees are in the same place at the same time, sharing the same experience.

Brain Power Management

I talked about this idea of managing brain power with Dane Atkinson, president of SenseNet, a major provider of network solutions located in New York City. He told me, "Much of what we at SenseNet do for our Fortune 500 clients is to build intranets that outsiders never even see, which supports the efficient deployment of brain power already on staff." He went on to say, "For example, we put into place a system that can access a calendar through a company's intranet. Most of the employees of that company can access who's doing what, when, and with what skill sets. A project manager at another end of the company may need those skill sets when a person is scheduled to complete his or her current project. Being able to manage the skills and time of employees efficiently makes for a more competitive body of knowledge."

A company using this capability designed by SenseNet can also observe when an employee is sick by noting the occasion and later reconciling it against the amount of time the employee has accrued in sick days thus far. In addition, with this system, one can view by date to see who's doing what, or view the employee roster by skill set to see what abilities are available when and where, thus allowing for seamless scheduling. Any manager can see the availability of another person, or even an entire department, for a seminar or meeting on any given afternoon. I call this rapid deployment of *ad hoc workgroups*, whereby a project manager can easily configure a group of people to execute a project. It's sort of like time-sharing was in the old days, when you had to plan access to the much-in-demand mainframe computer. The difference now is that people are time-sharing on-staff brain power.

One of the dualities of the Net is that it performs a type of leveling effect on any given labor market. If the cost of writers in New York City is prohibitive, it can afford an opportunity for both the buyer and vendor of that service. If a writer lives in Plano, Texas, where the cost of living is much lower than New York City or Los Angeles, it becomes feasible for a contractor (or editor, in this case) to farm the work out to the writer in Plano, instead of to someone in New York.

More than likely, you're starting to read about telecommuting, if you haven't already. The Internet already does and will continue to play a substantial role in this major shift of workplace habits. I suggest you check out the Telecommuting Guide at http://www.svi.org/projects/TCOMMUTE/TCGUIDE/index.html (see Figure 2.5). This guide was one of the first sites devoted to this trend. Published first in October 1994, it has been updated with anecdotal and interesting success stories you can replicate in your own firm or field. Additional resources on telecommuting can be found at www.svi.org/PROJECTS/TCOMMUTE/webguide/ (Smart Valley Inc.'s Online Telecommuting Resources).

Outsourcing on the Internet

Once your company has embraced the idea of farming work out on the Net, you will most likely find yourself asking the next logical question: "Is it necessary to have this person on staff at all?" In many cases, you will indeed need and want that person on staff, for reasons of consistency, security, workload, and so on. If it's possible to stay open to the idea of simply outsourcing a function (which you may already be doing locally), then why not consider doing so over the Net? Again, the savings can be substantial. You may or may not pay a bit more for the luxury of having just-in-time help, but that is often easily offset by the downtime you have when there is no work for your staff who you usually would be paying. There you are, the clock is ticking, you have no work for them at the moment, and they're

Figure 2.5 The Telecommuting Guide is a great resource to consult if you're looking into this new trend.

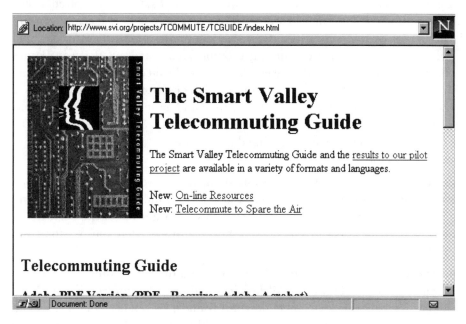

having a good old time buying "hotel art" in some auction site on the Net. Not only are those employees' job security at risk, but the overall health and welfare of your unit or company is at risk as well.

Another word of caution: If you're looking for someone to work with you on an ongoing project, it is advisable to first meet that person, or at least figure out if you both are temperamentally suited for each other. You can use the Kiersey Temperament Sorter at http://keirsey.com/cgi-bin/keirsey/newkts.cgi for this purpose, although be advised that it is not the be-all and end-all of "psychological" testing materials. People are indeed more complicated than a few simplified categories of reactions, but this can give you a general idea of how you might interact at a distance. Remember that email/Net interactions can be far different and more difficult than face-to-face ones. Think of how some Usenet newsgroup "flame wars" can start so easily over one emphasized word in a posting that in a letter or oral communication would have meant nothing at all. Interaction using the Net is a new medium, with its own pitfalls and advantages, and only time and experience will show you the differences.

In a small business especially, you will want to work with someone who has skills you don't have. This way, the most number of skill sets are covered by the fewest number of people. However, people with different skill sets are often drawn to those pursuits based on their character. The point here is to make sure you can work with someone who may well be your exact opposite in nature, attitudes, and values. I've been in a couple of working relationships that went down in flames solely because of core value differences that weren't fleshed out at the beginning. In addition, make sure that roles, expectations, job descriptions, communications, and so forth are spelled out clearly ahead of time and are continually refreshed as necessary, even more so than in an in-office relationship. The same goes for any offsite employees, if you are a manager handling contractors, as noted in the previous section of this chapter.

Also keep in mind that you will want to check out your potential partner's background via a résumé and references, and keep in mind that the price you end up paying may be closer to the usual contract costs in order to get the best. Using the Internet is not necessarily cheap. You indeed can get what you pay for, from both ends of the spectrum.

Internet teamwork is like dating: both sides tend to present their best sides at first. Similarly, the medium of email leaves much open for interpretation. Even though I get scoffed at by my Net-cognoscenti friends, I often use emoticons when writing email. This is to ensure the other side will know what I meant to say, since there isn't a common environment and they can't see my facial expressions or hear the tone of my voice.

Knowledge Cottage Labor

In the pre-Industrial Revolution days, work was farmed out to people's homes, where they had looms, spinning wheels, and cobbler benches that were used to turn out the products. It was the Industrial Age that centralized the workplace. Now, in the Information Age, we are shifting back again the other way; only this time, instead of looms, spinning wheels, and cobbler benches, we have computers, modems, faxes, and printers.

It doesn't matter if you're farming out programming, spreadsheet analysis, copyrighting, or graphics, it's all information that is more easily transported than actually moving you, your vendors, or your employees. If a vendor is working out of a home or small office, he or she often incurs all the costs of hardware, software, Internet connection, phone, electricity, and so on. While this flat-out Darwinian marketplace can be brutal on small firms and independents, many prefer it because their income is diversified across a number of clients and subsequent revenue streams. I remember I was once let go from an advertising agency because some "bean counter" in London said the New York office had to cut back 40 people. One of the most stressful aspects of employment is not having control over your circumstances.

Dianna Husum, one of my editors for *Web Digest For Marketers*, lives in San Diego. We have worked together for years, and it was only recently that we actually met in person. It was a funny encounter, having worked so closely together with someone, only to meet for the first time. We are not the only ones experiencing this "work-together-and-meet-later" phenomenon. It's happening everywhere. Keep an eye out for pontifical articles discussing how this phenomenon will alter social patterns in our society. The irony is that Nancy C. Hanger, my developmental editor, with whom I worked closely on this very book, lives and works in New Hampshire. No, we've never met. How did we connect? Through a mutual colleague, Daniel P. Dern. How do I know Daniel? Through the Internet.

Relocating People

If you're looking to relocate a person, department, or even yourself, you can do a great amount of advance work on the Net. Take a look at the Multiple Listing Service's (MLS) listings of the Central Region of Oregon at http://www .bendor.com/real_estate. I'm not suggesting that you can relocate people only to Oregon, of course. What I am pointing to is the fact that those particular services reflect a general trend. With some of the MLSs opening up to the general public, it must be that major shifts are affecting this industry as well. Take advantage of it as much as possible. The best time to access local real estate markets on the Web is before you even decide to enter that market. Real estate availability should be one of the contributing factors to making a decision on where to move.

 Use InfoSpace's City Guide lookup (http://in-132.infospace.com/ mytown/mytown2.htm) to find out demographic information about an area you are thinking of moving to before you go. Be sure to check the area listings for businesses, shopping, weather, local government information, town facilities, and so forth while you're there. MapQuest also has a section called MoveQuest (http://www.movequest.com) to help you plan your move, too, including school information and home buyers' MLS listings, plus more (see Figure 2.6).

Figure 2.6 Before you move there, check out a neighborhood on the Net with MoveQuest.

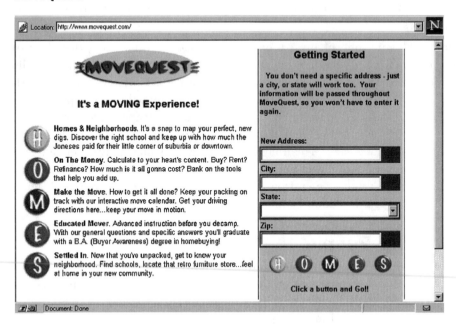

HomeWEB (http://www.homeweb.com) offers a relocation services directory, home search services, relocation managers, and professional real estate listings. If you're going to put some of your employees up on a temporary basis in a given city's rental units, you should check out Rent Net at http://www.rent.net. If you're in the market for commercial real estate, check out RealBid (http://www.realbid.com). It offers companies the opportunity to place a bid online for commercial real estate. One of my clients, Cushman & Wakefield, is the handling broker.

Finally, there is the Homebuyer's Fair (http://homefair.com/home/), which provides nearly everything you or your employee needs in order to plan a relocation. One of the tools available on this site is the "relocation wizard," which helps you map out a very specific timeline of what to do when: when to start packing what to pack, when to fill out change-of-address forms, and so on. If you are a compulsive list maker, you'll love this function.

Another tool found at the Homebuyer's Fair is the salary calculator, which will tell you if you or your employee's salary is competitive with the local job market. Wouldn't it be terrible to go to the trouble of moving new employees, only to find out they are underpaid compared to the rest of their ilk in that locale? They could relocate with you, then realize their mistake, and switch jobs shortly thereafter. With this tool, you start by choosing your origin and destination. Canada and other non-U.S. countries are the last two options in each list. On the next screen, you will be able to choose specific cities and countries to move to. The moving calculator lets you determine approximately how much your move will cost by asking how many furnished rooms you are moving, your point of origination, and your destination. Finally, with the relocation crime lab, you can even get an idea of how your current city stacks up against the city you are moving to, in terms of the crime density.

Distance Training/Learning

If you have to train a widely distributed group of employees, it can turn into a costly proposition, since you have to bring them to a central location, house, feed and, of course, teach them. Many companies use intranets to distribute educational materials across an enterprise. Distance learning/training can be most easily implemented over corporate intranets, as the actual bandwidth is apt to be greater and, therefore, the Net connection rates much faster. This will be especially beneficial if there are video components in the curriculum. A sales force can also be trained by way of extranets (an extranet allows a company to give restricted access to users around the world, often with the use of a password). Here again, the knowledge itself is more easily distributed than the people to whom you wish to distribute this knowledge.

The American Society of Training and Development did a study on corporate training in 1996. It found that companies offering Internet and network-based distance training rose from 12 percent in 1994 to 33 percent in 1995 and finally to 53 percent in 1996. According to the MASIE Center (http://www.techlearn.com/release5), a training and technology research group located in Saratoga Springs, New York, 82 percent of companies polled are planning on utilizing some form of distance learning, while only 15 percent of those groups polled have actually selected the tools they'll use to carry out this task. This indicates a huge opportunity for the development of such tools. Look for this industry to mushroom in the very near future, if it hasn't already by the time you read this. Who knows, it might even get more attention in the media than Java!

International Data Corporation (IDC), a global consulting and research firm, has reported that by the year 2000, $1.75 billion will be spent on distance learning and training. With that much being spent, imagine how much will be saved in gas, time, insurance, and so on. "Competitors, tools, and technology are emerging and rapidly defining the look of training and learning via the Web," said Ellen Julian, a research manager at IDC, in a recent press release. "The potential of this new delivery system for both IT- and non-IT-related training is enormous; in particular, the ability to provide tools that enable individuals to learn as needed means a giant leap forward for the cause of just-in-time, continuous learning in the workplace . . . Presently, some fine information technology training Web sites are up and running, but there is work to be done in the development of full-service Web sites with varied, desirable features. The key for suppliers who plan to offer training over the Web is to make it possible for customers to tailor the site for their individual learning needs."

Oracle's Oracle Learning Architecture (OLA) offers developers a Web-based training environment in which they can take courses at their own pace, while keeping up with vendor technologies. The OLA Library holds over 75 training modules. Topics range from Oracle 7 Server-based administration to writing KORN shell scripts. Students, and their employers, are able to create their own curriculum, and course offerings are available in numerous languages.

Southwestern Bell uses its SBC Town, an intranet that employs a bevy of technologies to train its technicians by using Virtual Reality Mark-Up Language (VRML) modeling (3D models) and Java applications, along with the Web. Designed by EDS (Electronic Data Systems), this extraordinary system is called dVISE. The implementation of the project started in early 1997.

Here's how it works: A technician receives a simulated service request that outlines the difficulty level. She then grabs her virtual toolbox and "drives" to the physical location with her mouse. Everything behaves as it does in the real world. A technician opens a terminal box on the screen by clicking on it and is presented with an array of different actions that can ameliorate the problem. Then the technician sends test tones through various terminals to see where the line break is. The system faithfully represents the sounds on the computer the way they sound in the real world. If that technician comes down from the virtual telephone pole without paying attention, she's apt to be run over by a virtual car! Once the technician thinks she's found the fault, she enters the diagnosis into the system to see if she is in fact correct. Throughout this process, the technician is being tracked, so she can later be evaluated on how quickly or how slowly she solved the problem and the accuracy of her results. This is a vivid example of online learning in that it loosely models reality.

Now let's take an example that isn't from a high-tech company. The Illinois Association of Realtors is making its courses available over the Net to its 36,000 members. Instead of having to take a day off from work to travel across the state to take a course in person, the broker can simply take the course at his or her own convenience. A broker is also able to communicate with instructors and other brokers through a number of different channels, either by time delay or via email. The "university" site is constructed and maintained by a company called Real Education at http://www.realeducation.com.

Although most corporate distance training and learning programs tend to be located behind intranets and therefore not viewable on the open Internet, it is useful to take a look at what some colleges and universities are currently doing in this field. Duke University, among many others, now offers a full-fledged MBA program online (http://fuqua.duke.edu/programs/gemba/index.htm). You must have a minimum of eight years' business experience and already be working for a company that is presumably picking up your tuition. The program takes 19 months to complete and is available in the Americas, Europe, and Asia. A sampling of courses for the North America module includes Decision Models, Managerial Effectiveness for the Global Executive, and International Financial Statement Analysis.

For an example of a more mass-appeal distance learning model, check out Ziff-Davis' "Learn-It Online" (http://learnitonline.com). For an annual subscription rate of $29.95, a subscriber can gain access to tutorials for popular desktop software programs, such as Microsoft Office. The current catalog offers 14 courses. Each course runs about 10 to 20 minutes and covers about 15 applications. Students can design their own study tracks with the help of a skills assessment feature.

Shrink Rap

Not all learning comes out of a book, or from the mouth of a professor, for that matter. Some types of knowledge are born out of realization. That realization may come from experience or possibly therapy. At the time of writing, online therapy has just turned the corner into reality. Wilson Banwell offers Shrink Rap, which is led by Dr. Jim Ricks (http://www.wilsonbanwell.com/shrinkrap.htm). Shrink Rap offers free, live, weekly chats with leaders in the mental health field. All sessions are provided by doctoral-level licensed clinical psychologists or psychiatrists with demonstrated experience in the area of treatment. The online chats are merged with a simultaneous call-in radio show. This will enable both speakers and listeners (or online lurkers) to access the content from two different media at the same time.

Also on the Wilson Banwell site is PROACT. This area offers services such as confidential career assessment, therapy for entire organizations going through personnel crises, and personal therapy sessions on self-esteem and eating disorders. One must wonder if sessions addressing online addictions are coming soon.

Just as the Internet is having a profound effect on workers, companies, students, and the population at large, expect that every aspect of human resources will somehow be affected by the Internet, either centrally or peripherally. Many of those trends have been identified and discussed in this chapter. Many more will emerge as the Internet seeps deeper and deeper into the fabric of our lives and beyond.

Resource Center

E.span   **http://www.espan.com**

People searching for jobs as well as those looking to fill jobs should visit E.span. This site houses one of the largest employment search and candidate databases around, and the programming behind E.span makes its searches fast and precise. Job candidates can submit résumés, register for email notification of new job listings, and conduct thorough searches of available positions. E.span has also simplified things for the individual charged with finding the right candidate. The site's Model Employment Ads houses a collection of more than 200 professionally written recruiting ads designed for the Internet: Recruiters simply adapt the ads to fit their needs. Recruiters can also tap into Descriptions Now!, which is a service that provides ADA-compliant, professional job descriptions online. Clients choose from thousands of job descriptions, answer a few questions, and are rewarded with a customized, detailed job description within minutes.

CareerCast   **http://www.careercast.com**

This site offers a single point of access for quick and thorough searches of several Web- and Usenet-based resources for job listings. CareerCast uses a robot to update its own database each time a job listing or résumé is posted to corporate or other Web sites. The CareerCast site is very spare—offering only the search fields and a résumé submission form—and assumes a certain level of sophistication on the part of the user. Information about CareerCast's services is not available on the Web site; however, the persistent will find email links that provide additional sales and service contacts. According to a press release dated 10/22/97, CareerCast automatically emails résumés from qualified candidates to employers or notifies candidates via email when jobs fitting their criteria are posted.

International Assessment Network   **http://www.assessment.com**

International Assessment Network, Inc. (IAN) offers a nice blend of free resources and paid services for individuals and human resource professionals. Particularly helpful is a searchable database of more than 12,000 job descriptions compiled from the Department of Labor's *Dictionary of Occupational Titles.*

The Top 100 Electronic Recruiters   http://www.interbiznet.com/eeri

This is the first place to stop when searching for a job or trying to fill a position. A metasite for electronic recruiting, the Top 100 Electronic Recruiters does a nice job of addressing three different audiences: job seekers, human resources managers, and third-party recruiters. Of particular interest is a comparison price list for popular online recruiting services and reviews of tools and resources for all three audience groups.

ZDNet University   http://www.zdu.com

While lots of people talk about the amazing long-distance learning potential the Web offers, Ziff-Davis has quietly built its own impressive online "university." For a mere $4.95 a month, the virtual student can choose any number of Internet or computer classes from over 50 offerings taught by industry experts and book authors. Whether you need to brush up on C++, implement an intranet, or learn to do some online marketing, ZDU has the answers, plus a chance to meet and mingle with your fellow students in the Student Union or Resource Library. Traditional message board "teaching" has been boosted by the use of live, online classes using Virtual Places chat technology in the site's online chat area (http://www.zdnet.com/cc/chat.html).

MINING THE INTERNET
for All It's Worth

You are very lucky. Why? Because so many people and companies want your attention to such a great extent that they're willing to give you valuable information for free that you once paid dearly for, or at least mark down the price to what was unimaginable just a few years ago. And guess what? You will continue to get even luckier. In an effort to keep up with the increasing competition for your attention, those companies will continuously need to offer their constituents higher-quality information. How lucky you will be is determined by your ability to exploit this happy circumstance. In these pages, I will share with you some of the most delectable offerings out there. In addition, I will share with you the tricks of the trade to get what you want.

If the beloved American monologist Will Rogers were alive today, he might say the following about the Internet: "You know they're telling the truth when they say there are over 100 million Web pages on the Internet because when you do a search for something, you get 95 million of them back." Here you'll discover how to separate the wheat from the chaff and learn how to whittle down what seems like millions of search results to a meaningful few that deserve your attention and focus. Maybe you're not looking for a piece of information that's on the Net, but rather an answer to a question. I'll show you some places where you can get those questions answered.

Information is like oil. You have to know how and where to drill for it. That knowledge gives you two competitive advantages: First, if your cost of gathering information is lower, you can run smarter and leaner than your competitor. Second, unearthing information your competitor doesn't know about opens up doors of opportunity that he or she can't even perceive. Imagine if your competition didn't use computers today. He wouldn't be a competitor very long, would he? The same is quickly becoming true for finding and using information on the Internet. If you can't find information quickly and easily, you will not be a competitor in your field, whether that information is statistics, government regulations, market research, or customer feedback. If you get to those nuggets of knowledge first, you're that much ahead of everyone else. After reading this chapter, you'll be armed with information about:

- Search strategies
- Push
- Boolean searches
- Filtering agents
- Sweet spots for information
- Soliciting customer input
- Selected sites to see

Search Strategy

Focus: It's what you need to stay on mission. Before you dash off, randomly looking for what you want, think of how you might filter out the "noise" that can easily distract you from finding the gold. First, think of a few keywords that might succinctly express what you are looking for. Take all the articles, such as "the" and "a," out of your search phrase. Remember to remove all of the conjunctions, such as "and" and "or." Now, look at what remains. Try putting that phrase in the search engine of your choice and see if it narrows the field a bit. It should. If it narrows it too much, which I doubt, try inserting other descriptive words that could conceivably be found on the Web pages or newsgroup archives you're trying to unearth.

Since no one search engine has a complete database of the entire Web, you should try this with a few different search engines. Even if there was such a thing, it wouldn't be completely up to date, since Web pages and newsgroups change daily.

The next thing I want you to do is take that search phrase you've created and go to AltaVista at http://altavista.digital.com. Look for the Advanced button on the homepage and click on it. There you will find one of the most useful and under-utilized tools of the Internet (see Figure 3.1). Paste your search phrase in the text field and put quotes around it. By doing this, you ensure that those words within your search phrase will appear within 10 words of each other on the pages AltaVista digs up for you. This should help you zero in pretty fast on what you're

Figure 3.1 AltaVista Advanced is the most sophisticated search tool for searching the World Wide Web.

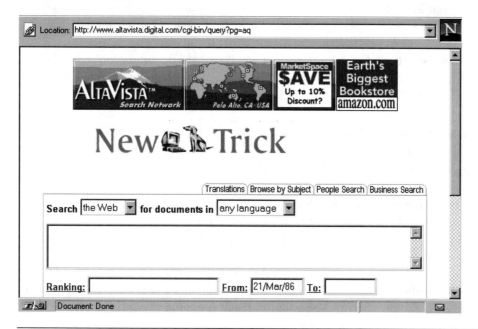

looking for. Even if you still get back 23,000 pages, click on the Refine button and you'll then be able to easily toggle on and off various words that AltaVista found on the sites returned. Those words will indicate to you whether that segment of the search is either on or off track. Tell AltaVista to get rid of those that are off track, and then press Search again. Bingo! You've got a much finer grain of a search this time. If it's still too large and you wish to refine it some more, you can always do so.

That Refine feature is essentially a user-friendly way of letting you write *Boolean search strings*, without even realizing it. To get an idea of the extended Boolean search phrase that AltaVista wrote for you based on your refinements, press the Back button and look at the text field in which you entered your original search phrase in quotes. You'll see that it's much longer and more complex. By comparing that much-extended search phrase to the refinements you checked off, you'll begin to get an idea of what an advanced Boolean search phrase looks like and what you would have had to write yourself in order to get the same results.

If you've hit pay dirt, then save the actual results as a document to your hard drive. This way, you don't have to redo the entire search the next time you're looking for the same thing, or if you can't finish your search in one sitting. Remember, saving that Web page of the search results is like saving a snapshot of a horse race: The results you get tomorrow may well be different than the results you got today. If you're going to come back to that same search in a few minutes, hours, or maybe even days, you will probably get similar results. If you wait weeks or beyond, you'll probably want to conduct a fresh scan of what's out there, unless you're looking for footprints of pterodactyls etched in stone. Even those have a tendency of moving around on the Net.

> **Boolean search strings.** Searches based on Boolean programming logic. Boolean logic is based on two-valued logic, which has two results (True or False) and three values (AND, OR, and NOT).

The search capacity of the AltaVista Advanced search tool is so large, you could write a book on it; as a matter of fact, someone already has. Richard Seltzer penned a 274-page book on neat things one can do with AltaVista called *The AltaVista Search Revolution: How to Find Anything on the Internet* (McGraw Hill, 1998). If you choose not to read the book, at least take a few minutes to look at the help file in the Advanced section of the Web site. Make sure you're in the Advanced section, as the help file for the AltaVista Simple Search engine is considerably different and much less comprehensive.

Now, take the same search phrase AltaVista Advanced wrote for you and go to HotBot (http://www.hotbot.com). In addition to mining a different database, it also provides different search tools. For example, you can conduct a search and then search the search results. You may wish to try several different search engines, all using the same phrase, and compare the results.

Search Engines versus Directories

Most of the major search engines have their own databases, created by *spiders* or *crawlers* that go out on the Web periodically (varying from engine to engine, meaning some engines are more up to date than others), updating and adding information. Another type of engine is a *directory*, such as Yahoo! In this type of database, the information is created and maintained by humans. Directories are available in a strictly browsable format, rather like a library's vertical card file, where traditional search engines can be searched only by keywords. Finally, there is the hybrid search engine/directory, which has become more and more popular. Excite's WebCrawler—categorizing its database, as well as allowing for searches—was one of the first and is still perhaps the most complete hybrid. InfoSeek's search engine is separate from its directory, which has its own searchable catalog. InfoSeek has a database for general searches. Finally, *Wired*'s HotBot will search the entire Web or center in on particular areas, such as the Usenet, news services, people, classified ads, or shareware, using its spider-created database or portions thereof.

Doing a Metasearch

Another way you can search is to use the metasearch engines. A metasearch engine searches other search engines. For example, you can search AltaVista, Lycos, WebCrawler, Yahoo!, and others by simply going to CNET's http://www .search.com. While you'll get a snapshot all at once of what each engine has on your search subject, it can be pretty huge, like the size of Wyoming. Additionally, search.com can't perform advanced searches on each of the search engines, only one big simple search on one engine at a time. This may be all you need or want. If you are looking to get a very specific piece of information in your crosshairs, it's going to be pretty hard if your gun sight is as large as all outdoors. You can also try searching *all* of the major search engines at the same time (simple searches only) at Cyber 411 (http://www.cyber411.com), which can speed things up for you, but can also be overwhelming if your search isn't highly limited in scope.

Each search engine offers different "slices" of the Web and usually Usenet newsgroup postings as well. I personally use AltaVista, HotBot, and WebCrawler, in that order. You may ask, "Why not Yahoo!?" Well, Yahoo!'s Web searches use other engines, not one of its own. Remember, it's a directory, not a search engine. AltaVista is the first on the list of Yahoo!'s search engines, but I've already been there and done that. However, I do like Yahoo! for its indexed directory. When I don't know exactly what I am looking for, I like to browse Yahoo! by category to see what attracts me. I also tend to use it when my searches come up dry.

When you don't know the name of the site or source you're looking for, attempt a *ricochet search*, where you find a site that points to other sites of the ilk you're looking for. This tactic was used often for researching this very book. For example, when Becky Rich, who did a great deal of research for me, went looking for examples of sites that were holding promotions or events for Chapter 7, "Online Events, Promotions, and Attractions: How to Make a 'Scene' and Draw Them In," she first located promotions on a site-by-site basis. This was time consuming and tedious. Furthermore, the nature of promotions is that they're time sensitive, so they may or may not have made it into a search engine during the time frame in which she was searching. She then triangulated by locating sites whose sole mission is to keep track of new promotional campaigns on the Net. It was a bonus, as each of those sites had comprehensive category breakdowns of contests, while others offered search engines that specifically looked for contests according to chosen parameters. At Chase Online, we refer to these category- and function-specific sites as *link piles*. This isn't exactly a high-tech-sounding term, but it is a descriptive one nonetheless.

I can remember another instance in which a reporter asked me where I uncovered a particular statistic. The statistic in question was that a typical business-to-business phone sales call can cost between $250 and $500. To be honest, I had forgotten where I read this. I asked my colleague, Dianna Husum, to investigate and find the source. Diana used a search string of "$500 sales call" and finally found it was attributed to Booz-Allen Hamilton. However, it wasn't even on the Booz-Allen Hamilton site! It was found as a quote on an unrelated site, where someone was using it as a support point, similar to my own usage of the quote.

 TIP Always verify information you find on the Net using a *primary* source. In other words, don't ever take someone else's word for it. If you find a page of government statistics, go to the government page and confirm those numbers *there*.

From there, I called Booz-Allen Hamilton, had it confirmed, and then told the reporter. The point here is that whether you're looking for a site or a specific piece of information to be corroborated, you won't always get it first from the horse's mouth. Instead, you might get it from an intermediary source, such as a link pile or a quote from an unrelated site using the information for its own purposes.

 TIP Know when to get off the Net. Sometimes it's just faster to pick up the phone and call the PR department of a company for information. A colleague of mine was once looking for the name of the European CEO of a company. After having difficulty finding it on the Net, she called the U.S. counterpart and had the answer in less than five minutes.

Hit a Bull's Eye with a Boolean Search

Until now, Boolean searches were mostly found in the domain of librarians; in fact, many of the original Internet publications were aimed at librarians. In this age in which we're constantly filtering information, these skills are becoming more and more useful to a greater number of people. You can get much more out of many databases if you know some basic Boolean techniques. Although search engines such as AltaVista make it so you don't really need to know how to construct a Boolean search string yourself, it's a good idea to know how to anyway.

> **TIP**
>
> AltaVista and some of the other major search engines already have AND as a Boolean search parameter built into their Simple searches. Be sure to use the + (plus sign) when in Simple mode to automatically get a Boolean AND query. If you put quote marks around your query, you also narrow the search to those verbatim words (in other words, it will search for exactly what you type in— no more, no less. So, "rubber chicken" will give you Web pages that contain those exact words. Remember to leave off the plural "s" if you want a better list of hits: "rubber chicken" will also give you pages that say "rubber chickens.")

Basic Boolean search parameters follow the two-valued logic system, where there are only two answers to any query: True or False. The query can use three parameters, or values, in order to reach an answer: OR, AND, and NOT. OR means both or either can be included in an answer. AND means that both values must be included in an answer. NOT excludes a certain parameter from the answer, narrowing it even further. The following list shows typical Boolean search parameters using both two and three values. For example, if you wanted to find quality rubber chickens online, you could set up a query string as follows:

- "rubber AND chicken" (AND statement, which would yield anything with both rubber and chicken in the text)

- "rubber OR chicken" (OR statement, which would yield either just rubber or just chicken in the text)

- "rubber AND chicken NOT cheap" (NOT statement, which excludes anything including the word "cheap" in the text, yielding, we hope, a quality rubber chicken Web site for your needs)

Each search engine on the Web has a slightly different syntax for wording personally created Boolean strings, using different symbols to represent the three values. Be sure to check the help file of the Advanced section of any search engine before you try to create a Boolean search statement of your own.

> **TIP**
>
> Keep your search skills tuned by subscribing to the Search Skill of the Day list at http://www.tipworld.com.

Filtering Agents

Instead of going to the search engines and letting your fingers do the tapping, you can have *agents* scan the Net for you. You tell these agents what you want to see. They, in turn, scan the newswire services or the Web itself for documents that contain those words most important to you. These agents can deliver the documents to you via email or on the Web.

According to the preferences you set up, NewsHound (http://www.newshound .com), Knight-Ridder's news and customized information service, scans newspapers and wire services, such as Reuters, Knight-Ridder Tribune Business Wires, and the Associated Press. Once it finds relevant articles, you can choose to have them emailed to you, or you can view them yourself at NewsHound's Web site. There is a monthly or annual subscription fee, and you can test the usability of this service with a 30-day free trial.

My Yahoo! (http://edit.my.yahoo.com/config/login) is essentially a way for users to create listings of favorite sites, Yahoo! categories, and keyword searches. There are also areas for custom news, quotes, sports, and contacts, plus the FireFly service (see more about FireFly in Chapter 6, "Retail: Setting Up Shop on the Net"). For the novice Net user or Yahoo! devotee, it's a way to keep information and news nicely organized in a familiar, friendly interface.

My Excite Channel (http://nt.excite.com) is best described as a digital clipping service (see Figure 3.2). The Excite NewsTracker service monitors material published by more than 300 digital news sources and packages them by topic, which the user can then modify, pick, and choose, to create an individualized daily news folder, available on its Web site when you surf to it.

Individual Inc. NewsPage (http://www.individual.com/services/newspage/ newspage.htm) is an online news service providing access to categorized news stories from 19 different industries. NewsPage claims more than 25,000 pages refreshed daily. There is a charge for usage, and there are premium sources it will search as well, but those will cost you more on a pay-as-you-go basis.

CRAYON (the acronym for Create Your Own Newspaper) at http://crayon.net is another service that assists users in navigating the wealth of Web-based news sources. Users build personalized newspaper editions using sources linked by CRAYON. Users can select either a frames or nonframes environment and can decide whether they want others to view their personal editions. The frames version comprises a personalized navigation bar that runs down the left margin of the page, a personalized masthead running across the top of the page, and a large window for viewing the news pages.

Figure 3.2 Excite's NewsTracker presents articles of interest to you based on preferences you give it.

Sweet Spots for Information

While you're quite apt to find the "Top 100 Sex Sites on the Net" or the "Top 100 Sport Sites on the Net," I've yet to find the "Top 100 Databases on the Net." In this section, I want to draw your attention not only to free databases that will be valuable to you, but also to other sites that frequently post new information. Let's start with databases.

Databases

Aside from search engines, which are essentially searchable databases of Web pages and Usenet postings, you can search for a myriad of more specific information elsewhere.

For example, take Trade Show Central at http://tscentral.com. You used to have to pay hundreds of dollars for a book that listed trade shows, events, and conferences; now you can gain free access to similar information. However, on the Net there is a new added value because this information is updated daily with 3000 new events (see Figure 3.3).

Figure 3.3 Trade Show Central's database offers over 3000 conferences, meetings, and events.

Every 10 years, the Census Department collects demographic data on the United States. Check out the Census Lookup Service (http://cedr.lbl.gov/cdrom /doc/lookup_doc.html), which allows free searches of U.S. census data and reports. This is your consummate location for U.S. demographic, social, and economic statistics. Nice touches include an email alerting service to keep users on top of new releases, a thematic mapping system that allows you to create statistical maps on the fly, and other data extraction and visualization tools.

SalesLeadsUSA (http://www.lookupusa.com) offers a cheap and efficient means of finding information on just about any U.S. company, from its phone number and address (free) to a more in-depth profile at a cost of $3. Mailing lists, business credit services, and similar products are also available for a fee.

AT1 (http://www.at1.com/index.html) lets you simultaneously search several databases of publications via a single query. Databases covered by the free service include the *Congressional Quarterly*, *Complete Drug Reference*, *Consumer Reports*, Court TV, *Communications Today*, Charles Schwab, *Help Wanted USA*, Hoovers Business Resource, and more.

IBM Patent Server (http://patent.womplex.ibm.com) allows you to search over 26 years' worth of U.S. Patent & Trademark Office patent descriptions, as well as the last 23 years of images. Care has been taken to make the tedious job of patent research and status fast and easy. The server supports simple keyword, phrase, and patent number services, as well as field searches by title, abstract, all claims, assignees, inventor, and attorney/agent. Results are bidirectionally hyperlinked so that you can follow the creation chain. A complete copy of a patent can be ordered online for a nominal fee, delivered by fax or snail mail. (Note: *Current*, in-process, patent information is not available through this service.)

SAEGIS (http://www.thomson-thomson.com) Trademark is a collection of 16 international trademark databases featuring two powerful search engines: custom searching and AutoQuery (see Figure 3.4). Custom searching allows users to quickly conduct sophisticated trademark searches by name, owner, design, or other fields found in a trademark record. AutoQuery defines the best possible trademark search strategy, producing results that only the most experienced trademark researchers would have previously found. SAEGIS charges 25 cents per hit on trademark searches, but offers several valuable free services. The SAEGIS Trademark Alert and Visual Gazettes enable you to search the most recent four weeks of pending U.S. Federal Trademarks and trademark information published in the USPTO's *Official Gazette*. The SAEGIS reference library allows you access to a number of Thomson & Thomson publication sites, such as the TRADE-MARKSCAN *Design Code Manual* and the *International Guide to Trademarks*, as well as ample links to intellectual property resources on the Web.

Stanford University Copyright and Fair Use Site (http://fairuse.stanford.edu) has a fully searchable location devoted to statutes, cases, issues, and other resources for copyright law.

The Security and Exchange Commission (SEC) FreeEdgar Database (http://freeedgar.com) offers free, unlimited access to fundamental financial data as it is released to the SEC. Corporate financial reports created from EDGAR filings, downloadable Excel spreadsheets of all SEC filings, and financial analysis and reference resources are a mere mouse-click away. Be sure to review http://beta.freeedgar.com for the site's newest tools—which is an excellent way to memorably house and track your site's newest offerings as well.

Creating Your Own Database Gold Mine

Over the years, I myself have used the Net to create a database of value. *Web Digest For Marketers* (*WDFM*) has a list of over 12,000 subscribers. As any publisher will tell you, that list is one of the most valuable and measurable assets to a publication. To me, the list is much more than just a pile of email addresses. In order to become a subscriber,

Figure 3.4 SAEGIS is a collection of 16 international trademark databases.

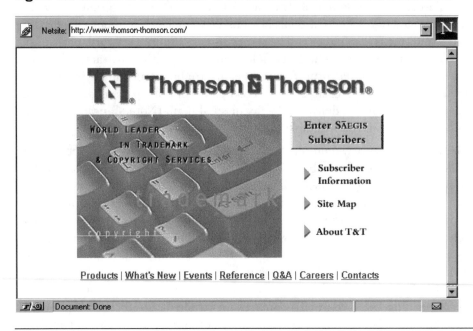

the surfer must fill out a brief form telling me his or her name, the company he or she works for, business title, email address, and where he or she heard about *WDFM*. This is valuable information. It's a swap of one kind of value for another.

I've been mining the *WDFM* database for years now. I look up companies, publications, EVPs—you name it. I even used the database to help gather examples and information for this book. I find it astonishing that so many companies go to the bother and expense to promote a Web site and then just let the surfers get away. Maybe they go as far as to capture their email addresses, but do nothing more. The higher the quality of content you provide, the more license you have to ask for more information to build this all-important asset. In addition to mining this database for my own purposes, it also comes in very handy when selling ad space. Instead of telling potential sponsors of *WDFM* that I have 12,000+ subscribers but have no idea who they are, I can say instead that I've got 27 VPs at Microsoft, 14 at 3M, and so on. This is not a theoretical asset. It's real money on the line . . . or should I say, real money online?

Free Advice

The old adage says that free advice is worth what you pay for it. The Internet is changing that theory. There are many high-powered consultancies, law firms, accountants, and a vast array of other professionals who are willing to entertain a query from you, in the hopes of turning you into an ongoing client. You see, the answer to one question usually prompts another one. Don't count on these professionals to endlessly answer all of them. It's a good idea to have one well-thought-out question when approaching sites such as these.

This approach reminds me of a technique practiced many years ago by a chiropractor. When he first came to this country, he used to promote his practice by going into shoe stores. While the patrons were waiting for the salesman to bring them their shoes, he would offer to adjust the bones in that patron's foot. When the patron liked what she felt, she would ask him to do the other foot. At this point, he presented his business card. This is exactly what's happening today on the Net. Professionals will help you part of the way, but do expect to turn you into a client if you want further attention.

Arent Fox (Arent Fox Kitner Plotkin & Kahn, Attorneys at Law, http://www .arentfox.com) specializes in technology and information law, and its site is a good starting point for Internet-specific legal information gathering. On this Web site, you can actually email a question to the various attorneys specializing in different areas represented by the firm. There's also a concise look at the legal considerations involved in conducting contests and sweepstakes on the Internet. Online discussion forums on advertising, contests, telecommunications, and more allow participants to explore legal issues and solutions. Browsers can also cut to the chase and email queries to the firm, which is surely an excellent lead generator.

With Arthur Andersen's Interactive Tools (http://www.arthurandersen.com/ firmwide/itools.htm), you can conduct an online assessment of your company and see how it compares to other businesses. Simply fill out an online, multiple-choice questionnaire, which should take only about five to seven minutes, and your answers will instantly be compared to replies of 1000 other small and midsized business owners and executives in a similar mail-in survey. You can also take part in online discussions and systems auditing. At the time of writing, the site offers a function allowing you to compare how your business manages travel expenses to what Arthur Andersen feels are the "Global Best Practices" of managing these expenses.

At Cushman & Wakefield's Ask C&W (http://www.cushwake.com/chall/index .htm), you can submit a question about commercial real estate valuations via email. Further information is available about whether the particular commercial real estate market in which you are interested is going up or down in value.

Court TV (http://www.courttv.com/legalhelp) gives you free legal advice on a multitude of subjects, such as the legal dilemmas one faces when getting older, small business legal information, and family issues, such as divorce and prenuptial agreements. Looking for a new lawyer? Court TV will help you find one according to the preferences you set up. You can even link to QuickForms, a service that provides agreements and policies for many of the issues we face on a day-to-day basis in the business world, such as running a company email system or purchasing hardware. Use one of their already-made documents or draft a new one yourself.

Outstanding Free Content

Another way for professional services to vie for your attention is to put up on their sites *whitepapers* that contain extraordinary amounts of well-considered and well-researched content. It is not easy to know or predict when and where these reports will go up, unless you subscribe to one of the agents mentioned earlier. Hopefully, they'll pick up a news story or press release that contains keywords that match the ones you were looking for. If these high-value whitepapers are indigenous to your industry, then your trade magazines and journals should carry news of them. However, you want to know before the rest of the industry at large does. If you are always the first one to have vital and pertinent information, you attract others to you, since you are considered a source and, by extension, a gateway of information. This can only help your company, your project, and your career.

> Traditionally, **whitepapers** are government reports on any subject, but in the Internet Age, they have come to mean any definitive documents or reports created by any company or entity, which are then posted as reports on Web pages.

The Morgan Stanley Internet Advertising Report (http://www.ms.com/misc .inetad/index.html) on the state of Internet advertising has just about everything in it: current trends, forecasts, rate card data, and measurement techniques. It is downloadable in four sections as *PDF files*. The report is dated December 1996, which is a few Internet years ago, but it is free and loaded with information.

> **PDF files** (Portable Document Format files) are standard files created by Adobe to create fully formatted documents from PostScript files. PDF files are ubiquitous on the Net nowadays. Adobe (http://www.adobe.com) offers a free application that reads these files, which is available for download on its Web site. Easy to both create and read, PDF files mean you can download fully formatted forms, such as IRS income tax forms, without worrying about them "not looking right."

Morgan Stanley's Internet Report (http://www.ms.com) follows in a similar vein. The future of Internet commerce, says this full-text report, will largely parody the history of mail-order commerce, except that Internet commerce will develop on a faster and much larger scale. The *Retail Report* goes on to project market size for Web commerce, as well as the industries that will be most successful in the new marketplace: insurance, financial services, computer hardware/software, travel, books, music/video, flowers/gifts, and automobiles—a must read for anyone venturing forth into the brave new world of Internet commerce. Morgan Stanley now also offers the Internet Quarterly: The Business of the Web, which combines highlights from all its major reports, including the Internet Report, Internet Advertising Report, Internet Retailing Report, and Technology IPO Yearbook.

Gartner Group (http://www.gartner.com) offers technology and marketing information. Current articles include salvaging a failed Internet marketing project.

Cyberdialogue/FIND/SVP, Inc. (http://www.cyberdialogue.com) provides data on interactive markets and provides online search capabilities for thousands of market reports. It offers services in research and consulting, market and industry studies, and an information catalog and produces books and newsletters as well as creating seminars on market information for businesses.

Even if you're not a Forrester Research client, you still can have access to a select group of Forrester Research reports and briefs, such as Desktop Data Merges With Individuals and Mixman Simplifies PC Music, at its site (http://www.forrester.com).

Dataquest (http://www.dataquest.com) from the Gartner Group packs facts, figures, and interpretation into this research-oriented site. Search through Dataquest research reports, register for the news alerts service, set up a customized page, or just browse through the highlighted research. It's all free, unless, of course, you want a full-length report. Then you'll have to give Dataquest your credit card number.

Trade Publications

No longer do you have to wait for your trade news to come once a week or once a month. Nearly all major trade publications are on the Net now, as well as some that don't even exist in print. The majority of trades seem to be moving toward a daily update model, such as *Advertising Age*. Some publishers will give you a daily update free on their sites, while others may charge you for the convenience of pushing it to you via email. Here are some of the better examples:

Advertising Age (http://www.adage.com) was one of the first marketing publications to hit the Net and continues to stand out in its category with its constant innovations. These include a daily update, chat boards, and a search engine that lets you look for jobs, local or national, within the advertising industry.

Bookwire (http://www.bookwire.com), the online home for *Publisher's Weekly* and much more, features a news section, original reviews and features, and a "behind the scenes" column written by industry insiders. The site is simple to navigate, provides all the necessary weekly news for this fast-moving industry, and keeps visitors entertained with whimsical features such as Flap, a voyage into book trivia. Other notable sections include Soapbox and its lively discussion areas; Bestsellers, a weekly list of bestsellers from *Publishers Weekly*; and a calendar showing a comprehensive listing of book industry conferences and meetings.

Meeting News (http://www.meetingnews.com), published by Miller Freeman Inc., provides you with updates on what's new in the travel and meetings industries. You can also search the Meeting Site Selection Service, featuring more than 7000 meeting and event facilities, or ask *Meeting News* for an answer to a problem you might have planning your company's annual conference in Spokane. Not enough for you? You can always subscribe to the print version of *Meeting News,* or peruse ads provided by the sponsors to get more ideas on possible locations and meeting areas.

The *Internet Advertising Discussion List*, moderated by Adam Boettiger, is a good place to expand and share one's knowledge of the world of Internet advertising. Started in January of 1997, it has become a hit among its over 12,000 subscribers in 77 countries. The list often includes newsworthy tidbits of direct interest to online marketers. You can take part by going to http://www.internetadvertising.org.

Soliciting Customer Input on the Net

Except for the section on where to get free advice, I've mostly concentrated on secondary research, which is information already compiled and packaged by others. However, the Net is an excellent medium for gathering primary research as well. You can engage your customers in a dialogue on a range of issues, such as their likes and dislikes of your product or service, or their thoughts on a proposed product. You could even ask how they might improve an existing product. Here again, you can use the Net to save much time and money. However, be aware that this is not a substitute for traditional methods of user feedback.

An interview with Nick Nihan revealed that issue. Mr. Nihan is the managing director of Decision Tree (http://www.decisiontree.com), a market research firm that heavily employs both online and offline market research for many of its Fortune 500 clients (see Figure 3.5). Decision Tree is often approached by its clients to do their research online because it is seen as being faster and less expensive than traditional methods. Even though one can interview 1000 people by phone overnight, this practice is a lot more expensive than doing the same online. In some cases, the Net is actually better than a face-to-face encounter, since there is a distance/anonymity factor that allows people to be more revealing. In other cases, as Mr. Nihan points out, there is no substitute for old-fashioned focus groups.

Online versus Offline Data Gathering

Depending on the scenario and its objectives, Nihan feels online qualitative and quantitative methods are better than traditional methods; however, he contends an online focus group system isn't adequate if it's done completely in lieu of traditional methods. A moderated enclosed Internet discussion using chat is not as good as traditional focus groups because the conversation is staccato. People are always rushing to catch up to comments that are scrolling off the screen. If they're struggling to keep up, they're going to write truncated expressions, just so they can keep pace with the rest of the group. Also, the moderator doesn't necessarily have as much control online, so it's not as easy to shut Joe up if he's dominating the session. You

Figure 3.5 Decision Tree is one of the pioneers in conducting online product research.

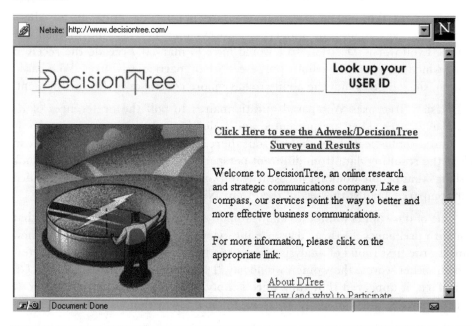

can also lose the quick give-and-take and chemistry that you would get face to face, in addition to the lack of body language and facial expressions. Finally, it's impossible to gauge silence online, which is often more telling than words. A focus group is a qualitative practice, and you're indeed sacrificing the quality of communication for this. Online chat environments are better used for concept testing and creative feedback such as, "I'm going to give you three benefit slogans. Which do you like the best?"

Nihan also points out that people don't usually write as well as they talk. If you're not a particularly good writer, you often lose intonation, feeling, and translation of what it is you actually want to say.

Online Methods

Nihan doesn't use bulletin boards because he believes many onliners aren't familiar enough with how they work in order to participate. His clients usually ask him to reach out to as wide a sample as possible. Bulletin boards would constrict that audience. However, it is a good practice for a high-tech audience that is already wedded to this technology.

I asked Nihan about using email, since it's ubiquitous and the time pressures faced in chat are then lifted. Nihan pointed out to me that email becomes a self-administered questionnaire. Using that methodology, you open yourself up to getting a lot of bad data. Why bad data? A respondent can put his or her answers anywhere in the email document. The tabulation process may not be able to read the answers. Even worse, Decision Tree would have to manually recode the received email, which defeats the whole purpose. Nihan particularly likes Web-based research, since it gives him the ability to have more control over the environment.

Decision Tree uses Web-based questionnaires to poll the preferences of its clients' audiences. They are presented and coded in such a way as to seamlessly pour into a sophisticated database. From there, the people at Decision Tree can look at the resulting data from different perspectives. For example, they can look for things that people wouldn't necessarily tell you directly, but are in fact revealed when compared against the rest of the group. Nihan told me:

"One of our clients wanted to know women's attitudes towards Web sites that dealt with pregnancy. In three days, we interviewed 450 pregnant women or new moms. In the first round of analysis, we got the impression there were site preferences. In other words, the women would say, 'I like this site versus that site.' On the surface, it appeared that they were simply just sites the women frequently visited. However, upon further analysis, we found out why that was. One group was product focused and the other was information focused; therefore, the two groups had very different profiles. Each of these segments were loyal to different sites. We at Decision Tree can then, hypothetically, tell a brand like Pampers to have a two-tiered marketing campaign, whereby one tier is aimed at moms who are brand loyal to Pampers, and the other tier is an information-based marketing campaign on a baby's diet."

A definite positive to online research as opposed to face-to-face research is that nobody judges the answers of the people being surveyed. The people filling out online questionnaires don't have to worry about anyone else's opinion; it is an objective, neutral environment. Nihan says he can see people's stereotypes coming out online because they're more apt to let their guard down when they're not being confronted by others' opinions.

One thing that Nihan particularly emphasized was the integrity of samples and where the samples originated. In the real world, telephone-based researchers use random digit dialing (RDD) in order to generate a *good* random sample. Decision Tree has created the online equivalent to building scientific samples. It runs a banner advertisement that spans a network of 70 Web sites. Depending on the number of respondents, Decision Tree buys a certain amount of impressions. Those impressions are spread out across that network, which covers a wide variety of interest groups. The banner might say, "Decision Tree, Take 10-Minute Survey, Get $10." Click on the banner and you go to the Decision Tree site, where you are asked to identify yourself for screening purposes. If you make it through this screening process, you can then enter into the survey. You fill out the survey, submit it, and have a check sent to you for $10.

Nihan admits the process is imperfect and always will be, but so is the traditional random digit dialing method. However, there is an element of trust that is integral to this type of online research. The Net is gender neutral, while the phone is not. On the phone, you can usually distinguish between a male and a female. To try and work its way around false replies, Decision Tree places its banners on topic-specific sites. It's not a fail-safe method, of course. If you're interviewing working women, for example, you might get a male mixed in, if that male happened to be visiting that site and clicked on the banner.

Another method Decision Tree users to filter an audience is to ask specific questions during the screening process. For instance, Decision Tree recently did a survey about high blood pressure and screened out people who couldn't answer a very specific medical question that only someone with high blood pressure would know.

Sampling Methods

Subjects in a research project are often *order biased*. That is, if you ask for their preference on three different logos, many will choose the first one, simply because it's the first, or the third one, because it is the last one they saw. To compensate for this order bias, Nihan's company automatically changes the ordering of the examples.

In order to make sure its findings truly mirror reality and to put them in the right context, Nihan also does correlation analysis between phone surveys and online surveys. For example, Decision Tree recently surveyed 500 onliners and 1000 people via telephone. It found there was a .98 correlation, which means the results were almost identical. In this case, even though the demographics between the online and offline samples differed slightly, the attitudes did not.

It's abundantly clear that the Internet is quite appropriate for some kinds of research and not for others. Because of its quick turnaround and potentially large savings, there will undoubtedly be many more companies coming into this space, competing with each other. Another firm to watch and explore is Decision Analyst (http://www.decisionanalyst.com). It boasts a market research service that taps into the opinions of more than 20,000 U.S. households with Web access. Called American Consumer Opinion Online, the service surveys panelists over the Internet on such topics as copy effectiveness for online, television, radio, and print advertising campaigns, as well as product market testing. Decision Analyst forms panels from its database, works with clients to develop online surveys, conducts the surveys or market tests via a private Web site, then tabulates and analyzes the results. Pricing depends on the project.

Customer Feedback

Undoubtedly you've heard the expression, "If you want to make a friend, ask his or her advice." The Web is no different in this respect. In fact, its instant interactivity serves as a perfect feedback loop to conveniently solicit your customer's, and perspective customer's advice. The product users can be queried for any amount of information you may want in order to improve existing products, or even develop new ones—often with only a little incentive for their time.

Pinging the Product User

Digital Equipment sells its Alpha server, a very powerful computer often used as a Web server, through both direct sales channels and third-party vendors. Even though Digital doesn't always make direct contact with its customers during the sales process, it solicits customer input via a feedback form on the Web (see Figure 3.6). It asks the users what they like about the computer, in addition to what they'd like to improve upon. This is a classic example of field research paying off.

In addition to getting critical feedback from its customers, Digital is also making a statement: "We want to hear from you. We're going to the trouble of setting this site up, administering, maintaining, and promoting it, in order for us to hear what you have to say. You, the customer, are important to us." It becomes a bonding point with Alpha users. Most of the users of this product who I know are fanatical about the product, and it's easy to see why.

Finally, the customer is incorporated into the actual design process. When a new Alpha server is released with the improvements suggested by current users, it's a good bet they'll be repeat buyers. This form of customer feedback is classic individualized marketing, the kind that Martha Rogers and Don Peppers talk about in their book, *Enterprise One to One: Tools for Competing in the Interactive Age* (Currency/Doubleday, 1997). It's also the sort of practice that turns customers into evangelists for your product or service, thus making each and every one of them a potential reseller for you.

Figure 3.6 Digital's customer feedback form helps create a bonding relationship with firms that purchase its Alpha servers.

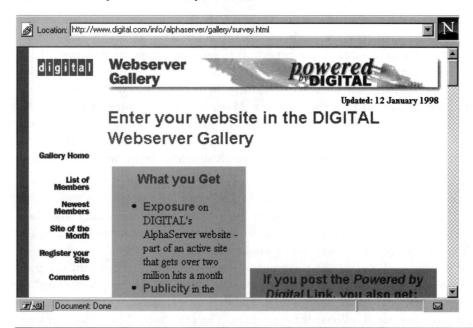

Vogue's Reader Panel Web Site (http://www.karli.com/vogue) provides a way for *Vogue* magazine and its marketing partners to tap directly into reader attitudes and demographics. Individual advertisers offer discount incentives for answers to brief surveys. For example, at the time of writing, Champion was doing a survey to find out if certain advertising would appeal to *Vogue* readers, as well as get a handle on the recognition of Champion's men's underwear line. The incentive was a pair of boxer shorts.

Discussion Lists as a Straw Poll Medium

Another very quick and simple way to solicit customer feedback is through email discussion lists. These can either be private or public lists. If they're private, you can control who joins and have an easier time authenticating potential subscribers. You may create a list explicitly for a given product and urge the users to join Will this protect you from your competitors eventually catching on? No. You must keep this in mind when soliciting input. For this reason, you may want each of your respondents to reply privately, rather than in front of each other. You can even run this type of list right from your email program, until you get into a few hundred participants. At that point, you'll want to consider more elaborate systems to manage the load. I'll talk more about managing and using these mailing lists in Chapter 8, "Direct Marketing and Sales Support."

Using a public list leaves you wide open to both your competitors and cranky customers. Nevertheless, you might choose this route if you're simply looking for a quick read of a niche market. It's important to remember you might tip your hand to your competitors as to what you're up to. If you're using an already existing public mailing list, controlled by someone else, be sure to ask the moderator's permission before posting your queries. Many lists have protocols for just this purpose. For example, in the subject header (assuming they allow you to do this in the first place), you might have to put the word "SURVEY," so that readers instantly know your post to this list is expressly for the solicitation of feedback.

If the moderator doesn't want you to ask the list about a product idea, offer to run an ad soliciting participants on the list. You can offer people an appropriate incentive for their feedback. Don't offer T-shirts unless you're selling T-shirts. I once saw a major New York ad agency offer a T-shirt as the incentive for coming to its Web site three times over three weeks and filling out three questionnaires. What was on the T-shirt? Why, the name of the advertising agency! If my company ran such a campaign with the moniker "Chase Online Marketing Strategies" on that shirt, I don't think I'd want to be associated with those people, let alone have them serve as human billboards for my firm. The offer must have drawn in large numbers of kids and people with too much time on their hands who thought it was an attractive deal. This is not what you would call a "scientific technique."

Although doing a public solicitation exposes your ideas early in the game, it also has the advantage of quickly testing the waters to see if you should continue to proceed with your idea. It also happens to be very inexpensive.

The Usenet can also serve as a barometer of people's opinion on a given topic. However, these Usenet groups are a more public venue, as one need not subscribe to participate in the discussions held within these groups.

Selected Sites to See

I've selected a few Web sites in seven different categories that I believe you'll find useful. These sites are by no means the only sites to see, nor are they quintessential sites that serve the needs of all people. There is no such thing, and don't let anybody convince you otherwise. However, these are good places to start. For thousands more sites, I suggest you go this book's companion Web site for a comprehensive listing of them. But since you're within the pages of this book right now and presumably not online, let me get you started with a few select sites.

Financial Sites

The most efficient use of space here is to point you first to invest-o-rama (http://www.investorama.com), a good *link pile* for investors and investing, which you can pick apart to your heart's delight (see Figure 3.7).

For free, it's hard to beat StockMaster at http://stockmaster.com. You can get up-to-the-minute stock prices and performance graphs on demand for free. There cannot be any better financial Web resource out there. Caveat emptor: Due to user overload, this site is nearly inaccessible between 4:00 P.M. and 5:00 P.M., Monday through Friday EST, which serves as a testimony to its popularity and relevance.

The *Wall Street Journal* (http://www.wsj.com) site requires a fee of $29.00 if you subscribe to the print edition and $49.00 a year if you don't. This online subscription gives you the current print *WSJ* edition, access to the past two weeks of the Dow Jones archives, and the *Barron's Online* edition. Additionally, you have access to the Asian and European editions, as well as frequent updates throughout the day, stock quotes, and nearly every imaginable financial index you can think of (see Figure 3.8).

The International Weekly Journal of News, Ideas, Opinion, and Analysis Web site, otherwise known as the *Economist* (http://www.economist.com), offers about 15 articles each week from the current print issue. Those who enjoy the magazine's

Figure 3.7 Invest-o-rama is a comprehensive collection of links to all things financial.

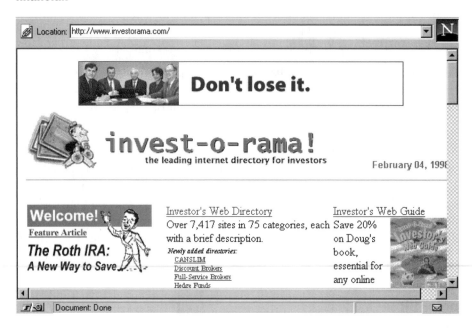

weekly summaries can register at no charge to receive the "Business This Week" and "Politics This Week" columns via email. Searchable archives, unfortunately, contain material only back to February 1996. If you're looking for an intelligent overview of an industry or market, *Economist* surveys can't be beat.

Personal Mining

Sometimes you're looking for people, places, or things. The Net is excellent at helping you find all of these. The key is knowing the places to go where you can find what you're looking for.

Switchboard, at http://www.switchboard.com, can help you get in touch with people you've lost track of over the years (see Figure 3.9). Of course, it isn't complete, as nothing on the Net is, but it is very deep. I know people who have no listed phone number or address and no magazine subscriptions or property, yet they're in there. You can also search for businesses and email addresses.

Four11, at http://four11.com, is another good place to try and track down people's email addresses. It started out as an email directory service and then branched out

Figure 3.8 The *Wall Street Journal* Interactive edition delivers extraordinary value for $49.00 a year or $29.00 if you're a print subscriber.

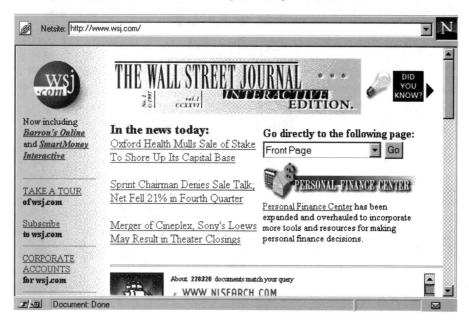

to include White and Yellow Pages directories, maps and directions, and even access to your favorite celebrity's email and local address.

Learn Everything (http://learn2.com) is an incredible "how to" site. You can learn how to jump-start a car or how to wrap gifts without getting the tape stuck to your fingers. This is the perfect site if your mantra is, "Every day, I'm getting better in every way."

The lost and found at http://lost-found.org is a nonprofit organization that provides people and organizations, including police departments, a venue for locating lost information and items.

Did you ever have a question and you didn't know where to get the answer? Maybe you wanted to compare the cost of building a PC versus buying one already built. What was the population of Boston in 1863? If you're an early riser in the morning, check out Ask Any Question at http://www.findout.com, where answers will be emailed to the first 100 questions submitted daily.

Figure 3.9 Looking for someone's contact information? Start with Switchboard.

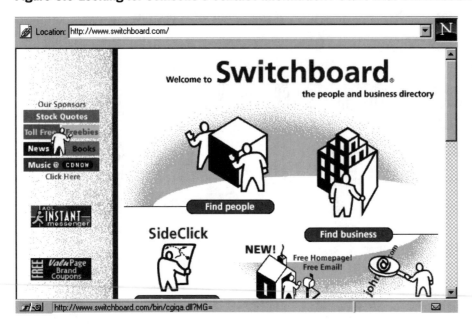

©*Switchboard Incorporated.*

For Your Business

American Business City Journal, at http://www.northernwebs.com/set, updates local business news daily for dozens of American cities.

The *Thomas Register* (http://www.thomasregister.com) is a printed and CD-ROM-based catalog of information about 155,000 U.S. companies, featuring products and services, company profiles, and catalog information (see Figure 3.10). After registering, Web users can search the large database for companies, products, and services.

With the Right To Know Web site (http://www.righttoknow.com), you can easily order, either over the telephone or the Internet, your public and private records to be delivered straight to your doorstep. You cannot order anyone else's, unless you have his or her key personal information. Choose from three packages: Basic, Plus, and Premium, and get as little as three credit reports, an FBI disclosure form, and a mailing list removal letter, or as much as your education, employment, medical, motor vehicle, and Social Security records.

Figure 3.10 *Thomas Register* Online contains information on over 155,000 companies.

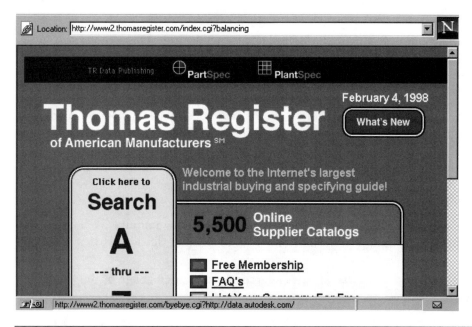

Net Mechanic (http://www.netmechanic.com) offers free tools to check your links (Link Check) and HTML codes (HTML Check), and now offers a service designed to test the reliability and performance of your Web server (Server Check). Simply enter the URL of the page you want to test, and the Server Check robot will monitor your server for the next eight hours. It accesses the page every 15 minutes and measures the amount of time required for each step in the retrieval process. After eight hours, an emailed assessment is returned to you, which includes a comparison to the Server Check average. If desired, a flash email message can be sent each time your server fails to respond to one of the tests, which can help pinpoint critical outages. This is a handy tool and a nice demo of the Server Check Pro commercial product.

Business Tools from ADP (http://www.adp.com/emergingbiz/tool) gives small business owners and managers a place to turn for sound advice on day-to-day management issues, such as finding funding, payroll obligations, and human resources management. This section of Automatic Data Processing's Web site has plenty of advice and articles about small business management. Can't find the form to apply for a federal identification number? ADP has it, and several others, available for download.

News

Say what you will about Matt Drudge's reporting, his homepage (http://www .drudge.com) is an incredibly useful "best of" news sources, many of which you can search right from there. From a single location you can search Reuters, AP, and UPI, plus regional and international wire services (see Figure 3.11).

Newslinks, at http://newslinks.com, is the oldest one-stop spot for a comprehensive, daily updated link pile to more online news outlets than you've got time to look at in your lifetime. It features newspapers, magazines, broadcast entities, journalist-related links, online 'zines, and some special reports (see Figure 3.12). Each type of resource is hierarchically categorized by type, subject matter, country, and title.

Crossroads (http://crossroads.krinfo.com) is a community Web site from Knight-Ridder that provides information seekers worldwide with a forum to

Figure 3.11 Search scores of news sources from the homepage of the Drudge Report.

Figure 3.12 One of the original and most comprehensive collections of links to every type of news site on the Web.

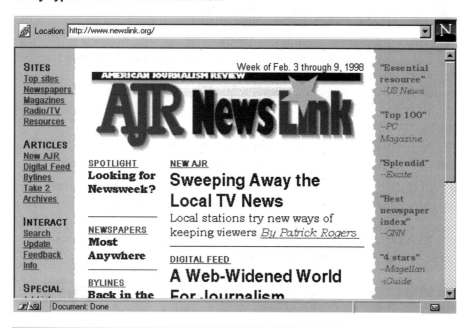

proactively share their expertise and knowledge. Visitors to Crossroads can participate in discussions, receive tips from experts, browse the latest information industry news, attend training sessions in their areas of interest, and even order the latest documents and tools.

Legal

If you know where to go, you can often get answers to your questions without consulting a lawyer. Even if you do have to consult a lawyer, in order to contain legal fees, it's better for you as a client to learn as much as you can on your own.

Free Advice (http://www.freeadvice.com) is designed to give the basic legal information people need to understand most situations arising in their personal and business lives. It provides easy-to-understand answers to thousands of the most frequently asked questions compiled by attorneys from leading law firms nationwide. It covers dozens of legal topics, from accidents, bankruptcy, and divorce to business, tax, and trademark law.

Venerable legal research source LEXIS-NEXIS (http://www.lexis.com) now allows its subscribers to tap into its databases via the Web. In addition to its subscription service, the site offers a free alert-type service called Hot Law. Sections within Hot Law include Hot Topics, an overview of important current cases in specific legal areas such as California criminal law or Florida family law; Hot Cases, a listing of cases most commonly requested by customers; and Hot Bill, a rundown of current legislation. There's just enough free information to keep it interesting and tease serious users into the paid services.

Internet

CyberTimes, at http://www.nytimes.com/yr/mo/day/cyber, is one of the Net's best resources for insightful articles about the Internet itself (see Figure 3.13).

At WhoIs.Net (http://www.whois.net), you can register and protect your domain name, change your current domain name, or search for other domain

Figure 3.13 An impressive collection of original columns and articles about the Internet is provided here from the *New York Times*.

names. It will also email you whenever someone registers a domain name that fits keywords you've ask it to track. Did you ever wonder exactly how many domain names there are worldwide? WhoIs.Net gives you a time-sensitive update for the .com, .net, and .org domain names.

CyberAtlas (http://www.cyberatlas.com) has tremendous depth and breadth and should be on every Net marketer's hot list (see Figure 3.14). It is one of the best spots around to find statistics about Internet usage patterns, demographics, and similar information. The site points users to recent Internet-specific reports from analysts and more.

Visit Iconocast (http://www.iconocast.com) and sign up for Michael Tchong's weekly e-cast of marketing analysis and news, in a style defined as cogent, convenient, concentrated, customizable, charismatic, and curmudgeonly. This former CyberAtlas editor hopes to streamline the information retrieval process by serving as your "data refinery," offering specific business recommendations based on data, not opinions.

Figure 3.14 CyberAtlas is a good source for recent demographics and statistics concerning the Internet's growth.

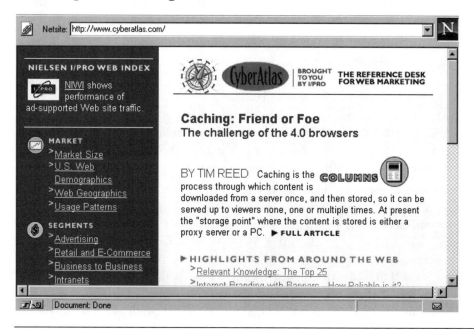

Statistics

The U.S. Department of Commerce Bureau of Economic Analysis (http://www
.bea.doc.gov) provides a wealth of current economic reports and statistics on U.S.
states, regions, and international trade.

The Bureau of Labor Statistics' Web site (http://www.bls.gov) provides you
with an overview of the organization; access to regional and national labor statistics,
such as employment and unemployment, hours, earnings, and productivity; the
Consumer Price Index and Producer Price Index; and details on BLS surveys, publications, and research reports.

 Always have the text field that lets you see the Web address
(URL) showing when you surf. On most browsers, it is at the top
of your screen. It comes in handy when you hit an error page and
get the dreaded "File Not Found 404." What do you do if this
happens? Well, if you were going to http://chaseonline.com/
marketing/articles.html and you don't see anything there, go up
to the URL box, highlight /articles.html and delete it. Then press
Enter. You'll be sent to http://chaseonline.com/marketing, where
you can navigate to all the subpages of the site. It's quite
possible the subpage still exists, but the specific address may
have changed.

By the time you read this, there will undoubtedly be more resources of all kinds
previously discussed in this chapter. That is the nature of the Net, a living, breath-
ing organism with tens of millions of people and their collective knowledge hanging
off of it. The Net is sometimes described as a giant CD-ROM. This isn't true, as a
CD-ROM is considered finite once it's manufactured.

For new sites that are rich with resources, I suggest you subscribe to my *Web
Digest For Marketers*, at http://www.wdfm.com. Furthermore, you, the owner of this
book, are entitled to one year's free subscription to the archives of *Web Digest For
Marketers*. Take advantage of this offer when you visit the *Web Digest For Marketers*
site by clicking on the Archives button. When you are prompted with a dialog box,
enter the word "Larry" (with a capital L) in the text field where it asks for a name.
In the text field that asks for a password, enter the name "Chase" with a capital
C. Once inside the archives, you will have access to thousands of mercifully short
descriptions of Web sites broken out by category, such as publishing, retail,
research, outstanding content, and so on.

Finally, know when to stop. The Net is an infinite place. Your life is not. I strongly suggest that you train yourself to set coordinates for that which you are looking for and then get out once you've found it. I say this with one caveat, and that is, be aware of what you don't know. You will find times where you are looking for something and inadvertently bump into something else that is entirely unanticipated and outside the scope of your search project. Don't be so slavish as to ignore the happy happenstance, but rather go with the flow until you reach a point of diminishing return down that path.

HTTP://007
Spying on Your Competitors and Yourself

There are fountains of hard-won knowledge that are directly relevant to you and your business on the Net. The providers of this intelligence can save you precious time and money. The value of this "unintended" shared learning is incalculable to you, yet it's absolutely free for the taking. All you have to do is keep tabs on these online resources—in other words, your competitor's Net presence.

Find out what your rivals know and what they don't know. If you do it right, you'll uncover far more than how sophisticated they are on the Net. You can peer into their plans and thinking. Your aggressive investigations should uncover holes in that thinking—those holes have your name on them. Your mission, should you decide to accept it, is to identify and exploit these holes to your advantage. Despite themselves, your competitors will teach you the best practices to adopt and what bone-headed directions to avoid. In short order, you will reap sizable dividends from a modest investment of time.

This chapter shows you how to get under your competitors' skin and how to prevent them from getting under yours.

Knowing Your Competitor's Shirt Size

You can get so close to your competitor on the Net that you're able to practically read his mind.

I once asked a search engine to show me all the available pages on a competitor's site. The search revealed an entire new business presentation, replete with cue cards and selling points. I then called the company that was going to receive that presentation and had a discussion about where the strategic thinking of my competitor was flawed. The prospective client was impressed by my reconnaissance and very concerned by the lack of discretion on the part of the competitor. The whole exercise took 15 minutes and instantly established my firm as a player in the prospect's mind.

Benchmarking

The most popular product we sell at Chase Online is our benchmarking surveys. We sit down with a client and establish what areas and companies are going to be focused on, then we set out spelunking into their competitors' sites based on that criteria. For Con Edison (a major New York-based utility), we wanted to find out who was offering the best customer relations, investor relations, and business-to-business relations on the Net in the utility category. We titled this section, *Best Practices*. We also reported on common mistakes in the category to avoid and called this *Worst Practices*. We called the third area *Next Practices*, which were typically good ideas found outside the utility category. For example, since the deregulation of utilities was just around the corner back then, this company wanted to look ahead at being competitive by adding value with online customer account information. At the time the study was conducted, there was no utility offering this service, as it is a historically risk-adverse industry. So we benchmarked financial companies, which are much more apt to lead with such services. In this way, our client can do more than simply tread water with its peers; it can actually set trends that will eventually become standard operating procedures for that industry (see Figure 4.1).

In these benchmark studies, a client usually likes to zoom in on a couple of arch rivals and learn all there is to know about them: Not just how they're using the Net, but hints at what they might do next and where there are chinks in their armor that might be exploited on or offline.

You should look for the following things at a competitor's site:

- Look and feel (the graphics and tone of voice of the copy).

- Any attempt to collect user information, done very often by offering content on a free subscription basis.

- Any attempt of your competitor's Web site to "plant a cookie" on your computer. Be sure to set your browser preferences to alert you when this is attempted, since this is an opportunity for your rival to collect additional information from you.

- Password-protected areas, and do anything you can, within reason, to get in there (this does not include hacking—you've got better things to do!).

Figure 4.1 By benchmarking Web sites in the financial category, Con Edison became one of the first utility companies to introduce online bill payment.

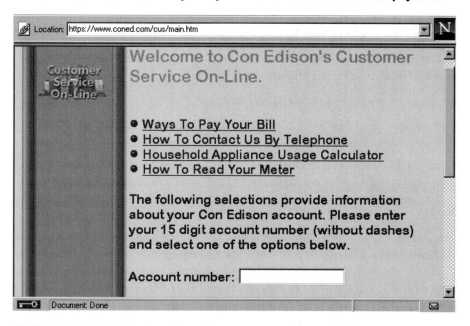

© 1996, Con Edison. Used with permission.

- The level of sophistication of the "hidden text," by asking your browser to view the source code.

- How smooth or rough the process is if you buy something at a retail site. Do they email you a confirmation of sale?

- The quality of the content offerings or the lack thereof.

  You should also make the following observations:

- Check to see if they offer a site-wide search engine available from every page.

- Notice if there are any fancy databases and how deep these databases go.

- Observe if they have Web pages that specifically reflect a banner campaign pointing to those dedicated pages.

- Keep an eye on the URL titles as you drill down into the site. See if they are using real words, made-up words, or garbage characters created by the Web server.

—If they are garbage words, you are being tracked closely.

—If they are real words, the search engines will notice and interpret them.

—If they are made-up words, they are ignored.

- Look to see if the text loads before the graphics, so you have something to look at while the rest is loading.

Finally, get answers to the following questions:

- Do they offer their complete contact information on every Web page for the user's convenience?

- How long do the graphics take to load?

- Is the information well organized?

- Do they offer free advice?

Next, put a microscope to their Web site. Go to http://altavisa.digital.com and enter the company's *URL* in the advanced search engine offered there. If AltaVista doesn't have the site listed, no problem. Just add your competitor's URL in AltaVista yourself, and come back a few days later after AltaVista has had a chance to examine that site and load its contents into its own database, where you can then slice and dice it into bite-sized pieces for analysis. This is exactly how I found that new business presentation I mentioned at the beginning of this chapter.

 URL is geek-speak for Universal Resource Locator. It's the address for a Web site. Many URLs have Ws before their name, as in www.chaseonline.com, while others don't. Make sure your Web address has it both ways, with and without the Ws. Some people just type in your company name, sometimes with the Ws, sometimes not. When you have it registered both ways, it increases the odds that someone can find you the first time out.

Have one of your techies examine the *hidden text* on each page of your competitor's Web site to see exactly how sophisticated your competitor is in coding Web pages (see Figure 4.2). If a good HTML person knows what she is doing, she can judge pretty quickly the level of sophistication of a Web page. If you wish to examine all 432 pages on a given site, that might take a while.

Looking at the hidden text will tell you how sophisticated your competitors are. It will tell you if they are trying to fool the search engines by loading up on

Figure 4.2 The hidden HTML text behind *WDFM*.

```
<html>

<HEAD>
                <TITLE>Larry Chase's Web Digest for Marketers</TITLE>
<!-- updated 11 Jan 98 by dhusum -->
                <META name="description" content="WDFM is a free bi-weekly ezi
cked with real-world examples you can apply now to increase the effectivenes
                <META name="keywords" content="World Wide Web, Internet, marke
 net marketing, seminars, tools, articles, reviews, retail, media, research,
                </HEAD>

<BODY BGCOLOR="FFFFFF">

<center> <a href="whatwdfm.html">
<img src="gifs/wdfm1.gif" BORDER=0 width=510 height=77
 ALT="Web Digest for Marketers...About...">

<center>
<b><a href="subscribe.html"><h3>Click Here for your
free subscription to the WDFM Early Bird Email Edition.</h3></a></b>
<p></center>


<table border=0>
<tr>
```

Making the Most of Hidden Text

Underneath the homepage are groups of HTML (HyperText Markup Language) codes that help your browser figure out where to place things and how to make them look. You can see what this looks like in many browsers under the option "View Source." It's like looking under the hood of a car. You can see much about how the page was constructed and even copy it verbatim. TIP: Many people browse with graphics turned off or with text-only browsers. In this mode, you have to know what those unseen graphics are saying and pointing to. META tags are made for this reason. Be sure to fill them in. Doing so will also help you achieve higher standing in search results, as many search engines look at META tags to help them figure out your standing. A company that sells cars will want the words *car* and *sales* prominently in its metatag in order for the search engine to "see" the site. When you go to look for a site using the keywords *car+sales*, that company should come up higher on the list if its META tag words are composed properly. You can see how important this would be for a new customer looking for your services on the Net!

keywords. If you notice they are not using *META* or *ALT tags*, they haven't done their homework in figuring out how to help the search engines rate their sites. Without ALT tags, people who are surfing with their graphics off in text-only mode will only see the words *graphic link* without knowing where it points to. The only way they can find out is by clicking on the link and actually going to it.

ALT or META tags. ALT tags are what a good HTML author inserts whenever there is an "embedded" graphic, sound, or video file on a Web page—these are simply lines of text that show up on a Web browser where the embedded object is, or will be. This not only gives site visitors with slow modems something to read (and look forward to) while a page is loading, but provides content information if the browser has images turned off, or if they are using a browser that doesn't use images at all.

META tags are codes, keywords really, that search engines look for in order to catalog a Web page. All Web pages should have them in order to get cataloged in the engines more properly. A good primer on the use of META tags and how search engines work is located at Northern Web (http://www.northernwebs.com/set).

You may find they're doing some naughty things, such as embedding keywords hundreds of times to fool the search engines into rating the site higher than it should be. I once heard of a major airline embedding the word *sex* into its META tags thousands of times. This tactic is not only crude, but ineffective as well, as it draws people who are looking for sex to the site. If the airline wanted to abuse the redundancy factor, it should have used the word *weather*, which many travelers search for prior to flying. Either way, the practice is easily exposed and can lead to bad public relations. You can help expose this if in fact you find your competitor *spamming* search engines in this fashion. The term *spamming* comes from an old Monty Python routine in which they chant "Spam Spam Spam Spam . . . " When you send send send all those emails to people who didn't ask ask ask to receive them, you get a reputation as one who sends "spam." Avoid this like the plague plague plague. Many search engines have been reprogrammed to not accept sites that abuse this privilege and, in fact, often send mail to the sites that try to trick their engines, exposing them as unethical companies.

By looking under the hood of your competitors' sites, you might also find that they're entirely clueless—not taking advantage of all the legitimate ways to mark up a Web site so as to actually help search engines and users themselves.

Think of the keywords that people are apt to use when searching for a site like yours. Then liberally use these words in the copy you write for your Web pages. When the search engines come with their virtual clipboards to inventory your site for their database, they'll see these often-used search words at your site and will therefore be sure to move you up in the search results accordingly when such words are asked for. Do you offer a service for window cleaning? Then your keywords should include *window*, *clean*, *cleaning*, and so forth. Again, see Northern Web's site (http://www.northernwebs.com/set) for a really good beginner's look at how to make keywords fit your site to a tee.

If your rival offers an email newsletter, subscribe to it. Remember what the "Godfather" said: "Keep your friends close, and your enemies closer." Of course, if you subscribe to your rival's newsletter, he or she will know who you are . . . or maybe not? Using an anonymous email address is one way to get around this potential problem; we will discuss this at more length later in the chapter. Getting an anonymous email address can cost little or nothing and is very easy. You can subscribe to AOL, Prodigy, and the like, or use a free email service, like RocketMail or HoTMaiL. If you want to do it right now, go to http://www.rocketmail.com or http://www.hotmail.com.

Finally, you can benchmark by looking at the credits for graphics and technologies used on your rival's site. Take these names down and contact the vendors later to get a handle on what your rival is paying for his or her site. Very often, these vendors, in their exuberance to get your business, will reveal what is currently on the drawing boards for the next phase. Getting "skinny" on a rival from one of his or her indiscreet Web vendors is a phone call or email away. Ask them for quotes on the sorts of things they did for that particular site and you will get an idea of what your rival paid. You might even get it for less, as it gives the vendor the chance to resell something that is already created.

The Klingon Cloak: Anonymous Viewing

When you're crawling over your rival's site, you should be aware that he or she can identify you as well. For this reason, I suggest a couple of tactics that let you check *anonymously*.

Get a separate mail account that has a fake name attached to it, such as bobf@zippy.com. Getting a cloaked account for $20 a month is well worth it if you plan on heavy snooping. This account will especially come in handy when you request email newsletters, sales brochures, or sales calls, to check the level of sophistication of your rival's sales force. There are also free email accounts available for the taking on the Web: Geocities (http://www.geocities.com), RocketMail (http://www

.rocketmail.com), HoTMaiL (http://www.hotmail.com), and MailExcite (http://www .mailexcite.com) are only four such possibilities, and at most locations, you can take out several different accounts under pseudonyms. New free Web-mail services are being offered every day, it seems. Be careful when you fill out the sign-up information, as many *spiders* around the Web are very good at tracking down the true owners of accounts—automated programs that go out looking for information, anything from new sites matching a particular format to who lives at what email address. Simply using one of your other screen names on AOL will probably not do the trick. I know a number of people who are quite upset that their email addresses can be found by entering their names in any number of people/address search engines. In many cases, you can even get a map to their houses along with exact addresses and fax numbers. Here's one solution:

- If you are only an occasional snoop, you may just need to cloak yourself at the Anonymizer (http://www.anonymizer.com). Passing through a site like anonymizer.com makes it much harder for a rival to identify you. It prevents him or her from knowing certain things he or she would otherwise automatically have, such as your domain name (i.e., chaseonline.com) and possibly your actual name (i.e., larry@chaseonline.com).

- Your current IP number (which tells your rivals exactly which ISP you use and where you are located).

- The kind of browser and computer you are using.

- What country you come from.

- What site you just came from (which Web page you last looked at). Instead, your rival's referrer logs will tell him or her that you came from Anonymizer, rather than some identifiable site, like your homepage.

You go in one side of this site and come out the other anonymously, so your rivals can't see your domain name when you hit their pages. What they see instead is "anonymizer.com" (see Figure 4.3). The downside here is that security-sensitive sites can and do filter out specific domain names, and you can be blocked access to the site you wish to snoop. I know a number of sites that not only filter out the Anonymizer, but also specific domain names that belong to their competitors. Some sites have a filter that can break through the Anonymizer's "network proxy" as well, revealing your true information. Of course they can and do get access through other accounts; it just serves as an inconvenience and makes it harder for them to stay right on top of you, unless you have a cloaked account.

Figure 4.3 When snooping on a competitor's Web site, you can first pass through Anonymizer.com, so your competition can't tell where you're really from.

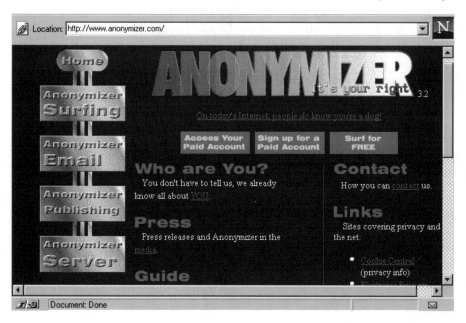

Look Who's Pointing at Your Rival

Once you've surveyed every inch of your rivals' sites, you can then see who has links pointing to them by going back to AltaVista or WebCrawler or HotBot and asking those search engines to serve up that information. When you go to a search engine, you are not asking the "virtual librarian" there to go out right then and look at every single Web page and archived Usenet posting that exists—that would be impossible. There are literally millions of pages and postings on the Web and Usenet. Instead, search engines sent out *bots* or *spiders* (a fancy name for an automated program) that catalog new stuff on the Web since they last went out and looked. They then add that information to the database that makes up the search engine site. So, when you go to WebCrawler to look up the words *purple+velvet*, the results you get are only the cataloged pages and postings containing both the words *purple* and *velvet* that WebCrawler's search engine has in its database as of that day. This is why searching for information on the Net can be more of an art than a science, at times. Your results depend entirely on where you look and exactly what keywords you use in your search. Take advantage of the online help information at the search engine sites—they can help you get far more accurate results by helping you learn how to narrow your search keywords.

Why should you check more than one engine? Because the Web is so big and changes so fast, no one engine can accurately catalog the entire Web. But I do think that AltaVista has the most sophisticated and up-to-date information of all the search engines. For example, I can look up a rival's site in AltaVista and tell it to exclude all the pages within the rival's site itself from the search results. Once you've filtered out all these internal links, you can get down to the business of seeing who's pointing to your rival and why. Go to these links and see why they're pointing to your rival's site. Are they pointing to your site as well? If not, why not? If yes, where do you stand in relation to your competitor in these other companies' eyes?

Perhaps some of these links are advertisements your rival is running, in which case you're now starting to unearth marketing budgets and strategies. You might find other links heavily concentrated in certain geographical or industry areas, which will reflect the direction in which your rival is pulling.

If your rival is a big company, you may turn up some "antimarketing" sites, such as www.flamingfords.com, where disgruntled customers publicly vent their misfortunes from having dealt with your rival. These people may well be low-hanging fruit for you to entice into your camp. Based on this, you could fashion a marketing plan that's solely aimed at the disgruntled users of your opposition.

If, on the other hand, you are one of those unfortunate firms that is the object of the ire of these antimarketing sites, you will most definitely want to contain the problem by addressing it head-on if possible.

Uncovering Your Rival's Strategy

Often these reverse-link look-ups will uncover ad banners that your rival paid for out of his or her advertising budget. Go to the site where that link is, find the banner, and note the message on it before clicking. You will be taken to your rival's Web site and shown a corresponding page. If that banner was a recruitment ad, that corresponding Web page will give you rich information about who your competitor is looking for, the job description, and sometimes salary ranges. You may even want to have someone outside your company go through the motions of applying for that job to see how the fulfillment and follow-through process works. Keep in mind that the ad running may or may not be drawing qualified leads. If the ad stays up forever, it may be a sign that it isn't reflecting reality when it comes to compensation, qualifications, or geographical expectations. Still, it's an indicator of your rival's movements.

What's in a Name?

Visit the InterNIC, the place that keeps track of all domain names (http://rs.internic.net), and you'll learn even more about your rivals. In addition to finding out when they registered for their domain names and who is responsible from an administrative and technical point of view, you can also enter the companies' names into the search field (http://rs.internic.net/cgi-bin/whois). This is a little-known fact. If you enter *Procter*, for example, you'll turn up all the domain names that Procter & Gamble has registered, when it registered them, and if they're currently assigned to a Web site—whether or not the Web site is currently being used is not listed; you will have to try to go to that URL and see if it is active. The very names themselves will give you clues as to what companies are planning for future sites and how long they've been in preparation.

Inside the InterNIC

You can think of the InterNIC as the central post office of the Internet. It knows who holds which domain names and will give you the names and physical addresses of the owners of each name, in addition to the technical administrator. The "NIC" can tell you how long someone has had a name and when it was last updated, as well as what other names that person or company has registered.

Go to WhoIs on the InterNIC site and enter your competitor's name in the text field to see what domain names he or she holds and when they were obtained. It may give you some insight into what he or she has planned for the future.

For example, if we check on Procter & Gamble's registered domain names, we see that it has pampers.com and vidalsassoon.com—both of these yield full Web sites dedicated to those two trademarked products. However, Procter & Gamble also has names such as sinus.com, badbreath.com, flu.com, dish.com, aleve.com, and dozens more "generic" names to do with diapers, cold and flu medicines, and household cleaning—all of these sites yield only a generic Procter & Gamble links page. The company, however, has reserved all these domain names for future development; no one else can use these domain names unless Procter & Gamble is willing to sell them.

Using the Usenet and Listservs for Undercover Work

As you probably know, the Web is only the most visible part of the Net. In addition, there are tens of thousands of Usenet *newsgroups*, which are essentially public discussion groups that you can read and/or post to yourself. Using the same search engines as mentioned before, you'll want to search the Usenet for any references to your competitor's name, products, services, or people. You may even want to contribute a comment or two when appropriate. There are several different programs available for reading and posting to Usenet groups, such as Forté Inc.'s Free Agent newsreader (http://www.forteinc.com/forte), or the built-in newsreader in most Web browsers, such as Microsoft Internet Explorer, Netscape, or Opera. Make sure you have information from your ISP as to what "news service" you have available. Most ISPs have their own news service—for instance, Panix may have a news service called news.panix.com; configure your newsreader to point to that service to get all the newsgroups your ISP subscribes to. There are literally thousands of newsgroups available; be prepared to take some time to find the ones your search engine adventure turned up for you to check.

In addition to the Usenet, there are mailing lists using either *listservs* or *listprocs*, which are usually discussions that are held by email. Instead of going to the Usenet, which is a bit more public, you'll want to subscribe to the email discussion lists that are relative to your industry and rivals. In fact, your rival may already be administrating a discussion list. If he or she isn't, you may want to *start one yourself.*

Both Usenet and mailing lists are good tools to have in your arsenal when collecting information. When you first join, just *lurk* for a while and do not post anything. *Lurking* is simply reading a Usenet group or mailing list and not saying anything. Most groups and lists are composed of mostly lurkers, with a comparatively small percentage of people who actively post. It's like talk radio in this respect: many listeners, few talkers. See who's active, what the nature of the topics are, and how they're handled. You may want to build good will by introducing yourself and offering up a valuable piece of information, in a few short words, or give the URL of your Web site. This is done to build good relations with the landed gentry who came before you.

There is a great deal written about proper Netiquette when posting to newsgroups or mailing lists; the culture that has grown up over the years is quite distinct, and ruffling feathers by asking typical newbie questions out of turn, or even asking basic questions about the topic at hand, rather than taking the time to read the group's FAQ (Frequently Asked Questions), can ruin your chances to get "in" with the mailing list group. Take your time and let them get to know you by posting a few polite and short follow-up statements to an ongoing discussion; test the waters. After a while, you might float a few questions that solicit the input of the members on a given topic. Don't say, "Hey, what do you think of my rival?" Rather, ask for discussion on points of disagreement between you and your rival. This is an effective and inexpensive way to *ping* your trade or marketplace.

As well as searching out the names of your rival companies, identify names of specific key people employed by your rival. Then do searches on these people. See

Minding Your Own Mailing List

Many firms find it very handy to stay in touch with their constituencies via broadcasting news updates and the like to those who have requested it. This is what my *Web Digest For Marketers* (*WDFM*) is. *WDFM* is a one-way mailing list (see Figure 4.4). Others are two-way and accept traffic from the recipients so that discussions between all can take place. If you start a mailing list, make sure the quality of content is high enough so people have a good incentive for filling out a brief form that includes name, company, email address, and where they heard about the list. Aside from knowing who you're talking to, you'll have an easier time mining your future database of subscribers for future business opportunities. Those four basic pieces of information are also invaluable if you find yourself in a position to sell advertising on the list, as advertisers will first ask who your audience is.

what trade shows they're speaking at, what articles they've written, and what they said in those articles. These articles may have heretofore been customer newsletters that are now, in part, posted at your rival's Web site. Some sites may have the key parts of the newsletter in a passworded area, while the accessible parts of the newsletter are out in the open and can be read by search engines, increasing the site's standings in any search for those industry's keywords.

How much does this cost? Not much at all, except for your time or that of some whiz kid from a computer science school who is interning for you and understands your search criteria. Unfortunately, whiz kids are not always available, as they have their studies and are not always as keenly tuned as a seasoned business

Figure 4.4 Offering quality content serves as an inducement for the reader to give you more than just his or her email address, which will serve you well in database mining.

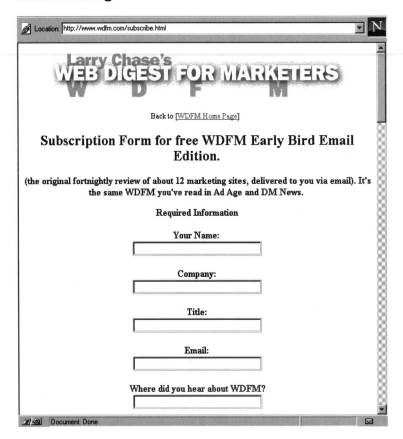

professional. So be prepared to spend between $20 and $70 an hour for a business and net-savvy pro who can get it right the first time (that hourly rate is an approximate range—your mileage may vary). Ask for his or her search strategy, and be prepared to compare it against another's in order to determine the right professional "sniffer" for your needs.

Touching Base with Databases

There are certain databases you can mine for free, or for very little money, and obtain rich information on your target companies.

If you go to Trade Show Central, shown in Figure 4.5 (http://www.tcentral .com), you can look up who's exhibiting at over 30,000 conferences, trade shows, and seminars worldwide. Are your competitors there? Should you be if they are? Are they advertising an aggressive promotion to bring traffic to their booths?

You can go to American Business Information's SalesLeadsUSA (http://www .lookupusa.com) to get a top-line Dun & Bradstreet rating on over 10,000 companies

Figure 4.5 Use Trade Show Central's daily updated database to see where your competitors are speaking and exhibiting at your industry trade shows.

Copyright Trade Show Central, LLC.

and then retrieve deeper information for $3. Dig a little deeper with an Experian report and you'll find out who gets paid first: the phone company or the landlord. From LEXIX-NEXIS, the P-TRAK database (http://www.lexisnexis.com/lncc/general/subscribe.html) contains information from a national consumer reporting agency, limited to a person's name, address, birthday, and sometimes alternate names, previous addresses, and phone numbers. It is marketed to law enforcement, legal offices, businesses, and government agencies. The cost as of this writing is $125/year for a subscription (available by telnet), plus a per-transaction charge (averaging $85/transaction). Many rumors about how much information these databases contain have circulated on the Net over the last few years, revealing an underlying fear of how easily personal information can be disseminated over the Internet.

Of course we haven't yet touched on basic tracking by way of press releases and statements to the press. There are dozens of options for employing the electronic version of Beryl's Clipping Service. Or, you can do it yourself. It really depends on how much this information means to you versus the time you spend doing it yourself. I myself tend to spot-check every now and again. I feel it's good for sharpening my research skills, as well as adding knowledge to my business relationships.

There are also services that will monitor specific newsgroups and Web pages for you, alerting you to any changes in the page's content or to the mention of your rival in a newsgroup, for instance. One such service, eWatch (http://www.ewatch.com) costs very little: between $300 and $500 per month.

I've also used electronic news-clipping services to good effect. NewsHound (http://www.newshound.com) is a pay-for service (usually with the first month free), but allows you to fine-tune your information and draw from a more elite selection of wire services and databases (see Figure 4.6). NewsPage (http://pnp.individual.com) offers a free news-clipping service, as well as more sophisticated levels of information gathering. With NewsHound and others like it, you can dial up the selectivity of the words, so that you only get stories in which those words appear most prominently in the document.

A free and lighter surf of the daily outpouring of *info-glut* are My Yahoo! (http://www.yahoo.com), PointCast (http://www.pointcast.com), Netscape In-Box Direct (http://www.netscape.com), or other similar services that either save your preferences for your next visit or push them at you as often as you request—it all depends on your tolerance and endurance. It is interesting to note here that what is charged for at the time of writing may well be available and pushed out to you for free by the time you read this, as the cost of content over time is starting to resemble Moor's law of Computing Power: every 18 months, the power doubles and

Figure 4.6 NewsHound will filter through a myriad of wire services looking for articles of interest based on your preferences and will then email them to you.

the cost halves. There was a time not too long ago when it was unthinkable that the *New York Times* would give its content away for free. Now it's taken for granted. With higher and higher quality content becoming available for free all the time, cutting-edge companies will use every additional centimeter made available as grist for weaponry against its marketplace foes. In other words, it will be a field day for those who realize that information is power.

Spying for New Business

If you're on the prowl for new business (and who isn't?), you'll want to employ all of the tools in this section to strengthen your chances to score that win. You probably have companies in mind for new business leads. Start by targeting them. Even more than a brochure, a company's Web site speaks volumes of how it perceives itself. The closer you can get to them before making first contact, the better. Subscribe to any online mailing lists they offer. See if they have members of the department you're targeting listed on the site. If so, grab their names and do a Net-wide search for information. It can come in very handy when you bump into someone in the hall when you're first visiting.

Say, for example, you visit the sight of a client that you are planning on pitching. You can use some of the information gleaned from your visit to this site as a reason to make contact. An opener for you might be an email gently pointing out that a few links on the site are no longer working or are dead. He or she might email you back and thank you for that helpful information, and you pick it up from there. You may also find that this company has interests in an area in which you excel. You might call or email the company saying that you vend a solution that is integral to what it talked about on its site. I've also found that if I email such a company about having found some very interesting sites pointing to it, it always elicits an eager response: "Who is it?" "How did you find them?" "What are they saying about us?"

Remember the example I gave at the beginning of this chapter in which I pointed out to a prospective client my competitor's presentation that was publicly available for anyone to bump into? When I mentioned it to the prospective client on the phone, he had to stop and listen, then go to the site online, where he and I critiqued the positioning the rival had in mind. This prospective client got a number of messages from me in one burst:

1. My rival was not being discreet.

2. I was sophisticated enough to detect it.

3. I was aggressive enough to mention it.

Knowing a prospective client's business that well has to be respected. He or she will think about the value you can bring on a sustained basis and quite possibly, by inference, the lack thereof by your rival. It's a very potent selling message.

Spying on Yourself

One of the very first things I searched for on the Web was my own name. Everybody does. I found eight other Larry Chases out there. I'm sure there are more by now. What that told me to do was register larrychase.com as a domain (at http://rs.internic.net). I suggest you do the same for both your name and all or some intuitive part of your company's name.

Just as with your competitive reconnaissance discussed earlier, you can use many of the Web's search engines to sniff *yourself*, as it were. Pretty much the same applies when trolling the Usenet groups and mailing lists for your company or self as you did for your rivals. Using the very same techniques, you can see whose Web page links point to you, and why.

When people consider advertising in my *Web Digest For Marketers* (*WDFM*) newsletter, their comfort level goes way up when they see big, blue-chip names pointing at it and saying nice things about it. Think of it as a hyperlink seal of approval . . . unless, of course, they are saying negative things about you. The very same search engines that search the Net can also be used to troll Usenet groups. If you are a large company, this can give you an early "heads up" about potential problems before they get out of control. This voyeuristic technique is especially effective when you want to find out what your constituents really think about you. They are more apt to speak freely if they are not prompted by you directly. Some people ask other members of a Usenet group or a mailing discussion list to mention your product or service so that you can get totally honest input. Unfortunately, at the time of writing, there seems to be no one resource that scans all publicly accessible mailing lists—the search engines on the Web catalog only Web pages and Usenet groups. Therefore, it is best that you simply join those mailing lists that are relevant to you.

You can also install referrer logs at your own site, which aren't expensive at all. They'll tell you where the person who visited you was last and how many referrals you got from that site. I had Mike Laskin, a University of Pennsylvania computer science student, set mine up for a few hundred dollars. No work has been done on it for one year. There are more sophisticated packages, of course, but for many companies, plain old referrer logs that are focused on a few key pages on your Web site will do just fine. It seems every week there are new tracking packages out there that do more for less money. I personally prefer AccessWatch (see Figure 4.7) and Wusage (http://www.accesswatch.com and http://www.boutell.com/wusage).

These two software packages cost very little and tell you how many times each of your pages has been accessed, provide bar charts showing usage over 24 hours, and offer weekly flowcharts comparing one day to the next, and so forth. Fancier packages will give you more information, such as referrer logs. They may range from $700 to $7,000 or more. My pick in this category, at the time of writing, is Microsoft's Usage Analyst (formerly Intersé, http://www.backoffice.microsoft.com/products/features/UsageAnalyst/SiteServerE.asp). Most of these packages will give you the basic information you want to know about your Web site's traffic:

- How many people hit your homepage
- Which domain names hit your site the most
- Time of day when traffic is heaviest and lightest
- Overall access numbers to the site, including dates and times
- The average pages viewed on your site by a visitor
- Which pages were viewed most
- Which pages were viewed least

Figure 4.7 AccessWatch.

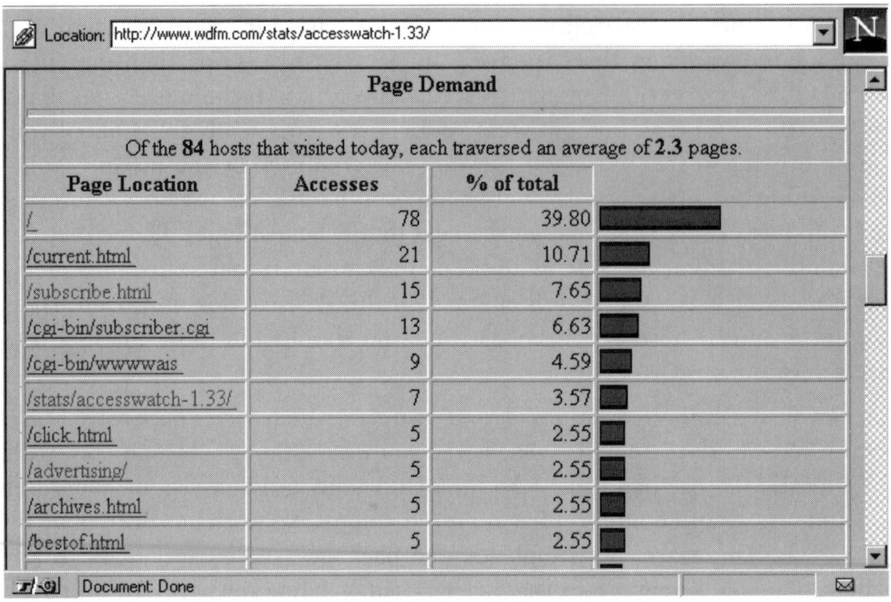
Location: http://www.wdfm.com/stats/accesswatch-1.33/

Page Demand

Of the **84** hosts that visited today, each traversed an average of **2.3** pages.

Page Location	Accesses	% of total
/	78	39.80
/current.html	21	10.71
/subscribe.html	15	7.65
/cgi-bin/subscriber.cgi	13	6.63
/cgi-bin/wwwwais	9	4.59
/stats/accesswatch-1.33/	7	3.57
/click.html	5	2.55
/advertising/	5	2.55
/archives.html	5	2.55
/bestof.html	5	2.55

Document: Done

When we talk about marketing in the second half of this book, I'll demonstrate how these high-value, inexpensive techniques can give you on-the-fly feedback on how well your offers (notice I didn't say *ad banners*) are pulling. Very often, I notice the highest numbers are coming because of a very favorable review that *Web Digest For Marketers* has received. I then get permission and reuse the kind words from the likes of *PC Week* and AT&T on the site itself. I found all these kind words by going through the referrer logs and following up on the addresses that were delivering significant, and sometimes not so significant, traffic.

Increasing Your Chances of Being Found

There's a right way to move your standings higher in the search engines and there's a wrong way. Spending your time trying to dupe the search engines is a lose/lose proposition, as I mentioned previously. Some engines take what some consider to be punitive action by deleting your URL should you continue to attempt to abuse the parameters they lay down for fair and reasonable placement. Furthermore, your time is much better spent being more proactive and aggressive, grabbing mindshare by devising campaigns that rewrite the rules so that your competition gets caught up in a game of "catch up to the leader"; namely, you. Packing your site's code with thousands of keywords to trick the search engines is not a productive use of time in the long run.

Having said that, there's no reason why you shouldn't know your standings in the search engines by using handy tools at places such as did-it.com (http://www .did-it.com) and PositionAgent (http://www.positionagent.com). Both of these sites systematically check the popular search engines when various search words are used to call up companies (such as yours). If you want an idea of what keywords are most commonly used, you can get a real-time view at Lycos (http://www.lycos.com) and Excite's WebCrawler (http://www.webcrawler.com). I'll tell you right now, it isn't zinc alloy or gallium arcinide. Nevertheless, it will give you an idea of how people go about looking for things on the Net using search engines and keywords.

Since search engines are hotly competitive with each other, the race is always on for delivering better results, so the changes here are fast and furious. In fact, there's a superb free monthly newsletter that keeps up with the latest changes that can and will have a direct impact on your standings. You'll learn which engines are collecting the entire page and what portion of that page is used in determining your standings in search results. *Danny Sullivan's Search Engine Report* (http://www.searchengine-watch.com) recently reported that Yahoo! was going to cease rating companies based on name in favor of weighting words across the site (see Figure 4.8). So much for AAAA Tool and Die being at the top! You might also want to check out *Web Developer.com Guide to Search Engines* by Wes Sonnenreich and Tim Macinta (Wiley, 1998), which, in part, compares the features of several of the major search engines.

It's a good thing to stay on top of your standings in search engines, but I wouldn't put too much effort into it; there most certainly is a point of diminishing return. In my case, the engines account for maybe 30 percent of my traffic, with the rest coming from advertising, press coverage, trade-outs, and referred links from sites with resource sections for marketing.

Curiously enough, there's another way you can increase your standing in the search engines: Put keywords in your *signature file* at the end of your email. When you submit postings to newsgroups and mail to some discussion lists, it tends to get archived on the Web. Your post is archived with many other documents with similar words. That means something to the search engines that come around with their virtual clipboards. Furthermore, you easily and automatically create a higher incidence of coincidence. If you're an online marketing consultant, and that fact is in your *sig* file, which has been sorted on some discussion list of authors and agents, it might very well come up when someone submits a search for "online marketing" as well as "online advertising." I've had people contact me who read a newsgroup post I made years ago.

Figure 4.8 Stay on top of how search engines affect you and your competitors with *Danny Sullivan's Search Engine Report*.

What's in a SIG File?

Sig is short for *signature*. At the bottom of every email you send out, you should have a sig file that gives your contact information and what you do or an offer. Many email programs let you write this standard "outro" once and then automatically send it with every email you send. This sig file should not be more than six lines long, after which it is considered overkill, and many Usenet groups will truncate after five lines. I suggest you use the horizontal space across the page as much as possible. Here's my example:

Cordially, Larry Chase/Pres, Chase Online Marketing Strategies
Email: larry@chaseonline.com | http://chaseonline.com
Voice: +01 (212) 876-1096 fax: +01 (212) 876-1098
Free subscription to *Web Digest For Marketers* http://wdfm.com
See my "Selling Websites to a Reluctant Boss" in *Ad Age's NetMarketing*
http://www.netb2b.com/cgi-bin/cgi_article/monthly/97/07/01/article.3

Knowing how people look up your kind of product, service, or company is important when you are writing your copy for the site. Be sure to use words likely to be searched upon nearer the top of your homepage and every page thereafter. In fact, consider every page a homepage, as search engines are just as likely, if not more so, to offer up a sublevel page that has more keywords in its copy than your homepage. I noticed this when I saw that some of my third-level pages had higher traffic than my second-level pages. This is also a good reason to write your copy in an *inverted pyramid style*, where the most important thoughts and words are likely to surface in the abstracts just behind the links that the search engines turn up on queries.

> **Inverted pyramid writing style.** This is a journalism style that puts all the important information at the top, with details further down. Much newspaper writing is done this way, so the story can be cut at any point for space considerations. On the Net, it isn't space that's in short supply, it's people's attention spans. In short, get to the point!

Seeding your presence into the Net by way of search engines is a long-term proposition that is further discussed in the second half of this book.

Client Focus

Thus far, we've talked about casting nets out to pick up snatches of information about competitors and ourselves. But what about knowing the users of your products or services better? Just as you should troll the Web, Usenet, and mailing lists for individual competitors and yourself, you should see what you can turn up on your clients. I remember a company I was working with was coming out with a new product. The company was extremely sensitized to the prospect of other companies coming out with something similar. When one of these competitors showed up on my radar screen with a product directly pitted against this company, I immediately gave my client the heads up. This told him to put more manpower behind his product to market it sooner than later. The pricing of this newly founded competitive product told him what he could charge for his. He could also adjust his marketing copy to accentuate this stronger aspect of his product, while he quickly moved to improve upon those areas in which he was weaker.

We've found other bonding points for our clients on the Web. Many don't even realize they're mentioned on the Net until we tell them; it makes for great conversation. I remember one was amazed to find out he was listed by the New York Road Runners Association, while another had a yen for fly fishing. As a consequence, whenever I see something in my cybertravels on fly fishing or road running, I pass it along to them via email so they can surf over. It only takes a few seconds, but it consistently builds a stronger bond over time that will be less apt to be broken by a lower bid, or what have you, from a competitor.

You might also want to capture intelligence on behalf of your clients, whether you are providing Net-related services or not, especially if they are less Net savvy than you. It adds value to your relationship and keeps you tuned in to your clients' businesses.

On-the-Fly Focus Groups

There's a win/win proposition with online focus groups. Since the cost is a fraction of what it would normally be, you could make it worth your customer's while to participate by offering a good cash incentive or something of value out of your inventory. Right now, you can download free server software that will allow you to have real-time chat back and forth in text mode between customers—some even include file transfers, whiteboards, and the ability to surf the Web together. Free Jat from SenseNet allows up to 12 people to chat on your site using a Java-based client you can download for free from its site (http://www.sensenet.com). NetMeeting, packaged with Netscape Communicator, can be activated from a Web site as well, opening up a client that allows for chat, a whiteboard, and even shared applications. ICQ (http://www.mirabilis.com) has business chat groups set up for small businesses that want to start a focus group from their Web pages— both the ICQ pager/chat program and this setup are free.

You can also set up an Internet Relay Chat (IRC) client on your site and register it with an IRC "network" such as TalkCity for free (the software is provided for free, if you are interested) and have your company's site listed as a business chat area on its pages (http://www.talkcity.com). Several business groupings are already set up that way, such as a small network of automotive dealers who have auto chats listed. For about $1,500, Ichat (http://www.ichat.com) or EAChat (http://www.eachat.com) will also create a server-based chat for your customers. Ziff-Davis (the Cobb Group) has set up a Virtual Places chat client for its online publications and ZdNet "university," in order to draw in customers and provide continuing online focus groups for its own marketing feedback (http://www5.zdnet.com/cc/chat.html). For a few hundred dollars, you've got instant feedback on your product or service before it comes to market. You can test pricing, positioning, branding—you name it. At the very least, you've increased the velocity to market—a competitive edge.

By including the end users by asking them to share their impressions, you're also incorporating them into the actual design process. If you're able to collect data in this fashion, you will simultaneously move the product cycle along while reducing overhead.

My own *Web Digest For Marketers* is something of a testing lab. Every time it goes out, I make sure there are new offers in it from myself as well as other advertisers, to see what works and what doesn't. I tend to test offers for services I provide. Some are incredibly successful, while others do nothing. There's only one way to find out. This is why it's good to have a channel to a significant segment of your target audience. You keep them in place with quality content, which they and you need, while trying to figure out what sort of deals are attractive to them. A small offer on one site yielded an ongoing advertiser for another, while a large offer from another site drew no serious leads. The message for all of us is: keep testing.

Investment Investigations

At the time of this writing, publicly held companies are just starting to get into the swing of offering jazzy financial reports online. IBM currently offers a Java applet that lets you build your own charts of its historical performance (http://www.ibm .com/ibm/ar95/AR-dynamic), while Microsoft's tables can be converted into local languages and currencies. Financial tables can be downloaded as Excel spreadsheets at 3Com's site so that you can manipulate the numbers and overlay them over other firm's performances, as you please. Schlumberger's 1994 annual reports were made available for download in both Excel and Lotus formats (http://www.slb .com/ar94). For all-around chart information, I recommend Stockmaster (http:// www.stockmaster.com), which gives you 52-week running averages of the most publicly traded companies in chart form, all for free.

Once you have this information in such a flexible format, you can do all sorts of neat things with it; for example, you can compare stock and dividend performance between two, three, or more companies over the past five years. More and more information is constantly being made available in more sophisticated formats— take advantage of it.

Taking the Pulse of Your Competition

In addition to Web and Net applications, engines, and pages to utilize in your reconnaissance, there are a number of things you can do with off-the-shelf software and customized software that can get you hovering right over your competitors.

Customized Software

To get right down to tracking clients who have been on your site, there are long-standing applications built into Unix and NT servers that are now available on Web pages as well, such as Traceroute and Dig. Both of these utilities will track back to where the IP number originated from and whose ISP it uses, so you can find out not just where a customer is located, but also which Internet Service Provider he or she uses. Two very good sources for Web-based information on such utilities are http://kryten.eng.monash.edu.au/gspamt.html, which is a site devoted to anti-spam information, and http://www.akweb.com/singles/tracerou.htm, which allows you to perform a full traceroute while on the Web. An interesting site is the Latitude/Longitude locator at http://cello.cs.uiuc.edu/cgi-bin/slamm/ip2ll, which pinpoints an IP address's location in the world using the InterNIC's domain records—maps are linked to this site, if you want to see a push pin designating on a world map where your target is located (see Figure 4.9).

If you have written for you the same sort of tracking software that you can find on the shelf, you can get even more information. Is it legal? In most cases, yes. Is it worth your time and money? Only you can decide that. But you can gather additional information about where those visitors to your rival's Web site are coming from. You can't determine exactly how many page views are being served up, but you can make some educated guesses by looking at the rival's site and figuring out an average of what each visitor might pull off the site. If that site is offering streaming video, then the chances are there are fewer page views, since each connection is more apt

Figure 4.9 Pinpoint the geographical location of any Web site with Latitude/Longitude.

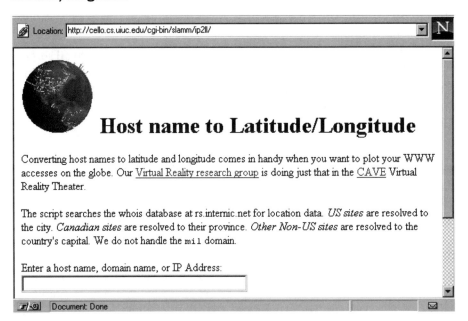

to be concerned with funneling those moving images down the pipe rather than serving ad banners, which are minuscule by comparison.

How to Protect Yourself from Your Competitors Sniffing You

The bold truth is, you can't do much about it. The same way that it's an opportunity for you to grope your competitors, they can do the same to you. Nevertheless, there are some precautions. Be sure that all of your staging areas are password protected; neither the search engines nor your rivals will penetrate this easily. You can stop competitors from sniffing you out when you put up new information on your site by using some HTML code (<URL-MINDER-IGNORE>). This prevents the sniffers from seeing that new info (see more information on this at http://www.netmind.com). The downside is, if you have customers who use this software to alert them as to when you update your pages, they will also not be able to see it!

When you send out your newsletter, do not put all of the recipients' email addresses in the "To:" or "Cc:" fields if you are using a basic email program. If you do, everyone on your list (assume your competitors are in there) will see who the other subscribers are. If using a simple email program, put all the recipients' names in the "Bcc:" field. That way, the names appear as "list suppressed." This is a paranoid-sounding phrase, but at least it protects the anonymity of each and every recipient. Or, you can create a "group name" and put all the addresses under the group; only the group name will show in the "To:" field (such as "All Customers"). A majordomo program can also be employed here that will send everyone your newsletter, but the "To:" field will have the name of the list, rather than the recipient. This will need to be set up on your ISP or server by a technician. If you don't mind this, it may be the most cost-effective way to go, next to using your own email program and a group name.

You can't prevent your competition from scanning you closely, but you can at least know they are doing so. Hopefully, they are not as sophisticated as you are, so you'll be able to identify them (since they will not be cloaked or anonymized, as explained earlier). In this way, you at least know what they know about you or know what they don't know about you. You can also block entry from specific domain names. So, for example, the search engine InfoSeek may prevent its competitor Lycos from checking out its new interface or technology by simply disallowing entry from anyone from Lycos.com to its site. Of course, the Lycos person can simply bypass this block by going into InfoSeek via his or her own AOL account. You can just make it more troublesome for your competition to get information about you.

Caution: Don't Get Carried Away
While Carrying Out Your Spy Mission

The naked truth is, snooping around can be loads of fun; in fact, you can have almost too much fun under the guise of a work-related project. This is particularly true of obsessive types, of which there are teeming hordes on the Net. Just like surfing the Web itself, you can more easily than not get sidetracked or go far deeper than is necessary. In other words, if you take it too far, it can actually prove injurious to the health of your project or firm. Know when to stop.

You can get pretty far down in the trenches with gathering information on yourself, your rivals, your clients, and prospective clients. As more and more information becomes available and the tools to perform such tasks become more sophisticated and cheaper, you'll be able to go even further. The question is: How far do you want to go? Do you really want to gauge the traffic flow hitting your competitor's site? Some of you will find this extremely relevant, while others will consider it overkill. The true answer is: How valuable will the information be to you once you've mined it? If the upside is great, then go for it. If it's questionable, then forget it, or have someone else do it, or perhaps assign a piece of software to the task that regularly checks patterns and notifies you when things are noticeably different.

The Net has made information practically infinite, but there is one commodity that is very finite: your time. I suggest you set up an information-to-time ratio, or information-to-money ratio, matrix so you can identify that point of diminishing return and not exceed it. If your corporation is large, then it may well pay to have someone on staff trained to snoop around regularly. If you're a smaller firm, say a consultancy, you might consider disciplining yourself to do only as much as you can reasonably manage on a periodic basis. You might also consider farming out to an outside source some of your specific recon missions on rivals or new business prospects. How can you find these companies on the Net? Well, just do a little digging with some of the practices learned in this chapter. You'll turn something up.

PART TWO

INTEGRATING THE INTERNET

into Your Marketing

YOUR BRAND IMAGE
and the Internet

Just because you're not Tony the Tiger or the Jolly Green Giant doesn't mean you shouldn't be concerned about your branding—quite the contrary. No matter who you are or the size your company, you should think of yourself, your firm, and your products as brands in this age of one-to-one branding. You may have the best intuition about where the marketplace will move to, or the best technology, or the most cogent advice, but if you don't package yourself and your firm correctly, it'll be your own little secret.

In this chapter, we're going to start with presenting you as a package on the Net, with lessons you can use offline as well. Whether you work in a small or large company, the reality is that you actually work for yourself. Then we'll examine how existing brands offline are migrating online, and vice versa. What should you obsess over? What should you ignore? Where and how should you spend your money to promote your brand? We're going to look at new types of brands emerging on the Net, such as intermediary brands. Perhaps you should be one. But right now, I want to talk about just one thing: You. In this chapter, you'll learn all about:

- Your personal brand on the Net
- Address for success
- Your company's image and the Internet
- Marketing professional services on the Net
- Starting a brand online
- Online intermediary brands

- Marketing to yourself
- Building brands with online communities
- Web page, design, and your image

Your Personal Brand on the Net

Since you have your own unique destiny, skill set, and character, it's in your best interest to present yourself as a package or a brand. It's your responsibility to identify what 1950's advertising legend and author of *Realities In Advertising*, Rosser Reeves called the *Unique Selling Proposition* (USP) for that brand called *you*. The Net will help you, if it doesn't force you, to concentrate on what benefits you offer to which constituencies. Whether you're in manufacturing or modeling, the key to establishing your personal brand on the Net is *reputation*.

If you do work for another corporation, you will want to carefully measure what is appropriate for you to do with branding yourself, as it may be in conflict with your company. If you're queasy about asking your managers what they think, just try putting yourself in their shoes (assuming they fit) and see how you'd feel if a subordinate did what you want to do. It may actually be helpful for the firm you work for, or it may be counterproductive. Tread lightly.

Big Place, Small Place

"The Internet is a very big place. The Internet is a very small place," observes long-time Net columnist Daniel P. Dern. What does he mean? In the aggregate, the Internet is a huge environment, now too large for any one person to fully comprehend; in fact, it's kind of intimidating in that way. However, you shouldn't be concerned with branding yourself to every being on the Net; that's too unfocused. Your mission is to laser-target one, two, or three niches within that huge biosphere and concentrate your power, your expertise, and your brand within those spaces. In this way, the Net is a small place, kind of like a village. Unix wizard Chris Graham calls this "Tribal Marketing." In this tribe or village, reputation is everything. You don't want to risk ruining your reputation for short-term gains at the expense of losing your long-term face. Contribute to your tribe. Figure out what your target tribe needs, and then fill it if you can—whether with a Web site, an emailed newsletter, or a moderated discussion list. John Audette moderates the I-Sales discussion list and has garnered a reputation that goes far beyond his 8000 participants.

Go to where your constituents *aren't*! It's very well and good to talk to your peers, but, if they're like you, you'll learn from each other, and you may not get many closing deals. That's why new media lawyers, such as Jonathan Ezor, belong to online ad discussion lists, as well as law lists. They have affinities with marketers because they're intellectual property lawyers. They establish a presence with potential clients, which is very smart on their behalf.

Personal Branding Strategies

Begin your personal branding by asking yourself the following:

- What groups do you want to market your personal brand to, and why?

- What sets you apart from anyone else like you?

- Who is like you and what are they doing out there to promote themselves? What can you learn from them? What mistakes of theirs shouldn't you make?

- What do you want from each constituency? Referrals? Sales? Leads for jobs or potential clients? Maybe you simply want to grow your *colleague-set*, as Tom Peters suggests in his landmark article on "Brand You" in *Fast Company*'s August 1997 issue.

Colleague-set is a network of your peers. You're apt to learn from them, get referrals from them, but are less likely to see direct business from them since they do things similar to what you do. It is referred to in Tom Peter's article in the August 1997 issue of *Fast Company*.

These strategies are all very valid reasons to employ the Net to propagate your brand with its USP.

Getting Your Name Out There

To further illustrate this, let me give you a page out of my own book (so to speak). I started my biweekly newsletter, *Web Digest For Marketers*, in 1994. It was a $50 subscription service at the time. When *The Wall Street Journal* put its entire paper online, and then some, for $49.95 per year, I realized that the boom had been lowered on the cost of content for the consumer. So I made the newsletter free. However, before doing so, the legendary Dick Rich (cofounder of Wells Rich Green Advertising) advised me to change it to *Larry Chase's Web Digest For*

Marketers. Now my name is seen, at a conservative estimate, by over 80,000 marketers every month. Over 500 Web sites point to my publication. This is about a hundred times more than the number of sites that point to my actual company Web page. What's the branding lesson here? Give something away of value and put your name prominently on it. *WDFM* accounted for more than 60 percent of my consulting and seminar work last year. Obviously, personal branding on this level can and will pay off.

WDFM gives me a "sphere of influence," which is all-important to establishing your personal brand. People ask me to review their Web sites, and over 12,000 people receive *WDFM* by email every two weeks. I must admit I am delighted when people come up to me at trade shows and seminars and tell me how much they appreciate the service. It opens a dialogue through which potential business can and does flow.

I try to have a wide range of services or products my readers can purchase; in fact, you're reading one of these products. It may be a $25 access fee to the *WDFM* Archives (which you get *free*, having purchased this book—an example of personal brand cross-merchandising), a seminar, or a retainer relationship. I try to let the customer buy whatever type package of me that he or she can afford. If they can't afford, or don't want to afford, anything right then, fine. They get a free subscription to the email edition of *WDFM*. Sometime later, when they're ready to buy something, they'll be reminded of me by that free newsletter.

Whenever people do subscribe, they get an email back from me, confirming their subscription and a little bit about the other products and services I offer. Notice how the welcome message, shown in Figure 5.1, informs the reader about things he or she will predictably want to know about *WDFM* while at the same time embedding information about me and my services.

Another example of personal branding is the practices that journalists employ. Their reputation is always on the line. This is why they jealously protect their integrity and reputation, as you should yours. Once a journalist loses his or her credibility, it is lost for good.

There are also big offline personal brands that have been migrated online, such as Martha Stewart (http://www.marthastewart.com). At the time of this writing, this site supports her offline products and services, such as her latest book and television/radio programs. There are personal brands such as the Drudge Report (http://www.drudgereport.com), which was spawned entirely online. Matt Drudge has tens of thousands of people who visit his site faithfully to see what gossip is coming out of the political, entertainment, and general news rumor mills—very controversial, very political, and a very smart way to make a mark for himself.

Figure 5.1 *WDFM*'s subscription email.

***

Greetings,

I'm Larry Chase. Thank you for subscribing to my Web Digest For Marketers(WDFM). Every two weeks you'll get WDFM via email. Each issue contains 15 short reviews of the latest business-oriented sites. Each review (usually not longer than 120 words) offers a constructive critique of a site that might be useful to you. Some of the categories covered are Finance, Media, Consumer Goods, Advertising, Research, Automotive, HiTech/Telecom, Recruitment, Outstanding Content, plus about seven categories. I've been publishing WDFM since April 1994. It was the first publication of its kind and is currently syndicated to Ad Age and Business Marketing Magazine, among others. Over 80,000 people read WDFM reviews monthly. The irony is that more people read it offline than online.

WDFM's parent company is Chase Online Marketing Strategies, which offers Internet seminars and consulting. I speak in the U.S. and Europe mostly, but will go anywhere. Just ask me:). My most popular seminars are those in which I customize the presentation for the audience I'm addressing. I've spoken at Internet World, The New York Times, PG&E, LegalTech, and many others.

My consulting clients include Con Edison, EDS, New York Life, and 3Com. My clients often ask me to help them determine what a company like theirs should be doing in a medium like the Net right now and down the road. I call this market-mapping.

I could go on, but I won't. If you do want more information on my consulting and seminar services, please visit http://chaseonline.com, or email me at larry@chaseonline.com. In the meantime, enjoy my Web Digest For Marketers.

Cordially, Larry Chase/Pres, Chase Online Marketing Strategies
email: larry@chaseonline.com | http://chaseonline.com
voice: +01 (212) 876-1096 fax: +01 (212) 876-1098
Free subscription to Web Digest For Marketers http://wdfm.com
See my Selling Websites to a Reluctant Boss in Ad Age's NetMarketing
http://www.netb2b.com/cgi-bin/cgi_article/monthly/97/07/01/article.3

No, But I Saw the Web Site

Very often, people will visit a book site on the Internet and not buy the book, or a movie site and not go to the flick. Nevertheless, they are left with an impression of your "brand" from offline, migrated online. Perhaps they didn't buy the product that time, but that visit to the site for the current Batman movie may well serve as a preconditioner for the next sequel. In other words, the visit today may help next year's sale. Think of it as a placeholder in a future customer's mind.

Respecting Your Tribe

One of the most critical keys to branding to your constituency is to respect people's time. Since many of us don't have the reputation of Procter & Gamble or IBM, we're obliged to tell a visitor to our Web site what we do, why we do it, and how we do it. Although it's not intentional, I've noticed that many personal and small company Web sites come across as being oblique when it comes to telling the visiting surfer what exactly it is that they do. I often run into a flowery mission statement that sounds too self-absorbed: "This company was founded on a deep-seated philosophy that everything is everything . . . " Readers may just get bored and end up going elsewhere. This is why it is imperative to predict what visitors to your Web site want and when they want it. In short, be your customer, or potential customer, then create a Web site that you would want to visit.

You are probably more at ease when a telemarketer says, "Ms. So and So, I know you're busy, so I'm not going to take much of your time." The exact same thing is true on the Net, both on the Web and in email. The A&E cable TV network has a great tagline: "Time Well Spent." Adopt this principle in all your online and offline communiqués. Is my time on your Web site well spent? If I have to grope around to find your point, it isn't. If I have to wait for your graphics to load on my slow or average modem connection, it isn't. But if you give me a "time experience" that pays off in adding value to me, it is. Figure out what "it" is and serve it up sooner than later.

This goes for email, too. Get to the point fast. People respect focus and speed. When I see an email from someone who always is asking for something, I tend not to open it right away . . . if ever. The old cultural protocol of the Net still holds: Give in order to receive. This doesn't mean you have to give the family farm away, far from it, but do give something if you expect people to give to you—either their time spent in looking at your Web site, or later, perhaps, a favor you may need from them that falls in their purview, even if all it is a reciprocal link to your site, or, heaven forbid, a sale.

Whether in a discussion list of your peers, a one-to-one email, or on your Web site, people in this medium respect you for having done your homework. This is rarely explicitly stated, but definitely is a truism. If you ask questions of a discussion list that could've been found elsewhere with ease, you're either a newbie or lazy. If you're a newbie, that list will hopefully treat you with respect and point you to the information, usually in the form of the list's Frequently Asked Questions (FAQ). If you're lazy and repeatedly take without giving, you start to tarnish your personal brand in that community, which consists of people you wish to influence. It is to your advantage to be prepared. Be patient with newbies once you're no longer one—as with everything on the Net, it can and probably will pay off down the road. You never know where a potential contact lies.

Be Memorable

Put your name, contact information, and USP or some offer of value in your signature at the end of all your email messages as well as your Usenet newsgroup postings. I have booked seminar engagements simply because someone read my signature file.

When naming your firm or Web site, give it an obvious name from a branding perspective. "Larry Chase's Web Digest For Marketers" tells you exactly what you get. It's also helpful for the search engines, as explained elsewhere in this book. Clever names are too cryptic for this day and age. KN2KB Inc. may look cool today, but you don't want a trendy name that will look like a has-been tomorrow. In five years, you don't want people saying, "Oh, that's a name from the late 1990s." People like names that spell out exactly what a company does, such as Danny Sullivan's Search Engine Report (http://searchenginewatch.com), or Eric Ward's URLwire Service, or John Kremer's Book Marketing Tip of the Week.

Address for Success: What's in a Domain Name?

Branding for individuals and companies begins right here, with your domain name. If you're an individual and your name is still available as a domain name, grab it. If it isn't, then get something close to it, such as your first initial and last name before the .com, or use a hyphen between first and last names. You may not use the domain name right away, but it's good to have it reserved for you. At the time of writing, this costs $50 per year, and you must register two years at the same time. When I found eight other Larry Chases on the Net, I went directly to the InterNIC at http://rs.internic.net/cgi-bin/whois (see Figure 5.2) to see if any other Larry Chases had registered larrychase.com. They hadn't. So I did. You can also check for domain registration at WhoIs.Net (http://www.whois.net), and even set up a free weekly email report of who registers a domain name close to yours.

Figure 5.2 A WhoIs query will help you narrow your choice of a domain name.

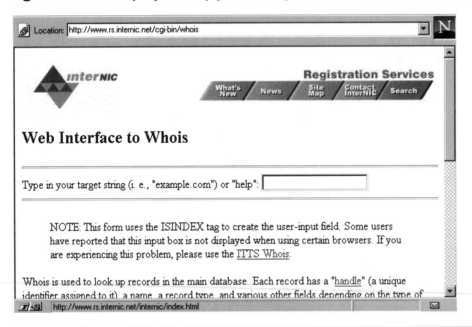

Try not to obsess over your domain name. Yes, it is important and pivotal to everything you do with regard to branding, but if someone has already registered your last name (more than likely), or your first and last name, or your company name, relax. It isn't the end of the world. Netscape was called Mosaic Communications in the beginning. Its domain name was mcomm.com. The company was pressured not to use the name of the original Web browser developer. It agreed and—*poof!*— it became Netscape Corporation at http://www.netscape.com.

Be as Accessible as Possible

Keep in mind, when choosing your domain name, that people are going to get to your Web site from a number of different directions, just as they travel to your company or house using different routes. Some people will come in by the search engine route, while others have already bookmarked you in their browsers. Many will try to go directly to you by typing what they think your Web address is in their Web browser's address field. For example, if you wanted to go to Fidelity Investments, you might assume you know what its domain name is and simply type www.fidelity.com—and you get there. However, this easy route wasn't always the case for Fidelity. Its original address was www.fid-inv.com. I once wanted to write an article that included the wide array of calculators Fidelity offers on its Web site. It was after business hours and I was on a deadline. For the life of me, I couldn't find it even using my extensive expertise with search engines. Therefore, Fidelity missed out on a great free reference due to an arcane domain name. It did recently add the "fidelity" domain name, which stands in its favor.

Remember to be that unknowing person who's trying to get to your Web site. Think of every conceivable way that person might enter your site's name into the browser. Not only do I have www.chaseonline.com, but I also have www.chase-online.com. Have your address with and without the www. prefix. Those Ws are not necessary to make a Web URL connection, even though many think they are.

Keep in mind that many people are still fuzzy about the difference between a Web site address and an email address. You must communicate your email and Web address in the lowest common denominator when talking to your constituents. Simply saying, "Go to chaseonline-dot-com" can and does confuse your audience. Clearly specify that larry@chaseonline.com is the email address and that http://chaseonline.com is the Web address. S-p-e-l-l i-t o-u-t! The general public doesn't yet understand any sort of shortened approach to email or Web site addresses in advertising, correspondence, or any other sort of communication from you. Don't lose your audience by taking what you think is a simpler route. Using yourname.com for a Web address is premature and is considered shorthand.

If the name you want is already taken as a domain, think of a "solution name" that people can remember, such as www.NoBugsNow.com if you're an exterminator. In retrospect, you may even find it was a better way to go. Once you settle on your domain name, keep it. I can tell you, from personal experience, that it's a nightmare to change it after you've let it propagate online and offline. For example, *WDFM* used to reside at http://advert.com/wdfm. When I moved it to its own domain name at http://wdfm.com, I had to tell hundreds of sites to change their links. There are still those wayward souls who bookmarked the old URL and found out about the change over a very long period of time. I have had to set up pages that redirect them to the new site. My logs show that every day, people still go to the old address, even though I changed the domain name years ago. Remember, then, you also have all your stationery, business cards, collateral, and advertising materials you have to change. The lesson here is you must think very hard before you change your domain name. It's like changing your street address or phone number, but worse.

Putting Your Domain Name to Good Use

Once you have your domain name registered, use it across everything: your Web address, email, mailing lists, and so on. Remember that conformity is the key. If your Web site has one domain name, such as RedSledCompany.com, and your email address is BigBobMan@aol.com, you have a few options to marry the two to prevent branding confusion for your clients:

1. You can get a Web server provider to house your domain name on its server.

   This server may hold hundreds of other Web sites, each with its own domain name, which is called a *virtual domain*. At the time of writing, this option costs between $40 and $75 per month for a relatively small site. Some few sites still do it free or a smaller annual fee, but they are getting increasingly difficult to find. Make sure you can edit your site from your own desktop so you don't get tied in to using the provider's services for each and every change you wish to make to your Web pages, unless you want to buy their services and let them do that work for you. Then, ask your provider how much it will cost to forward email addressed to your domain name to your other mail account (such as in the previous example, in which the person has a domain registered and housed on a server under the domain name, but has email going to AOL). It shouldn't be much. Some providers may even throw in this option as a deal-closer.

   Keep in mind that when you reply back to those who have sent you mail to your virtual domain name, they will see that you're coming from AOL. You can set up another system in reverse with your provider to prevent this from happening. This means that your mail sent back will first have to be routed to your provider, and then sent out from there to the recipient. The extra routing shouldn't take much longer than going directly. By employing this option, your Web server provider is doing more for you than simply housing your Web site with your domain name. It is hosting your domain name entirely.

   > **TIP**
   > A **virtual domain** is one that resides on someone else's Web server, but the address is the domain *you* registered and own. In other words, a client will type in http://www.yourdomain.com into his or her browser, and arrive at your site. However, if you are housed as a virtual domain on, say, panix.com's server, it's really going to panix.com, even though the URL shows your domain name.

2. Instead of setting up this labyrinth, you may want to simply have an Internet account with a provider that houses your Web site with your domain name, as well as provides you with Internet access with an email account that uses your own domain name. (For instance, you could be both http://www.RedSledCompany.com and bigbob@redsledcompany.com, using that method.)

Many Internet access providers offer you 5 or 10 megabytes of space on a Web server when you get an Internet access account. The downside is that although I may have an email address of larchase@blueclambox.com, my Web site will be http://www.blueclambox.com/user/chase/index.html, unless I pay to have a virtual domain created for me on my ISP's server. This is a cheap way to go (between $20 and $35 a month usually), but try giving someone a Web address like that verbally! It's like subleasing a post office box. If you can possibly afford it, be your own person with your own domain name.

If you have a mailing list, use a service that can *spoof* your email address. Spoofing or faking your email address is done to make it seem as though your email is coming from you when in fact, it's coming from a third party. This is helpful if you outsource your mailing list and want it to seem as if it is coming directly from you when, in fact, it's coming from your provider of the list service. In other words, pretend your company is called Red Carpet, and your mailing list address is admin@RedCarpet.com, but Spark List is housing and sending out your mailings for you. You want to make sure that the return address as well as the originating address shows as RedCarpet, not Spark List! Remember to use branding to prevent, not cause, confusion.

 You can start a mailing list for free! Cool List (http://www
.coollist.com) will let you send your mailings to your subscribers
for free in exchange for putting one of its ads at the bottom of
each message. Cheap? Yes. Confusing for the reader? Very. But
if you alert your subscribers about what's going on and it's all
you can afford right now, go for it.

Protecting Your Domain

If you choose a name that you believe someone else will challenge, you should protect yourself. Right now, if another firm challenges your right to a domain name, the InterNIC informs you that you've got 30 days to vacate the domain while the dispute is settled. At that point, it will be in a type of stasis until the dispute is resolved. In order to prevent this, you may want to quickly protect yourself by trademarking or servicemarking the letters or words that make up your domain name. If you register it through the U.S. Patent and Trademark Office, your potential adversary may pick this up on a standard trademark search if he is looking for such things, and many do. The InterNIC recognizes many government trademark offices. It recognizes the Tunisian Trademark Office, which just so happens to offer 24-hour turnaround trademarks. If you register it there, it's much less likely the other guy is watching the Tunisian Trademark Office. In this way, you can avoid getting displaced from your domain name. At the time of writing, you could get an overnight trademark from Tunisia for $800 from http://www.iprop.com.

Okay, enough about you; let's talk about your company's image on the Net.

Your Company's Image and the Internet: Migrating Your Current Company's Image Online

One of the first things you have to ask yourself is if you should keep your brand name as the domain name or "Net-ize" it. Columbia House (music company) uses its name as a domain name. Its mission online is quite clear: Sell music and entertainment products. But what about a company that makes detergent? Do you really expect Tide to sell its detergent on its Web site? If not, then what is its *raison d'être*? Procter & Gamble answers this challenge well. Tide's detergent site is at http://www.clothesline.com. (Yes, P&G owns http://www.tide.com as well.) Rather than showing the obligatory old print ads and TV commercials from the 1950s, Tide brought utility to its site by offering helpful tips on stain removal and other laundering tips (see Figure 5.3). Ask the "Stain Detective" for help by choosing your stain, fabric, and fabric color, and the online program does the rest. This brand smartly made the migration from offline to online. That's not a bad impression to leave with a consumer. Who says you can't do good branding for "low-involvement packaged goods," such as laundry detergent, on the Net?

Another brilliant example of taking a "low-involvement product" onto the Net is Ragú spaghetti sauce, which features a made-up personality called "Mama," who nags you and tries to get you to eat right (see Figure 5.4). It's an engaging site that packs an entirely new personality into a jar of spaghetti sauce. You also have the option of giving her your email address to be reminded of any coupons, updates to the site, or new products. Its success is proven by the thousands of Netizens who visit each day.

Some publishers have grappled with whether it's better to migrate their traditional brands online as they are, or to morph them into something completely

Figure 5.3 Tide Detergent is a good example of an offline brand brought to the Internet.

different. Time Warner's magazine division is represented online by Pathfinder, one of the oldest and deepest sites on the Net. It contains all of Time Warner's magazine properties and then some. However, in the early days, I remember being confused; I thought Pathfinder was the site for Toyota's Pathfinder, which actually was established soon thereafter. Once I understood the difference, I was amazed at the breadth and depth of Pathfinder's content. I did have to wonder though, if someone looking for *Time* magazine might otherwise miss it. Time Warner smartened up and linked www.time.com so that it goes to the Pathfinder site automatically. All of its magazines are now double entries like this, which is good branding procedure, even if done retroactively.

If you do expand your online offerings, make sure they all support each other in some way. I use management and sales consultant Barney Zick's "Three-Legged Stool" analogy. Each line or leg of business helps the next one. My publishing activities help my consulting and speaking lines of business, and vice versa.

Another way to extend your brand is to ally with a complementary line of business. For example, the *Ad Age* magazine site (http://www.adage.com) has a "jobs"

Figure 5.4 Ragú takes a whimsical approach to online branding with great success.

section. *Ad Age* didn't want to actually get into the jobs database business, so it set up a cooperative arrangement with The Monster Board jobs database (http://www .monsterboard.com, also http://www.monster.com—another example of registering two site domain names that refer to only one URL). The *Ad Age* site delivers added value to its readers, while giving some exposure to the Monster Board database. Trade Show Central (http://www.tscentral.com) has a similar arrangement with Ziff-Davis at http://www.ZDnet.com.

One way you can raise the barrier of entry for your competitors is to excel so far ahead of them that the cost of entry to leap-frog over you becomes prohibitive. In fact, the worth of your brand may well be assessed by how much it would cost to duplicate or exceed it.

Marketing Professional Services on the Net

Let's face it, a lawyer or highly paid consultant is going to have image problems if he or she starts sending out coupons in those Carolyn Wright card decks you get in your regular mailbox. On the Internet, however, professionals and their services are right at home with expanding their reach to new prospects. Why? Because whether you're a lawyer, accountant, or highly paid consultant, you're in the information business. The Internet handles information very well, as you know.

Arent Fox is a prestigious law firm in Washington, D.C. Its site features the wide array of attorneys it employs, complete with pictures and email addresses. In fact, if you want to ask one of the specialized lawyers a question, you can. Click on the picture and send him or her an email. That attorney will get back to you, free of charge. Indeed, you may be a candidate for an ongoing relationship with that attorney. The consulting firm of Ernst & Young not only represents all its divisions online, but also fashioned an entirely new product called "Ernie." Ernie gives you unlimited email access to specialists at Ernst & Young for $6,000 a year. From there, you have the option of upgrading to telephone access for more money. I must admit, I was very skeptical of this in the beginning, as it was my thinking that Ernie diluted the prestige of Ernst & Young's offline brand. I was wrong. In fact, quite the contrary is true; Ernie has turned into a success. Ernie has been instrumental in bringing in new business, not only at the email level, but also by upgrading services to higher forms of contact, including phone access, where the dollar volume is more substantial. This is brilliant!

Starting a Brand Online

Yahoo!, Excite, CNET, Amazon, Netscape . . . these names weren't in our vernacular just a few years ago. In fact, if you went back in time five years and listened to yourself today, you probably wouldn't understand much of what you're saying: "HTTP this . . . "; "email that . . . "; " . . . what about WWW?" Will your online brand become a household word in five years? Anything's possible. Yahoo! (Yet Another Hierarchical Officious Oracle) was started by two college students at Stanford University as simply a browsable search engine. Today it gets 40 million page views a day. I think it's more likely that your brand will resonate within a specific category; so while your brand may not turn into a household name, it should be a well-respected brand on key desktops.

If you're going to start up a brand, you must practice due diligence. In other words, use the cybersleuthing skills taught in Chapter 4, "http://007 Spying on Your Competitors and Yourself," and find out everything you can about those who are already in that niche. Be hard on them and even harder on yourself. What do you offer that they don't? Is it enough to make a difference? Also, beware if there are no competitors. It may be that you've stumbled onto a niche first. Then again, maybe someone else found it and decided not to proceed. Why? What did they find out? Or was it just not right for them and might be for you? This is what I mean by being tough on yourself. Management and marketing consultant Mac Ross once told me, "Beware of having no competition: there may be a reason."

> **TIP** What I recommend here is blasphemy to Web site developers: If you have limited funds, spend less on the bells and whistles of your Web site and considerably more on marketing. By marketing, I don't mean one blast of marketing at launch, but rather an ongoing promotional program that keeps you in front of your target group on an ongoing basis. If you don't have the amount of gunpowder needed to do this, you may want to rethink your business plan. The world will not click a path to your Web page unless it knows about it.

If you do launch a brand that starts out online, you should seriously consider whether it "has legs." That is, can you extend the brand online as well as offline? Excite Corporation started out as a search engine. Now it has expanded into offering chat and email. This is something I would've never thought of: "Hey, let's go hang out by the search engine and chat." Wouldn't you assume that someone who gets to a search engine has email already? I would, yet I'm starting to see people subscribing to my *Web Digest For Marketers* from mailexcite.com. Perhaps people are using the mailexcite accounts as stealth accounts for competitive reconnaissance, heeding my own advice from the last chapter!

Look at how Yahoo! has extended its brand, both on and offline. My Yahoo! offers a filtering service for news and press release wires. A journalist recently said to me in passing that he likes to get his sports news from My Yahoo! Could this take away at least a little piece of "attention-share" from *Sports Illustrated*, or the sports section of a newspaper? You bet it could, and it does. Attention-share is otherwise known as *time*, which is a finite commodity. Therefore, this fight is a zero-sum game; if I get 10 minutes of your time, some other site, channel, station, or newspaper loses that 10 minutes. Successful online brands can and do take away customers and attention-share from offline brands, if utilized properly.

Additionally, the people working at Yahoo! have extended their brand awareness smartly offline. I heard a radio commercial here in New York City telling me to go to the Web page of "Yahoo! New York" for more details on its local retail outlet. While visiting Maidstone Arms, a country inn in East Hampton, Long Island, I saw free postcards with the name of the inn on it and the printed question: "Have You Yahoo!'d today?" *Yahooligans!* and *Yahoo! Internet Life* are online sites and print magazines. Yahoo! is so ubiquitous a brand now that it is oozing out of the walls. It's using branding the way it's meant to be used, as a preconditioner. When Net newbies come online, they'll check out Yahoo! because it's familiar from offline campaigns. They'll let their kids read *Yahooligans!* because, after all, Yahoo! has a reputation to protect. Therefore, it is a trusted product. That trust traces directly back to branding.

Online Intermediary Brands

It's commonly thought that the Net "disintermediates" middlemen. It's true, it does. Most people with the words *agent*, *reseller*, or *broker* in their names should take note. Indeed, the Internet is creating a certain amount of friction between manufacturers and their respective sales channels because those manufacturers see the potential for selling directly to the end user, without the help or commissions of the middlemen. Fortunately, the Net is also opening up new opportunities for middlemen. These middlemen don't usually need much inventory. Their job is to bring buyer to seller, just like in traditional terms.

A relatively new online brand is cybermeals (http://www.cybermeals.com), which offers the seller (in this case, a restaurant) more customers and the user a finely tuned selection of deals on meals in the near vicinity (see Figure 5.5). I tried cybermeals myself, even though I was skeptical at first. Why should I order online, when I can call a familiar restaurant to deliver? The cybermeal database turned up three Japanese restaurants near me that I didn't even know about. One offered a lunchtime special of chicken teriyaki, salad, dumplings, and rice for $5.95. (It was so good it had to be a loss leader.) Cybermeals took the order and faxed it directly to the restaurant, which in turn, called me to confirm four minutes after placing the order. As the food was coming up in the elevator, I got an email also confirming the order and letting me know I might get a phone call (already had) for confirmation. I ordered, I ate, I loved it, and I now eat more chicken teriyaki for lunch around here!

Quotesmith is a different kind of middleman brand, this time for insurance. Here again, it offers value to both buyer and seller. The seller—in this case, the insurance companies with whom Quotesmith has a commissionable broker relationship—gets prospects it otherwise wouldn't have. The browsing customer, who is probably doing research on what sort of insurance to buy, gets loads of good information to help him make up his mind. Now, insurance is a grudge purchase if ever there was one, but when you get down to doing your homework, you're going to appreciate someplace like Quotesmith assisting in that task.

Figure 5.5 Cybermeals is a good example of an intermediary brand linking a hungry buyer to a nearby restaurateur.

Some new middlemen are direct challenges to old middlemen. Trade Show Central is one such example. Before it existed, you had to buy a costly print directory of all trade shows in the United States that had to be frequently updated. Now, that information is not only free at Trade Show Central but it's also more timely, as there are 3000 updates made daily to the database of over 30,000 trade shows and events worldwide. This is an interesting example of what I call *contiguous cannibalism*, referred to in Chapter 7, "Online Events, Promotions, and Attractions." Succinctly put, contiguous cannibalism causes one man's core business to be another's loss leader. Trade Show Central gives away what the bound volume charges for so that Trade Show Central can get your attention for its advertisers. In the near future, look for online brands to expand into other lines of business that feed them income. It isn't too hard to imagine an overnight shipping company offering free catalog software and even Web site housing for your catalog if you give it your shipping business. We've already seen long-distance telephone companies offer Internet access as a loss leader in exchange for your long-distance business.

Marketing to Yourself: When Should You?

Years ago, I got into an argument with an ex-vice president of NBC. He said the Net would never become the norm. I said he had missed the point. The Net wouldn't be a single norm, but thousands of norms. In these niches, you are quite apt to be marketing to people who are just like you. When you're setting up marketing strategies and the Web sites thereafter, you should ask yourself if you would click on that banner. Do you like waiting 40 seconds for a screen to load on your computer? No? Then it's a good bet your target group won't either. But it goes much deeper than that.

As I mentioned earlier, be tough on yourself. If you aren't, your prospects and clients will be. Be predictive in what your audience wants. After all, they share many traits with you. Don't just give them what they want at the time they are expected to ask for it. Delight them by giving them something they didn't expect. Don't leave it entirely to market research to tell you exactly what they're going to want next, because they usually don't know! In 1939, when people in offices were asked if they would like dry copy documents, many replied, "What for? We have carbon paper." Remember, people by nature do not like change. However, if you can spark their enlightened self-interest, you may not only have changed their habits (the hardest thing for any marketer to do), but you may have also gained a devoted and passionate prospect or client. When Xerox finally did come out with its copier, people bonded with the brand, once they understood the impact of its value. This is something those people in 1939 couldn't have possibly projected from what was then an abstract concept.

So how do you find those nuggets that delight your constituency? Look to yourself. My *Web Digest For Marketers* originally had a market of one: me. Then I found other people wanting the same information. If you ever catch yourself saying, "Why can't I simply . . . ," write the thought down and see if you can "product-ize" it and deliver it on the Net. Maybe there's a newsletter for your industry that hasn't been done yet. Perhaps there are already six, but they're too long, or not in-depth enough, or have some other weakness that you can identify as the niche to fill.

Another idea is to visit other industry categories for ideas you can migrate into your category. This ingenious approach was given to me by marketing guru Jay Abraham when I visited the financial categories on the Net for my client Con Edison. There were no other utilities offering online customer account information at the time. One year later, Con Edison broke new ground by offering customer account information and online payment options. This was considered a breakthrough in the otherwise risk-adverse industry of utilities.

When Shouldn't You Market to Yourself?

There are times when we truly are only talking to ourselves and no one else. What I find fascinating is that some of these expressions turn into Web sites. Companies are like biospheres, each with its own culture. It's quite conceivable that an interface makes perfect sense to a group of people who live and breathe that culture day in and day out. This is like viewing your company from within the goldfish bowl. Remember, a Web site can be accessed by anybody. You need to look at your company from *outside* the bowl and create the interface accordingly.

I suggest you live in the shoes of your customer or prospective client. I remember visiting a Web site of a large brand of soda. As I hit the homepage of the site I was presented with a dialog box while the page was coming in. The dialog box told me that in order to fully appreciate this site, I would have to download some application that would let me play the audio that went along with the visuals on the screen. What kind of branding impression is the visitor left with after going to all that trouble? "Diet Cola: You're Inadequate"? To avoid this dilemma, ask yourself some questions: What sort of things will make visitors delighted they came in the first place? Is it appropriate for them to smile or laugh out loud, or be intrigued by a juicy news abstract or idea? What will make them bookmark you so they can return again and again? How can you keep them in your sphere of influence? Ask these questions for every page you create on your Web site, not just the first page. The average surfer stays through three to five clicks (or pages), if you're lucky.

Building Brands with Online Communities

There's been a great deal written about online communities. While they are an important component to some brand building, communities are by no means the end-all. It is important to keep in mind that just because you have some people in your community one day, doesn't necessarily mean they'll be there the next. For example, Auto-By-Tel doesn't need to build a community of online new car buyers. It is highly unlikely it would work if it tried, as that community of interest is ever-changing. New people come in, while those who have purchased, leave.

People also gravitate to that which ultimately serves them best. Adam Smith's invisible hand of capitalism is at work here. If another community sprouts up that better serves some, if not all, of its constituencies, the population will go to the new place—believe me. Brand loyalty off and on the Net is a fleeting thing that must be constantly nourished. Since the cost and barrier of entry are low, anyone can and does try to poach your community. I also remain very skeptical that these places can amass large enough communities to actually earn a great income from advertising and transactions created by inducing brand loyalty.

In addition, there is the added problem of how to induce *clickthroughs* on banner ads that are placed in chat communities. Why would someone who is talking to a group of like-minded individuals about, say, local sports teams clickthrough on a banner ad placed on his or her community chat page *and leave the discussion* for your site? It is becoming more evident in watching online community projects that it could be doubtful that advertising placed in such a situation will ever do anything other than act as billboard impressions for brands, as visitors to their sites are evidently *not* leaving the chat to follow through on an advertisement on the chat page.

Numerous online communities are built for the sake of the communities themselves. This is fine, and as it should be. But nowhere is it written that simply because you have teeming hordes of people in one place talking about raising kids, they are then going to buy Pampers in the next breath. I think it's too much to ask for.

When *Not* to Create Communities

There are points where it is actually in your best interest *not* to create certain communities. I recently heard of a major bank that is preparing to set up communities for its clients. It may not be in the best interest of that bank to have its high-level clients talking to one another about their respective relationships with that bank. I heard of another firm that did a similar effort and found that clients were sharing negotiating tactics with each other on how to get the best deal from the sponsor of said community. I caution you here not to be vulnerable to the latest craze. Remember interactive TV. It hasn't really happened yet. All these things have their places and, over time, will have an increasing impact on the Internet. I'm not saying to completely disregard community building, either. I simply urge you not to get swept up in the updraft of the latest phase of hype. Everyone and everything in the late 1990s seem to be adding community to their online Web sites. Typically, a new technology or concept hits the media fan and takes over center stage for a while. Then, the technology either settles down into a niche and stays there for the rest of its product cycle, or it fades away into its final resting place in high-tech heaven (or high-tech hell!). Sometimes, the technology does in fact grow out of its niche and creeps into mainstream use. RISC computing was developed by IBM in the 1970s, but wasn't in widespread use until the 1990s. Again, just be skeptical of any technology or practice that heralds itself as the great change or paradigm shift of the week, including much-touted chat community technologies and implementation.

Ask yourself before you get into the community-building business: "Do I *need* a community? If I had one, what would I do with it?"

Web Page and Site Design and Your Image

As you know, first impressions mean a great deal in business. That first impression frames how we're going to feel about a given company. More and more, people will get those first impressions of your firm online, where they can see your site and hopefully interact with it. Your thoughtfulness of the visitor's encounter speaks volumes in terms of how that person will feel about your firm. The look and feel of your Web site has everything to do with what people think of you and, therefore, of your brand.

The Web has done to interface design what desktop publishing did to page layout. Being *able* to use 10 different fonts and numerous unmatched graphics on one page doesn't mean you should! The same is true for a Web interface. Technology has made it easier than ever for self-proclaimed designers to produce bad layouts for both the printed page and the homepage.

Don't Fool Yourself with Fancy Graphics

There's often a big disconnection between designers and the sites they're designing. I've seen clients look at dazzling Web pages and watch them swell with pride at how beautiful the site looks. When the designer demos a new page for them, they'll notice how quickly the page loads . . . or does it? Many people don't realize that the desktop PC doesn't stay in constant contact with the Web server. It brings in the page and stops talking to the Web server until another page, which hasn't been previously asked for, is requested. The point is that many of those graphics that seem to be flying up onto the screen with alacrity are not coming from the server at all. They're already stored locally on the PC you're looking at—if that page has been viewed before. Even if you press Reload, you may not see or experience what a first-time visitor to your Web site experiences. If you want to be absolutely sure your computer is void of any images on the server, flush your cache, quit your browser, and yes, actually reboot the machine. This is the only way to guarantee that you're looking at something that is loading fresh right off the Web, in real time.

Visiting a Web site is not just a graphic experience; it's also an experience of time. Many site designers look at each page as a single experience, rather than one of many site views that are loaded onto the screen of an impatient surfer. I know of some art directors who are very proud of their design work and have hard copies of the screens laminated and put in their portfolios. However, a laminated page in an art director's portfolio isn't the primary reason a Web site should be designed.

I'm not suggesting that you strip out all your graphics. Far from it. When I hear people complain about how they hate to wait for the graphics, I tell them I can solve their problem in one second. Simply surf with graphics turned off. They sheepishly smile and say, "Oh, but I like the graphics; it adds to the experience." They will wait a small amount of time for a pleasant interface. For an example of a smart-looking, well-thought-out interface, check out http://www.magnavox.com (see Figure 5.6). Additionally, http://www.projectcool.com is a gold mine from a conceptual artistic and user point of view (see Figure 5.7). This site was started in part by Glenn Davis, who originated the "Cool Site of the Day" genre. We often look there for new sites to review for *Web Digest For Marketers*.

I advise clients that no homepage should be more than 30K in size, with secondary pages no larger than 20K. "This doesn't allow for much creative room," complain many designers. Tough. Those are the real-world limits, and even that is pushing it. There are survey statistics showing that an astonishing number of people don't know the speed of their modems. It's a reasonable thing not to know, when you think about it. They probably bought the computer with an internal modem, and the speed was just one more specification in a blur of megahertz, RAM, gigabytes, and so on. Many people are surfing at below optimal speeds without even knowing it.

Figure 5.6 Magnavox is a good example of a thoughtful user interface.

Figure 5.7 Visit Project Cool for good examples of online interfaces.

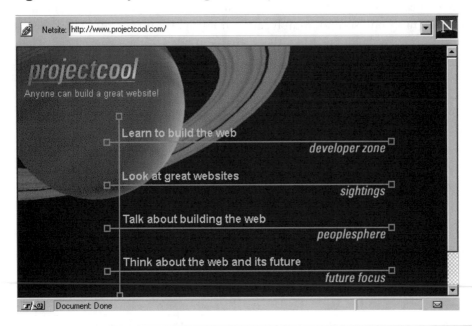

If your site has many people visiting from AOL, think about this reality check. When an AOL user logs on, he or she often gets downloads of graphics before he or she can navigate. It's sort of like an inoculation. What happens is that your computer receives graphic files at the beginning of a session, so they don't have to be loaded each and every time you go to that part of AOL. Therefore, most of the graphics AOLers see are already local on their machine; to them, AOL pages load quickly. When they go out onto the Net, though, the graphics are often flying in for the first time to their machines. When designing your pages, you must keep in mind that if you have many people visiting from AOL, they may think that your pages load slowly.

Other problems occurring on the open Internet can and do happen with regularity. The Net could simply experience a "bad hair day" in the entire Northeast for some known or unknown reason. Accessing U.S. sites from Europe after noon can take forever, too, as the transatlantic circuits are nearly always jammed. If you want an idea of how slow your site comes in from overseas, try accessing a site over there at the worst time of day for your region on the Net. That will give you some idea.

According to Media Matrix (http://www.mediamatrix.com), users' average time of involvement from the time they request a page until the time they leave that page is 1 minute. Therefore, if the page takes 40 seconds to load, you'll only have their attention for about 20 seconds. The lesson here is to design your page to load as quickly as possible, so that users spend more time taking in your message rather than sitting there on "mental pause," waiting for the page to come onto their screens.

Also, be sure to tell your designer to have the text files load ahead of the graphics files when your Web page is requested by a user. This lets the user read the text while the graphics are still coming in.

This medium clearly employs the design principles of the Bauhaus, where "less is more." Brevity is appreciated, if not demanded. Study how Helmut Krone, the incomparable advertising art director, brought these principles to advertising by looking at the original Avis and Volkswagen ads. I had the distinct pleasure of knowing this icon of advertising. He once said that an advertising page should be identifiable to you from 40 feet away. The impact and impression made on readers was that much greater when they were even closer. When someone approached Helmut, they would sometimes start babbling about themselves, out of nervousness. In that Bauhaus way of his, he would raise his hand and say, in that unmistakable low dulcet tone, "I don't want to know that much about you." Part of your job is to figure out when visitors to your Web site want "to know that much about you," and when they do not. Less is more. The following is a list of "design don'ts":

No clueless banners please. I want more than just a name; I want "Here's a darn good reason to stop what you're doing and click here" banners.

Making me wait is bad branding. It leaves a bad taste in my mouth. If that long download that I didn't expect doesn't pay off with a major paradigm shift, I'm out of here.

Don't force me through too many screens to get to the point. It's far too manipulative in this medium in which the customer is driving. If I have to keep clicking and reading and searching to find what I want, I'll go elsewhere.

Don't talk to me like I'm reading a brochure or watching TV. Those are other media. This is the Internet. Talk to me in your "online voice." Don't have one? Get one.

I'm more interested in me than I am in you. Remember that when I visit your site. "What's in it for me?" is what you must answer with every click.

Screen Real Estate

The browser window that you use to design your Web pages should look just like the majority of browser windows out there. The lion's share of surfers still have 14-inch monitors; yours may be larger or smaller. Average screen resolution is also set at 640 × 480 pixels (picture elements)—yours may be set to a higher resolution. Make sure all the toolbars of the browser are showing when you design a page set to that size and resolution—you don't want your visitor to have to scroll down vertically and horizontally because your Web page is just so big. Users may scroll down past that first screen if you've sufficiently captured their attention right in front of their eyes, or simply click on a link in that first screen. Yes, many people see more than that with bigger monitors and finer screen resolution. If you're sure your entire audience has that increased viewing window, then design to that. But I advise clients that you can't go wrong with designing to have the primary elements fit the least common denominator of viewing. Someone with a bigger monitor may then actually see your homepage without a vertical scroll bar. Have you ever seen the delight on someone's face when that happens? It says you are well organized and know how to design for a Web audience. Many firms simply won't be able to do this. Some will try to cram everything into that first screen, and that in itself is overwhelming, scrollbar or no. Use your best judgment when designing, then change your mind a few times.

You should also make available to a user a search tool that specifically searches only your site. That search feature should appear on every page of your site so the visitor can get from anywhere to anywhere quickly. A site map is also a good idea to give a bird's eye view to those who want it. When you have a search engine, clearly indicate it is for searching your site only.

We Live in a Low-Bandwidth World. Deal with It.

There are those who say that the Net won't be a true branding and mass medium until we have more bandwidth into the home and office. Not true. That's like saying TV couldn't be a mass medium until it was in color.

The fact that consumers can now be reached today via a two-way channel is a phenomenon of major proportions. You don't need full-motion video with quadraphonic sound and dancing holographic images to change people's media experience. Look what's happening already. Design for what's in place. Don't discount or dismiss our current technology as not being good enough. That kind of talk merely shirks the challenge to use what's here in ingenious ways.

Anyway, how do these high-bandwidth advocates suppose it's going to get to you? ISDN? At 10 cents a minute, that can add up. Some say satellite dishes will deliver higher bandwidth for less, but have you ever tried installing one of those things? Others insist the cable companies will move in. I can't get my cable company to get the wavy lines out of Seinfeld's face, so I definitely don't see it administering ISDN or broadband cable Internet access any time soon. In my opinion, the exponential expansion of the Net will continue, but it will go along the low-bandwidth route. This is just common sense: The lowest common denominator must drive the system in order for everyone to win.

Buying Media on the Net

Since branding budgets tend to be larger than other marketing budgets, I decided to park this aspect of marketing right here. Why? Because the dollar volume does start to get significant in this realm of media buying. You have five basic options when looking for media to purchase for your Web site, and, therefore, add value to your brand: search engines, content sites, discussion and mailing lists (which are covered in Chapter 8, "Direct Marketing and Sales Support"), and making your own channel of communication. You also have advertising networks, which I will address as well.

Search Engines

In Chapter 8, "Direct Marketing and Sales Support," I explain how to buy actual words on search engines that will increase your ad banner clickthrough rate, due to a more tightly targeted audience. That audience will see your ad come up each time they search for the words you purchased. Here, we'll cover *general rotation* buys, which means you don't buy anything but a general placement on the search engine page for any search word that hasn't been purchased and reserved by someone else. A search engine sales representative will like you much better if you come with a budget that will sustain over months.

Like any other media, the search engine companies have rate cards. These rate cards are a starting point for negotiations. Every scenario is different. Here are some basic negotiating tactics you can employ with the search engine companies.

Getting a Good Price

First off, you should know that they typically run loads of unpaid slots every day. They will sell out in certain categories, and they'll be sure to tell you that. For the most part, though, they have extra inventory. The key is to get that inventory for the best price.

If a sales representative from one of the search engines tries to come on strong (and some have) about how powerful his brand is and how he is selling out, listen patiently, as I do. Thank him for sharing the information and ask if he would like you to share your information with him. Of course, he will say "yes." You can then tell him that you have a budget—but quote him *20 percent less* than what you really plan on spending—that you're approaching three other search engines with that same budget, and you encourage him to offer a plan that will make the best of that budget. At this point, ask him if he would like to participate. So far, no one has ever said "no" to me. In this way, you've turned the tables. You make your needs the common denominator that the reps must cater to, rather than trying to untangle all their sales programs to figure out which one has the best value.

Getting the Right Number of Impressions

Once you've narrowed the field, listen to how your needs are being met. The keyword here is *impressions*. Make sure they are offering you real impressions. I've had sales representatives use an interesting closing tactic by telling me that extra impressions are had by people clicking on the Back button after they've finished looking at the Web page from a search result, and therefore, hitting the search results page again that has my client's banner ad still on it. I tell them that my client is paying for *initial* impressions. If a user happens to click "back" and see the ad again, that's great. But you cannot prove it, and I do not count that as an initial impression. If anyone is still trying to sell on hits, just leave. What you want are impressions. Hits are very misleading. Here's why: When you go to a Web site, you may see five graphics plus the text for that first page. Technically, that constitutes six "hits." You are interested only in your banner being viewed by your target audience and nothing else. Some sites will put your banner at the top and bottom of the page and may claim you are getting two hits or two impressions. Don't buy it.

An **impression** is considered to be one banner ad hitting one targeted user. Only proven impressions should be counted in a media buy. You should require proof of how many users from the target audience actually clicked through the banner ad to your site.

Remember I mentioned to quote the previously mentioned sales representative 20 percent below what you actually planned on spending? That extra cash can come in handy when you get down to the wire. Offer to up the ante by that extra 20 percent and see what the reps do in return. Make sure to ask if they offer an agency discount, which is typically 15 percent. Some do and some don't. If you're not an agency, become one quickly in order to take advantage of this extra margin. Some media outlets will want to see stationery or a bank account specifically dedicated to your agency or media-buying service function. If you're going to be buying media repeatedly, it's worthwhile. If not, try to get them to give you some kind of break on that end of the deal anyway.

Make sure that you have the opportunity to change your banners a few times a week, as you weed out the weak ones and replace with fresh attempts. See what the reports look like and choose the most successful ads to run again, and create new ones based on the successful ones. How often do those reports from the search engine company come out? The more often, the better, as it gives you a closer read on how your clickthroughs are coming. Remember to ask that of the representative when you're thinking about buying ad space. You do want clickthrough even though this is *just* branding, right? Getting your name up in front of them isn't enough. Don't you want to show them something slick back at your site, designed for this media flight especially? Of course you do.

TIP	Start your negotiations much earlier than you actually need your banner ads to run. Have the approval to purchase in hand, but keep that to yourself. At the opportune time, ask the rep if there is a signing bonus if the deal can be closed that very day. The bonus signing may come in the form of extra impressions or an additional discount on the purchase itself.

Get the Type of Contract You Want

Finally, it may be in your best interest to have short-term contracts, unless they really give you an incentive for going longer. I've noticed that clickthroughs will go up when changing search engine companies. I suspect it's because different users are seeing the ads for the first time, since users have brand loyalty to search engines, too. Having said all this about negotiating with representatives from search engines, I will say they are very good people to have on your side. If you ever move to buy words (as explained in Chapter 8, "Direct Marketing and Sales Support"), they can tell you which ones are most popular in your category. You may find some surprises. If you happen to be one of their favorite clients, you might just get a few more impressions than you bargained for as well.

Content Sites

There are many media buyers who prefer buying banners on content sites. This is usually due to the nature of the content. It's like buying an ad in what media-buying parlance is called "buff books," or high-interest magazines. High-tech and travel sites are often in high demand on the Net as these categories are now hot and heavy for consumers. Very often, these sites are related to print trade publications. If you're currently running ads in print, try getting the publishers to throw in some online impressions as well, to keep you happy as a print advertiser. If they avoid doing this for you, at least expect a very favorable discount on your online ad purchase. I know that some publishers divorce these two operations. I think that's nuts. They should be heavily cross-merchandising each other. Visit the site you wish to advertise on and see who is currently advertising there. Do this before contacting the sales representative for that site. See if many or most of the advertisers are those who also run in the company's print edition. If so, then it's a good bet that some added-value program is in place.

If your ad is going to rotate around the site, ask to see exactly where it rotates; you may or may not like parts of that rotation. By all means, get a guarantee on how many impressions will be delivered each month. I recently heard that some content sites wouldn't do this. I would never buy in that situation. After all, I'm guaranteeing them a certain number of dollars. I deserve a definable value in return.

Once you've purchased ads on someone else's site, it's only natural to want ongoing information. This can be handled in a number of ways. I/PRO is a third-party firm that audits sites to verify that the statistics the site are claiming are, in fact, correct. I have known some people who have mentioned that the delivery of information from I/PRO can take too long. In this medium of instant information, people want to know in real time what's going on. CNET gives its advertisers a password that allows them access to see charts that depict what's going on with their *avails* in close to real time. Other Web sites will simply give you access to their off-the-shelf referral log software, such as MS's Usage Analyst, which shows you in a more basic way what is happening: what pages got which hits from where, how many, and when. The rule of thumb here is, the higher the dollar volume, the more demanding you can be about feedback and the speed in which that feedback comes to you. For a comprehensive list of referral log options, visit Microsoft's Usage Analyst (formerly Intersé; http://www.backoffice.microsoft.com/products/features/UsageAnalyst/SiteServerE.asp).

Avail refers to an advertising availability. It is simply a space that is available for an ad. Think of it as an empty airline seat looking for a passenger. The term comes from the traditional print, audio, and video advertising markets.

Growth of Advertising on the Web

The general outlook on advertising on the Web is a skeptical one. At the time of writing, there are precious few sites that are solely supported by ad revenues. In addition, there are many thousands of new ad avails coming online every day. In the magazine world, you have about two new titles a day, so I figure there are maybe 120 new ad avails in the magazine world daily. Match that with the thousands of new avails coming onstream on the Web daily. What does this mean? It means ad rates will drop precipitously due to an open market. In fact, Web advertising may drag down advertising prices across all media. I can hear it now: "Why should I pay $30 per thousand readers in print when I can get it for $17 dollars per thousand on the Web?"

It's true the Web audience is growing at an astonishing rate. According to FIND/SVP—a research firm that studies a wide range of topics, including the Internet, its users, and its emerging patterns—19 percent of all American adults accessed the Web in 1997, 1998 will see 24 percent, and by the year 2002, 37 percent of American adults will surf the Web. This rapid growth is known in marketing circles as the *10 percent effect*, which we passed not long ago: Once a market has reached 10 percent of a population, it rockets to 30, 40, and 50 percent much faster than the initial growth rate. Remember VCRs? Once the price came down and the technology was standardized, everybody had to have one. So, yes, more people will come online to see more ads, but the growth of sites wanting to show you those ads is increasing at an unprecedented rate as well. Keep all this in mind when negotiating the media you wish to purchase.

Beyond Banners

Now that the Net is becoming omnipresent, big brand advertisers are asking themselves how to use this interactive medium as a branding tool. Are banners enough? I hear much talk about *going beyond the banner*. I think it's a lot of hooey. Banners are just fine, just like envelopes are fine. Both beckon you to click or open an envelope to see what's inside. You can't leave a huge impression on someone with a banner. You've got to pull him or her through to your Web site. Some mass merchants feel they don't have anything to say on a one-to-one level. I presented Tide detergent as an example earlier. Procter & Gamble found its online voice—so can the others.

The *beyond the banner* people now herald *interstitial ads* as the second coming. This is a bunch of malarkey. These advertisements are splash ads that come up between pages. You click on an icon on a Web site, and while the next page is loading, you get the interstitial. To me, it looks like subliminal advertising in slow motion. Much as some may try to convince me, I believe that ad takes additional time to load. Even if it really doesn't, I think the average user is going to think it does and will become irritated. I liken them to seeing commercials in a movie theater where I just paid $8 and all I want to see is the movie. The only site I've seen where interstitials work is something like the online "game show" You Don't Know Jack (http://www.jacknetshow.com), where between live game sets, you get what they are calling "interstitials." I'd call them commercial breaks, just like on TV, complete with animation and sound. But the growth of "static" interstitials that interrupt a Web site for no reason at all—those are interfering and only make the site visitor uncomfortable.

Advertising Networks

The challenge for big brand marketers is interesting. As more attention-share goes toward the Net, it must come from somewhere else. Time is a zero-sum game, as mentioned earlier. The source of that attention is other media. If big brand marketers still want to reach the people who have turned partially away from other media, it is becoming more apparent that they have to make impressions on the users in this interactive medium.

These big brands often are looking for demographics rather than interests. If you have a child, you will buy Pampers whether you're a techie or a teacher. Advertising networks have sprung up to deliver those demographics to brand marketers. DoubleClick (http://www.doubleclick.com) was the first and most known of these ad networks. At the time of writing, DoubleClick will sell you impressions only on the sites that it represents. In other words, it makes money two ways:

1. DoubleClick represents content sites, such as AltaVista, Travelocity, and Billboard Online.

2. The company makes money selling you a more specific demographic on those sites that it represents. For example, if you want to target women with graduate degrees from Canada, that will cost you a bit more than simply buying banners on those individual content sites.

Another company selling advertising through its services is Focalink Communications (http://www.focalink.com), which has a database called Market-Match, containing about 1000 sites, each offering a rate card and other information to help convince you to buy through them (see Figure 5.8). DoubleClick has only a few dozen sites from which it can offer you demographic fine tuning.

Figure 5.8 Ad agencies subscribe to MarketMatch's database. It provides information to agencies determining where to buy advertising.

Both DoubleClick and Focalink are well worth checking out and comparing. There are other ad networks as well, such as SoftBank and Petry. You can also buy ads across a wide network of Web sites in an auction, such as FlyCast (see Figure 5.9).

Channels

Finally, there's the prospect of making your own *channel*. By that, I mean a content site such as a PointCast channel, which pushes your information directly to the user's desktop, or maybe just integrates it as a part of someone else's site. What you need to weigh here is how much money you're going to spend on advertising versus how much money you'd spend creating your own media brand. It is not inconsequential. It takes manpower, lots of money, networks, computers, and a promotion budget. It may be worth it in some cases. Microsoft started Expedia and it's doing very well. Think of it: Microsoft is an advertiser that accepts ads on a media property—talk about convergence. It's impossible for me to advise you without knowing your specific circumstances, but if you think having a sphere of influence is key to your core business, then do seriously consider an advertising channel option.

Figure 5.9 Ad avails are auctioned off via FlyCast.

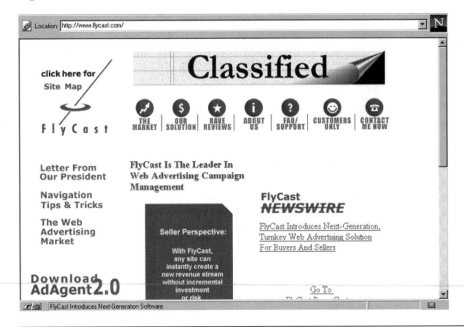

Conclusion

Comfort. That's what branding is all about, whether it is for you personally, your firm or organization, or a can of pineapple chunks. Whether people are going to buy your brand online or offline, they are going to want to feel comfortable in the knowledge that they are getting a product or service that has a reputation to live up to. You can think of it as a preconditioner. Very often, the most effective branding will hit the target audience using a number of different media at the same time. This causes a resonance in the target audience that often causes them to act. No single message may be responsible for that action, but rather a team-selling approach may be the order of the day. This team approach sets the target up with a brand image, then attempts to convert that target to buying the brand with some sort of incentive.

In this way, the target feels that he or she got high value (perceived as such by the branding efforts) for a good price (the financial incentive that lures customers into the buying cycle). The coupon without perceived value is value-less. Like it or not, you must have a branding strategy. Failure to do so will result in perception as either a pure commodity brand, whereby your price is forever headed downward in competition with others, or ignored altogether. To bring it down to a personal level, branding is the kind of suit you wear, the tie you select, and your watch that does more than tell time. Keep this is mind when you design your Web site and the out-bound communications to bring people back to your site. Remember, *everything* you say and do is branding.

Resource Center

ClickZ: The Daily Stop For Web Advertisers   http://www.clickz.com

Fans of the Online Advertising discussion list and Ad-Bytes will welcome ClickZ, a round-up of online advertising news, products, services, book reviews, and reports. A daily column from "people in the trenches of the Web advertising industry" makes the site bookmark worthy. My current favorite? "Quality vs. Quantity: Web Traffic and Genital Size," which tackles the issue of hit-to-sales ratio. Do you have a unique perspective or experience to share? A Web advertising war story? Add to ClickZ's collective knowledge (and your professional profile) by submitting a column for consideration.

Web Usability: A Designer's Guide   http://world.std.com/~uieweb

User Interface Engineering is keeping the buzz going about its recently released book, *Web Site Usability: A Designer's Guide*, by presenting a chapter at a time on its Web site. Based on over 50 usability tests of nine different sites, the book examines which popular sites work and which don't. Last time *WDFM* visited the UIE site, we browsed through a chapter comparing link structures used in the Disney site and the Edmund site. Earlier chapters evaluate navigation conventions, the use of tips, and more.

NetMarketing's Web Price Index   http://netb2b.com/wpi

This helpful tool from NetMarketing puts Web site development costs into perspective. Web Price Index is a monthly survey that looks at three hypothetical companies and their ongoing Web needs. Charts offer comparisons of site development and specific upgrades in six major U.S. cities. Each chart gives the national medians, and highs and lows for small, medium, and large projects.

WebTrack's Advertising Index   http://www.jup.com/
interact/data/adverts/adverts.shtml

Jupiter Communications has put together a rather nice database to track Web activity for companies that actively advertise on public Web sites. WebTrack actively monitors all companies with advertising expenditures greater than $0.5 million as defined by "AdWeek/Leading National Advertisers." Although last updated a year ago, the site still offers a quick and easy way to search for brand-name Web sites.

RETAIL
Setting Up Shop on the Net

The good news is, it doesn't cost much to start selling on the Net. The bad news is, it doesn't cost much to start selling on the Net. In other words, the barrier of entry is low. Anyone can enter—even you, perhaps. With everyone piling on to sell their wares on the Net, the cost of "one-upsmanship" in order to compete for attention will ramp up precipitously. One of my very first clients was Auto-By-Tel. President Pete Ellis said that when he started, it was much easier to exceed his expenses. Now, with all of the competition, he has to gross millions of dollars in order to clear a profit. Will you find that, in order to make money, you're going to have to spend some, or a lot, and then perhaps never make it all back? This chapter will give you the key elements you'll need in order to answer this and other critical questions. We'll cover the following topics in detail:

- Buying habits are hard to change
- Advertising: your Web site as a storefront
- Catalogs and shopping carts
- Design for retail
- Stretching your online ad dollars
- Unintended consequences

Buying Habits Are Hard to Change, But They're Changing

When I was a copywriter for New York ad agencies, I learned that the hardest thing to do is to persuade someone to change his or her routine. You could probably entice me to change the brand of paper cups I use more easily than which tooth-paste I brush with. My experience from working with banks and financial services taught me that the hardest habits to change are those centered around money. You probably intuitively knew this on some level; nevertheless, that's not to say it can't happen. It does all the time; it just takes a while.

When ATM machines came out in the 1970s, I wasn't a big fan of them. My main stumbling block was what I would do if it short-changed me. Then, late one night, I desperately needed cash. I decided to chance it, and I used the machine instead of waiting for the bank to open in the morning. Thus, a new habit was spawned in me and, eventually, in millions of other people, too.

When 800 numbers were introduced, allowing you to call toll free and purchase catalog merchandise, people did not immediately jump for joy and flood the lines with orders. Again, it took a while for people to incorporate this practice into their buying habits.

When I wrote ads for a computer company whose sole sales channel was in the pages of *Computer Shopper* magazine, I remember people scoffing and saying, "People will never buy computers from a magazine page. They need to touch the keyboard and see the screen in person." When it became apparent that people would indeed buy computers this way, the nay-sayers recanted by saying, "Okay, okay, so geeks and wonks will buy this way, but not Joe Consumer." Now that Dell and Gateway are nestled comfortably in the Fortune 500 club, these people have conveniently forgotten their nay-saying. Now they are proclaiming it about selling on the Net: "No one will buy from a page on the Web," they shout. History is merely repeating itself.

As found in the *Morgan Stanley Internet Retailing Report*, the online retail business will grow similarly to that of the mail order business, but probably at a faster rate. Why? Because the infrastructure needed to implement such buying practices is already in place. Although the telephone was invented in the 1870s, it wasn't until after World War II that we had universal service. In large part, this was because the wires had to be physically laid out and installed. That's not the case here, where there are currently 220 million computers worldwide, of which 35 million of them are used online.

Cyberdialogue/findsvp conducted a critical survey in 1997 that focused on those who shop online for personal, rather than business, reasons. This difference is key, since what we want to address in this chapter is sales to the consumer, rather than business-to-business transactions, the dollar volume of which is gargantuan when compared to the much smaller purchases made by a single user. You see, while Dell is selling over a million dollars a day on its site, a great percentage of that is to other businesses. One business may buy a thousand computers, but a consumer may buy one or two at a given time. This survey found that 27 percent of personal computer users purchased online in the past year, and 75 percent of them made multiple purchases. The median purchase amount was $150, and 65 percent of these purchases were made with credit cards. The types of products purchased were:

Computer software	41.0%
Books	29.0%
Computer hardware	18.0%
Gifts/flowers	16.0%
CDs/ music	10.0%
Travel	9.5%
Other electronic products	7.1%
Clothing	5.5%
Research	3.8%
Food	2.4%

Does this mean that if you own a bookstore and aren't very aware of the online impact in your backyard, you'd better get on the ball? Yes. Does it mean that if you sell clothing, you shouldn't bother exploring your options on the Web for a while? Not according to Deb Abrahams-Dematte, who's been selling tie-dyed clothing for two years on the Net at http://www.dyehappy.com (see Figure 6.1). She told me, "We started out by selling to 'Deadheads' (followers of the Grateful Dead) and now get private label orders to make thousands." Abrahams-Dematte notes, "I'm up to my elbows in blue!" It should be interesting to look back in on the Abrahams-Demattes in a couple years to see where their business leads them.

The point here is that you shouldn't ignore the Internet as a viable sales medium simply because the category in which you sell currently isn't the most popular on the Internet. Remember, you're not trying to sell to the entire universe, but rather a highly segmented audience.

What Stops Them from Buying Now?

As mentioned earlier, people's habits are hard to change, especially those centered around money. People are very sensitive about money issues, especially its security. So, even though the infrastructure is currently in place for millions of people to spend money on the Net, they won't. It's a matter of social reconditioning. Part of

Figure 6.1 You don't have to be JC Penny to sell clothing profitably on the Net.

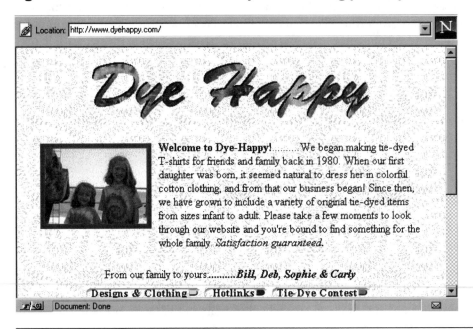

Web page design by Andrew Abrahams: DREW@citypost.com.

that reconditioning has to do with the comfort level of spending money in a new way; that is, online. Many people perceive this kind of Net transaction to be "out in the open," but the reality is we make less-secure transactions every day: after we make a transaction on the ATM, we throw away the slip with our account number on it; we give a perfect stranger, such as a waiter or a cashier in a department store, our credit card.

Indeed, people were not eager to use those toll-free numbers for a while precisely because they weren't comfortable about giving their credit card number to a stranger over the telephone. The reality is we have to wait for the social climate to catch up to the technology. We have to wait for the fear of using the Net to make monetary or credit transactions to subside. As I'll demonstrate shortly, it's not worth a hacker's time or effort to concentrate on grabbing just one credit card number at a time, because of the security features in place today. Keep in mind that even more sophisticated schemes for transactions will follow in the next couple of years. In short, the problem of reluctance to spend money online lies in the consumer's perception of what is *safe*.

However, this discussion of online commerce itself can be taken much too literally. The Cyberdialogue/findsvp survey revealed that 40 percent of those surveyed used the Net for some component of the shopping experience. That's why financial services, cars, and other "deep information" products need the Net to display information that's crucial to the sales process, even if the sale itself isn't made online. "How much money did you make online?" is often a naïve question, as it assumes that online is only a point of sale and not a provider of information leading to a sale, or a lead generator to a sale that is consummated offline. At the time of writing, the Dye Happy site doesn't accept online payments. They don't seem to be any worse for the wear for it.

What Will Make Them Buy Online?

There are three variables that converge in order for the consumer to feel comfortable and positive about purchasing online: *financial incentive, convenience,* and *added value.* These features are similar to the ones that moved people to change their habits and use ATMs and mail order catalogs.

Financial Incentive

Let's take the first variable: financial incentive. Just like the computers sold on magazine pages, online goods already sport attractive pricing compared to competing sales channels—this will get even better with time. The cost of sales online is less for a number of reasons: You don't have to own or rent bricks and mortar to house a store, there are additional savings in reduced inventory, and you are able to sell directly to consumers while disintermediating many middlemen. The savings are passed on to the consumer in this open marketplace, not because of any altruistic notion, but rather to stay ahead of the competitor's pricing. This self-service style of selling offers the consumer the option of completing the transaction online and making the purchase for less, by way of auctions and last-minute deals on vanishing commodities, such as airline seats. The other alternative for any savings is going through more traditional outlets and paying a bit more.

Convenience

The second variable is convenience. Instead of trundling down to the library to *access* the *Consumer Reports* that reviews lawn mowers, the customer looking for a lawn mower can simply pull the review up on screen at his or her desktop. Multiply that by a few hundred buying occasions in one's life and you're looking at saving an enormous amount of time. Even though users don't think of it on such a grand scale, the day they do in fact look up the information about a lawn mower on the Net means they have indeed initiated a new habit for one part of the buying cycle. Once in the environment of the Internet, users may or may not finish that cycle online, but may make the actual purchase offline instead. If consumers don't complete the transaction online, they' are still one step closer to doing so for a purchase in the future.

There are specialty food sellers out there who sell directly over the Net, such as http://www.pastrami.com, which originates from the Mill Basin Kosher Deli in Brooklyn. It is a robust and worldwide business selling New York deli food to homesick New Yorkers, shipping to Japan regularly—far more convenient than a plane trip to New York City! Another microniche player in the food category—especially if you're a salsa fan—is HotHotHot! at http://hothothot.com (see Figure 6.2). Note the low overhead and tight focus on the site's raison d'être. At the time of writing, I'm happy to report that HotHotHot! has not set up unnecessary chat groups or gone too far out of its way to build a community of "Hot Heads."

On the other hand, I've seen impractical and unsuccessful online food-ordering sites, such as one that will ship you canned stewed plum tomatoes via an overnight carrier. Somehow, I don't think that one is going to pan out! All of these sites may cater to the category of food, but it's really more a question of *how* you approach any given category and how to provide enough convenience for your customers.

Figure 6.2 HotHotHot! knows how to sellsellsell! on the Net.

Added Value

Finally, the last variable is added value. I have indeed tried to avoid using the overused Amazon Books site as an example, but I feel compelled to do so to demonstrate added value. I must have used its searchable database of "over 2 million books in print" a dozen times before I actually bought a book there. I remember I had to pay a few dollars to a research service that was housed on CompuServe to perform exactly the same search (using Books in Print) only a few years back.

SuperMarkets OnLine (http://www.supermarkets.com), which provides manufacturers' coupons for food and household items, directly addresses all three of the variables necessary to succeed in online sales. When you visit its site, you can fill out a profile describing your food preferences and household demographics; hence, you never receive cat food coupons if you own a dog. Then, you can print out the coupons that match your needs and take them to any supermarket where they can be redeemed. Here again, we can see that although Cyberdialogue/findsvp rated food products as a category having the least interest and success in online purchasing, this company offers a practical service that caters to an important—and large—niche.

Added value includes a number of services you can offer to customers, bringing them to your site again and again. Let's look at several of them now.

Adding Value with Personalization Services

I mentioned before that it will be necessary to add value to the online purchasing process by featuring items the user finds helpful and can't find in any other medium. Personalization is one such added value. FireFly, LikeMinds, and Net Perceptions are three of the better-known personalization engines employed on the Net.

These three work by what is called *collaborative filtering*. A user may go to a music site and fill out a form that asks questions about musical tastes. The user is helping the merchant to rule in or out possibilities that may be of interest to him or her. If I tell it I like Bob Dylan, it may come back and inform me that there is a tribute album to Jimmy Rogers he produced that I might not otherwise have known about. It could also tell me that Dylan figures prominently in the book *American Folk Lore Anthology*. Some of these collaborative filtering efforts continue to learn about you and compare your predilections with those of others who have similar tastes. As time goes on, they can make more sophisticated recommendations to you because they know you better. The collaborative "librarian" filter at Alexandria Digital Literature (http://www.alexlit.com) does just this, learning about preferences in reading through its "rating" questions for books and stories, then redefining and targeting reading choices as customers visit more often.

These filtering agents will become more ubiquitous as people realize the need for them. Since people are inundated with information now, they're apt to miss things that are truly of interest. At some point, people will want to be sure they're getting things that they otherwise might filter out. An example of this technology at work is at myLAUNCH, which employs the FireFly agenting technology mentioned earlier (http://www.myLAUNCH.com).

Another form of filtering is done by a company called Open Sesame. With this scheme, a visitor to your site doesn't have to fill out an extensive form. Its product, called Learn Sesame, actually follows users around a site and tracks behavioral patterns. At the time of writing, it costs about $25,000. It is a sort of Jiminy Cricket who watches over your shoulder. "Big Brother," you say? Well, the shopper has the option of turning it off. My bet is that most people will get over the Big Brother issues in favor of convenience and personalization. When you get advertising card decks in the mail, they're very often based on your buying habits reflected through your credit card usage. I don't hear anyone complaining about that.

Dana Blakenhorn, who publishes the *Get A Clue...to Internet Commerce* newsletter, suggests you watch which personalization scheme Netscape and Microsoft choose. Those endorsements and possible financial backing will be good indicators as to who will be around for the long haul. This is true for any plug-in, package, or technology standard on the Web today: The two big browser companies, as they duke it out to be #1, will decide for the rest of us which programs will become the standard.

Dane Atkinson, president of SenseNet, a major New York software and network solutions provider, told me that his company has also designed sites using personalization software. "We used personalization software recently for a cable network site. It observed the surfer's movements. It started making decisions by the fifth click and got more and more intelligent as the surfer returned and the profile grew. If the visitor had the tendency to visit the action movie Web sites, he would start seeing more banners for that genre."

At the time of writing, the initial cost of such personalization applications falls between $10,000 and $50,000, but it doesn't stop there. Since you're collecting a lot of information on a lot of people, you also have to pay for maintaining a large database that is ever increasing. This type of added value of personalization will thus be for major sites with major budgets, both initial and ongoing. Although these applications seem expensive now, know they will substantially decrease over time. I remember when SSL servers for secure credit card transactions were a rarity and quite expensive. Now, they're commonplace. As the cost of new technologies typically comes down precipitously, these added-value goodies will become more accessible to smaller players sooner rather than later.

Adding Value with Shopbots

Shopbots are those agents that go out and bring back prices and specifications on items that you are looking for, adding another sort of value-added service to your site. In some cases, these agents sit on your computer, such as Excite's Jango (http://www.jango.com). In other cases, they are Web sites that you visit and can either fill out a preference form while it searches in your absence, or you simply ask for a specific item during your visit and it scours its already accumulated database. Such a site is RoboShopper (http://www.roboshopper.com). Enter the item you are looking for and it searches its database of 3500 catalogs to see which one offers the item in question.

From time to time, I see attempts by these shopbots to locate the best price from myriad resources on the Web. Agent-type shopbots may not be the hands-down solution, as they require the cooperation of many retailers to hand over their prices. Most of these prices and specifications are in databases that are each configured differently from the next; some are shopping carts, while others are pages that are served up on the fly from diversified publishing operations. Just as the search engines can't pick up the contents of your database, neither can these shopbots see that information without your cooperation.

Adding Value with Cookies and Commerce

Another way to bring value to your customer is with the use of *cookies*. A cookie is a file that sits on the surfer's computer. It can tell your server a number of things, such as the domain name of the surfer's provider, such as netcom.com. You'll know the type of browser being used by the visiting surfer, such as Netscape 4.0. The cookie also carries with it a virtual trail of breadcrumbs that divulges which site the surfer visited prior to coming to yours. It won't tell you the actual name of that surfer, unless of course you ask him or her, then marry that information with the cookie to identify the surfer the next time he or she visits. Just using simple cookies can help you personalize your site.

Bill Mapp of Continental Airlines plans on delivering added value by way of cookies. He gave this implementation as one such example: "If we notice an interest in New York-to-LA flights, we're apt to notify that visitor when there are specials on such flights." If you're using the same computer each time you surf and go to the Continental Airlines site, it might say "Welcome back, Larry Chase. You might be interested in knowing that we're offering a 50-percent discount on a flight from New York to Los Angeles." Here again, people, for the most part, will accept this knowledge of who you are in favor of the savings, convenience, and intuition it offers as a trade-off. If surfers don't like the use of cookies and feel they are an intrusion on their privacy, they can actually turn off the cookie function in their browser's preferences.

| TIP | Using cookies as a form of personalization familiarizes your server with the surfer's PC, not the surfer himself. If multiple users use the same computer, your server will not have an exact fix on one person's profile, since numerous people are using that machine. |

Advertising: Your Web Site as a Storefront

There are many ways in which your online store is just like your physical store (assuming you have one), but this analogy can be taken too far. Just like a real store, you need to build foot traffic in order to generate sales. However, many sites make the mistake of designing their Web sites to merely simulate a mail order catalog or the physical space of an actual store. Like so many misconstrued notions about how online commerce and culture will unfold, these attempts will seem quaint to us in the coming months and years. While I urge you to see the similarities, be sensitive to where the analogy stops and the new way begins.

Cyberbait

You want to have some sort of ongoing lure, or *cyberbait*. It could be a database, such as Amazon's (which is a major investment to maintain), or it might be the attraction of coupons, like SuperMarkets Online. Whatever it is, it needs to flow naturally out of your product or service. I recommend you have this type of loss leader year round. You can also periodically have big blow-out events and sales, as discussed in Chapter 7, "Online Events, Promotions, and Attractions: How to Make a 'Scene' and Draw Them In."

I recently consulted for a company that sells liability insurance to health care professionals. I advised them to create an archive of helpful hints to reduce their target audience's liability exposure. The archive will be located at the company's site, while short tips on avoiding risk will be mailed out on a weekly basis to subscribers. An online and offline campaign will be devised to push the target audience traffic to the site to sign up for additional services. In the outbound tips, there will be lures put in to get the audience to visit the site again. The archive can work as one of these lures.

The key here is to promote one's added value on one's site, both online and offline, and then try to engage the visitor to your site for an ongoing relationship.

This can be done through a "Tip of the Week" service or via an updating service, like that of one of my first clients, 1-800-Flowers. An email reminder program was put in place, so a previous purchaser would be reminded two weeks ahead of an anniversary or birthday that the event was coming up and what was sent the year before.

These email tip and reminder services, along with large professional databases, like Amazon's use of *Books in Print*, cost a substantial amount of money to establish and maintain; however, it is the cost of business to build that all-important foot traffic. Bloomingdale's may heavily advertise a huge sale on canvas bags and may sell you the canvas bag at, or even below, cost. When you go to Bloomie's to get that bag, you see a blue sweater that's on sale for $185. You simply must have that sweater now. You wouldn't have known that you needed that sweater had the canvas bag special not gotten you into a position to see and want that sweater. Now, with bag and sweater in tow, don't you think those navy pants would . . .

Bloomie's takes a gamble on buying a bunch of canvas bags to sell at or below cost, and then spends even more money to advertise that fact. The canvas bags and the advertising to promote the come-on are the equivalent of your ongoing loss leader at your Web site. Amazon's investment in maintaining its database is equivalent to Bloomie's canvas bag campaign. You would be right if you argued that Bloomie's campaign constitutes a sale or promotion. What I'm suggesting here is that your online store needs an ongoing lure, where Bloomie's doesn't. It has people getting catalogs in the mail and walk-in traffic every day it's open. However, no one walks by your Web site or the umpteen others that pile into your category. Your competitive edge will be your ongoing loss leader campaign.

Another reason you want an ongoing loss leader at your site is that your timed promotion may or may not coincide with the buying cycle of your target group. More often than not, they'll go looking for some sort of information or utility, whether they know it exists on your site or not. Your mission is to make sure they know that it does exist.

Contiguous Cannibalization

One of the scary things about playing in the online arena is that the marketplace is *so* wide open. In this brutal environment, one man's core business can become another man's loss leader. For example, in order to capture your long-distance business, a large telecommunications company could offer you Internet access for free or at highly discounted rates. This practice puts enormous pressure on smaller ISPs. It wouldn't surprise me at this point to see an overnight shipping company give you a catalog or shopping cart software that lets you display your wares on the

Net for free, just so it can capture your shipping business. In other words, your competition could now come from anywhere. You may find yourself loss leader-ing something that a vendor or supplier next to you on the food chain offers for money. They could do the same to you. Make it your business to stay one step ahead of your obvious—and less obvious—competitors.

Search Engines Sending You Business

Having told you all this, it is important to remember that many of your prospects aren't even going to see your carefully crafted online and offline campaigns. They're going to first go to a search engine and enter in . . . what? What they enter into the search engine is all important because it determines how they'll find you, or not find you. Much of this information is covered in Chapter 8, "Direct Marketing and Sales Support"; however, I do want to address a few issues here about search engines as they relate to retail.

If you have a catalog, it is probably in some sort of database. Search engines typically visit your site and scan for words on the pages of your site, but not in your database. Once the search engine has catalogued the words on your Web pages, it makes determinations as to where your site should rank in its search results. If you've got 42,000 varieties of gardening tools in your database, the search engine may pick up only the specials you've listed on the few pages that are readily apparent to the visiting agent with its virtual clipboard.

Have available on your site a substantial amount of content that is readily accessible by the agents of the search engines so they get a better idea of what your site is about. You'll come up higher in the search results this way. One strategy is to include large amounts of content on your Web page for these agents to peruse and catalog when they come visiting.

There is a trade-off here that only you can decide to make. I charge access to the archives of my *Web Digest For Marketers*. My site would come up much higher in the search engines if the archives weren't password protected. As a result, the search engines account only for 25 percent of my traffic. If I didn't block access, the percentage would be significantly higher, as it would allow the search engine agents to examine the thousands of reviews and thus move the site higher up in ranking. Outside of paid advertising, most sites live and die by their standings in the search engines. However, if your loss leader is rich enough in value, prospects will find you through other ways. Editorial coverage in trade or general press, word of mouth, and other sites pointing at you will all send hard-core value seekers on their way to you.

Taking Transactions Online, or Transactional Analysis

Let's take a look at exactly what's involved in setting up an online store that accepts payments online.

Say you have an online store called "All Things Elvis." The first thing you need is a merchant's account with a banking institution if you're going to take credit card payments.

Getting an Online Merchant's Account

If you had a physical store, you would go to the bank with which your company has an account and ask to have a merchant's account set up in order to accept credit cards. If your firm's credit history is good, this shouldn't take too long or be a problem. However, even if your company's credit history is flawless, companies quite often have problems getting a merchant's account specifically for the purpose of online credit card transactions. For this reason, there are brokers who will match you up with an institution who will accept the risk. MerchantAccount (http://www.merchant-account.com) is one such service. These brokers are remunerated one time, often by the application fee you are charged by the sponsoring institution. Once these brokers are paid, they leave the process permanently. For a list of additional brokers, go to http://www.yahoo.com/Business_and_Economy/Companies/Financial_Services/Transaction_Clearing/Credit_Card_Merchant_Services/.

Now that you have your merchant account, there are basically three players: the buyer (with his or her browser), your Web site, and the clearinghouse that tells you whether or not the buyer's credit card is legitimate. Two examples of these clearinghouses are FirstData Corporation and FirstUSA. If yours is a big company, you're going to need a vast quantity of sales to support the huge infrastructure consisting of your server, industrial-strength connectivity to the Internet, and a full staff. More often than not, a company is apt to farm out this process to a Web service provider. There's usually a setup fee that can range from a few hundred to a few thousand dollars, depending on the scope of the store. Then there's a monthly fee that usually ranges in the hundreds of dollars as well. Depending on the pricing structure, that provider may also take a percentage of each sale or have a minimum charge per transaction.

When you're shopping around for a provider to house your store and take credit cards, try to figure out about how many sales you'll have per month, as the provider will often quote you a price based on predicted transactions. Dane Atkinson's SenseNet provides many different kinds of online retail transactions, to a wide variety of clients. I asked him to reveal his pricing structure. He told me, "We ask about the quantity of transactions. This amount will tell us how much bandwidth and computing power we're going to have to dedicate to that process."

For the sake of argument, let's say you have 50 Elvis-related products to sell online. Let's concentrate on the options you have to accept payment. It's easiest to accept orders through a toll-free number or by fax, but you'll also want to let those who are comfortable buying online do so. Here's what often happens.

A buyer selects an item to purchase. He or she proceeds to the checkout part of your site. Behind the scenes, this often means the buyer goes from your shopping cart or catalog into a more secure place where credit card numbers can be exchanged. All pages are not automatically secure, as secure pages run much more slowly. The buyer is actually transported from your site to what is known as a Secure Socket Layer (SSL) site at your provider's site. The buyer sees a dialog box that notifies him or her of this and sees either a solid key or padlock in the lower-left screen. When that key or padlock is made whole, you know you're communicating with the server at the other end in a much more secure fashion. Try this yourself on some sites and keep an eye on the URL to see if the domain changes. The actual appearance of the screen may look exactly the same as the rest of the catalog or shopping cart, while the URL is in fact different.

All information is heavily encrypted and is passed in a file. One of the key components of that file is a certificate that must be renewed annually. This certificate tells the surfer's PC that you are, in fact, the Web site that you claim to be. Breaking this file apart would entail decoding the encrypted information. This would take a hacker a very long time, even with the help of a supercomputer—all for only one measly credit card number. It just doesn't pay to steal credit card numbers this way.

Once the card number has been given in this secure area, one of two things will happen:

1. The card number is sent to a clearinghouse to establish whether it is a valid number and if there are enough funds available in the account to cover the purchase. This real-time checking of card numbers is a more expensive option, but is often worth it, as you immediately are alerted to insufficient funds or invalid card numbers. But since you are selling Elvis ephemera, you probably won't be making thousands of sales a day, the way Amazon Books does. In this case, it will be more practical to implement the next option.

2. The card numbers are simply stored and forwarded to you so you can check them all at once at the end of the day, or every few days. This is called *batch processing*, and IC*Verify* (http://www.icverify.com) is a program that will perform this task for you (see Figure 6.3). If you're taking in only a few orders a day or week, and you're not selling instant deliverables, it's probably more cost efficient to batch process the orders, rather than doing so in real time. However, if you batch process at the end of the day, having already delivered online software or content, you run the risk of parting with the goods prior to knowing whether you've sold them to a legitimate cardholder or not. On the other hand, if you're selling physical goods that must be delivered, you can simply withhold the sending of such items, until you are sure you're dealing with a legitimate customer. If someone is brazen enough to use a fraudulent credit card and have you mail him the merchandise, he's likely to mask his physical address, thus making it harder for you to track him down.

Figure 6.3 IC*Verify*'s credit card verification service saves you time by batch processing.

When dealing with online retail transactions, be aware of Post Office box numbers. The more information you have, the more likely you can track fraudulent customers down. If the dollar volume of the transaction is large enough, you may even want to confirm the authenticity of the customers by calling them. If you're accepting orders and payments online, be sure to check for redundancies, especially from those impatient customers who obsessively click the Submit button again and again to make sure the order goes through.

The higher the cost of a product, the more occurrences of fraud you're apt to encounter. It is especially important to keep in mind that even with real-time transactions, there is a risk on the merchant's part. You see, someone could be using a credit card number that is indeed valid and not stolen, but merely "borrowed," perhaps by a waiter who took the card the night before in a restaurant. When the real-time checking is done, it comes back saying that this card is fine and to let the purchase proceed.

However, some weeks later, the true cardholder sees this charge from you on his monthly statement and denies having made the transaction. Your merchant account is then notified that the money you thought was now yours must be returned. In fact, you're likely to be charged a fee, usually about $25, to reverse the transaction. As a result, you're not only short of the money you thought you had from the purchase, but you're also $25 in the hole! A credit card holder has up to 90 days to contest purchases. If you do sell instantly deliverable items online, you won't know for sure that money is truly yours until three months from when the purchase is actually made.

On a more positive note, fraud screening is getting better all the time. In the United States especially, it is getting faster and more accurate. Since Europe and points beyond don't have a unified standard for checking and reconciling such claims, it will be harder to limit fraudulent use from overseas at this time. You may elect to not accept credit cards from overseas for this reason, though it seems a shame to shut down markets that were heretofore not necessarily available to you.

As mentioned earlier, the barrier to teaming hordes of people purchasing online isn't really a technology hurdle, but one of social conditioning. By the time it is commonplace to purchase online, there will be an additional security feature that will further increase the average consumer's comfort level. It's called *Secure Electronic Transaction* (SET), and it's still a couple years away from deployment. SET will encode the user's credit card number so that even you, the merchant, won't be able to see it. The actual number goes through you and then travels over to one of the clearinghouses for validation. Through SET, an online transaction will be more secure than many other current offline forms of credit card purchasing.

| TIP | If you accept monetary or credit card transactions from outside the United States, always insist on the transaction being denominated in U.S. funds. This puts the burden and cost of conversion on the consumer, not you. Multicards (http://www.multicards.com) accepts in U.S. dollars or British pounds. It costs $150 to set up and receives 10 percent commission on each sale, at the time of writing (there is also a setup for larger transactions that will save you even more money on their commission). |

A Look Behind the Scenes from a Provider of Web Commerce

SenseNet provides two basic approaches to online commerce: transactions and subscriptions. Transaction-based transactions are simpler. Subscription-based transactions are more complex because selling occurs on a recurring basis. Let's look at transaction-based commerce first.

To begin with, you pay a Web service provider, such as SenseNet, a one-time startup fee. In the case of SenseNet, this fee is $1,000, in addition to a $300 annual certificate fee. Why so much? Dane Atkinson (SenseNet's president) says,

> If you only need a single shopping page, it'll cost $500. If you want to display a range of products, you'll need us to house a shopping cart. That costs between $1,000 and $2,500, depending on the scope of the product array. Of course, there are sites out there that hold 50,000+ items. This obviously would cost much more. So, if you want to set up an Elvis site that, among other things, contains a page that securely sells one product, an Elvis gold lamé jumpsuit and nothing else, the startup costs are nearly $2,000 and monthly charge of $250 for the housing of the site.

The up-front costs break out as follows:

- $1,000 to make your server commerce ready
- $500 to set up the management system that collects and manages the sales information
- $300 each year to renew your certificate

Whatever provider you settle on, make sure it can handle this labyrinth with consistency. A great price on putting up a secure storefront won't be such a bargain if it frequently crashes. SenseNet is a good benchmark to use as a rock-solid, major

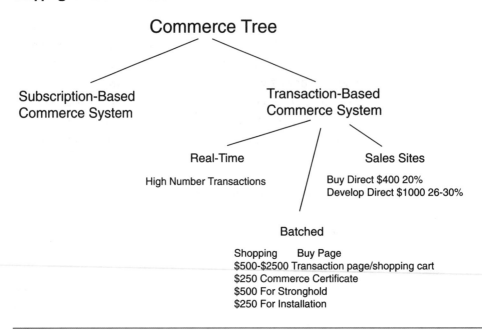

city Internet provider (see Figure 6.4). Its average monthly charges to its clients for housing Web sites run between $700 and $2,000, at the time of writing. Its clients include Pfizer, Procter & Gamble, and other Fortune 500 companies. However, SenseNet also houses many sites that conduct online transactions.

On the subscription side, Dane houses a few clients that actually do make money, some of which are niche content sites. His clients range from Shockumentory to India Abroad Online. From a gross revenue point of view, it profits between $5,000 and $10,000 a month. However, India Abroad just installed a commerce site, so that will undoubtedly increase total revenues.

Atkinson explains, "The reason that subscription-based systems are more costly and risk-oriented is because we have to maintain all the account and credit card information. Those numbers are online because the user wants access to his or her account number information at any time." One strategy around the security issue is to store the customer account information online, but keep the credit card number safely offline. If someone wants to have a subscription site at SenseNet, there would be an $8,000 one-time setup charge. However, there is no additional recurring monthly charge thereafter, assuming you have a site housed with SenseNet in the first place. Other providers may take a different approach by charging less up front, but then recouping costs by charging an additional monthly fee. Nevertheless, even with SenseNet's nonrecurring fee, you should put aside a few hundred dollars for the maintenance of the databases at your end.

Micropayments

The kinds of online transactions we've discussed thus far have primarily been credit card oriented. There are other approaches especially for smaller transactions. *Micropayments* are designed to fill a niche that covers small transactions that aren't worth putting through the credit card system. They work by having a virtual "purse" on your computer, out of which you can spend small amounts of money. However, as mentioned in previous chapters, the noise level out on the Web is deafening. Therefore, people are giving away things of higher and higher value all the time in order to get your attention.

Ask yourself, "Why should I pay next to nothing for something that I can get for nothing somewhere else?" You might answer, "Convenience. It might be worth 15 cents or $1.52 to pull up that article from a database while you are right there, on a deadline, rather than trying to go find it for free on the open Net, where it may exist somewhere else." True, I will spend small amounts of money while on a research mission rather than spend my time. This niche does indeed exist; journalists, librarians, research analysts, students, and so forth will find this useful. I don't see it happening for the masses at large, judging by their habits and expectations, which are forever increasing. Nevertheless, you should know the systems that are out there, in case they pertain to the particular niche you wish to serve.

Three of the companies presenting online micropayment systems are DigiCash (which is also e-cash), CyberCash, and Millicent. DigiCash is currently held in the United States by Wells Fargo Bank, which handles all the transactions from DigiCash tokens to dollars (see Figure 6.5). The interesting thing about DigiCash is that it actually acts as a separate form of currency. A merchant can trade DigiCash tokens in business-to-business transactions, after accepting tokens from a customer in payment for retail items. The customer buys the tokens by going to the DigiCash site on the Web, which is actually Wells Fargo, and presenting a secure credit cash transaction for a "purse" of DigiCash tokens, which can then be spent at DigiCash-accepting merchants. These coins, if not traded merchant to merchant for other goods, can be redeemed for a small transaction fee (like converting foreign currency) at Wells Fargo/DigiCash. Tokens can be verified by DigiCash as

Figure 6.5 For small transactions, put a purse on your hard drive using a system like DigiCash.

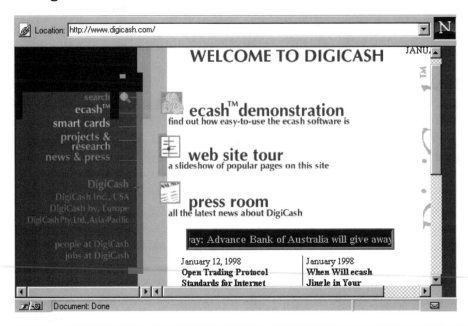

well, for no fee, so a merchant can make sure that the tokens haven't been forged or "re-spent" by an unscrupulous customer.

CyberCash is currently handling three types of transactions, only one of which is a micropayment scheme. CyberCash is an online credit card option (your credit card information is stored on your computer's "wallet" and transmitted in code to the banks handling the transactions for a merchant); CyberCheck is an online direct-debit option (debiting from your regular bank checking account); and CyberCoin is the micropayment baby of the group. CyberCoin works similarly to DigiCash, but instead of using only one bank, CyberCash has been courting many banks to buy into its system. Both merchant and customer therefore find a bank affiliated with CyberCash, and tokens can be bought or redeemed from these banks. Several large banks have already signed on with CyberCash; as either a merchant or a customer, it isn't too difficult to find one to handle your micropayment transactions.

As of fall 1997, Microsoft announced that its Virtual Wallet module for Internet Explorer (MSIE), which uses CyberCoin payments, will be integrated into its Web browser from now on. This endorsement of micropayments may open up a new chapter in this area of online transactions. Should you employ a micropayment scheme for your retailing online? The litmus test to use here is to ask yourself if your target audience is apt to use it themselves.

Millicent is a new system by Digital Equipment Corp. The idea behind Millicent is to cut back on costs of confirming transactions, confirming the veracity of a token (which is just a string of numbers, after all), and so on, by trading only monetary amounts up to *10 cents*. Verifying a Millicent is not an option so far, which reduces the costs even further; after all, who would bother stealing 3 cents? The name "Millicent" is therefore the amount of money it costs to transact as well: a thousandth of a cent. Not bad for the merchant in cost of transactions! However, Millicent is obviously limited in scope for both merchant and consumer: 3-cent page views for a specialized archive at your Web site, 10-cent newsletters, and so on will be the sort of retail items sold in this manner. All this said, Digital may develop Millicent to such a degree that these specialized uses will be *very* useful to a number of merchants and their customers.

Bill Presentment

You've probably thought about how tedious and wasteful it is to pay the same bills every month with checks being mailed inside of envelopes. You might imagine that others have also thought along these same lines. Whether the amount is the same or different each month, the savings in materials, time, and human resources are enormous. If you're in the position of billing someone monthly, or merely a frustrated bill payer, you should look into the possibilities of online bill presentment.

Microsoft is teaming up with First Data (one of the largest credit card issuers and processors) to make monthly bill paying easy on all of the parties involved (http://www.msfdc.com/default2.asp). The payee will use a program such as Intuit's Quicken to go on the Web and pay his bills online.

Sounds wonderful, right? This scheme, and others like it, requires the cooperation of many different players in the process; the merchant, creditor, bank, and customer all have to participate in order for the process to work. CheckFree has a system it is developing in this area, called "e-bill," at http://getbill.checkfree.com, while IBM has entered the fray as well, with its Integrion product at http://www.integrion.net. Many banks are going to their own, closed-system online bill-paying software packages. BankBoston, one of the early players, finds it necessary to invest in expensive television advertising in order to promote its proprietary system, thus convincing its customers that it is safe to use the Net to pay their bills. As I said before, social conditioning plays a big role in using the Net for monetary transactions of all kinds.

If everyone can standardize and agree on one system, it will make this process much easier. A typical customer is not going to learn and deal with a different proprietary bill payment system for each and every bill he pays. Doing it the old way would be easier than that.

Designing for Retail

Much like any other Web page, many of the rules remain the same for retailers. For a design checklist, you can look at Chapter 5, "Your Brand Image and the Internet." Keep in mind that the "prime real estate" of an average 14-inch computer screen is 640 × 480 pixels, with the toolbar turned on in the browser. You want to make sure that people see your special offers prominently displayed in this space. Make sure that your visitors see what they came for "above the scrollbar" at the bottom. I suggest you design a *slot* for the upper left-hand part of your screen, where you can slide specials or updates in and out of this space. Since the upper left of the screen has the most value, people often try to cram everything into that confining space. "Little Tokyo" is what my former associate Nina Rich used to call this graphic phenomenon.

Use well-orchestrated outbound messages that entice the user into your Web site. Being well orchestrated means a few things:

Timing. Not only should your online advertising efforts to build foot traffic be coordinated with your Web site, but your print advertising needs to do the same as well. Lead time on print is often longer than online lead time, especially if you are running color ads in magazines.

Fulfillment. Brace yourself for increased traffic and notify your provider. A typical commerce server can handle eight transactions at once.

Ask for the sale. It seems extraordinary how often Web sites neglect to close a sale. Don't be bashful.

In addition to co-op dollars with advertising, you should consider working with a promotional partner. Notice how the search engines are all making deals with bookstores, CD shops, and so on. You should think the same way on your scale. This may be as simple as setting up trade links or trying to bundle someone else's product with yours. In other words, try to sell the customer opportunity to someone else in order to bring more sales in for your own site. If that customer is in a buying mode, he or she may well be persuaded to buy related products.

When you are designing your retail site, you will also need to consider the presentation of your goods, using both (or either) catalogs and shopping carts. If you are working with a promotional partner, you may, in fact, need a more sophisticated sales area, cross-linking products from elsewhere. Let's assume, however, that you need to sell only your own product.

Catalogs and Shopping Carts

The terminology has become blurred between catalogs and shopping carts. For instance, CDNow entices you to shop its catalog online, even though it really is a shopping cart. Today, an online *catalog* is essentially a pile of pages that contain your wares. A *shopping cart* actually takes an item the customer wants and holds it until he or she is ready to proceed to checkout. Customers can then decide to remove any given item when he or she prepares to make a transaction. Dr. Ralph Wilson, publisher of the *Web Commerce Today* newsletter, points out that shopping carts also help you and the customer with critical parts of the transaction process. It can ask the customer what state he or she is from, so it can then figure out the sales tax. You can also set the shopping cart to a dollar threshold against shipping costs. For example, if the order is above $35, you may elect to absorb the cost of shipping. If it is below that threshold you set, you can charge the customer based on the distance and the weight of his or her purchase.

 Web Commerce Today, from Dr. Ralph Wilson, costs $49.95 per year at the time of writing, and I highly recommend a subscription. Look for more information about it at http://www.wilsonweb.com.

ICAT (http://www.icat.com/templates/) is a program that enables you to pour your items into a template that can hold graphics and information describing the products in question. The more sophisticated shopping carts can display items with specifications as well, then lead the customer to the checkout. One of the more affordable shopping carts is called ShopSite, made by ICentral. At the time of writing, the starting cost is $495. This program doesn't run real-time authorization, but it does let you update your site with the use of your browser's FTP capabilities. Nevertheless, it received a very good review in Dr. Ralph Wilson's *Web Commerce Today* newsletter.

Shopping carts do a number of things at once and need to coordinate with many different aspects of your operation. Let's say someone buys a pair of Elvis sunglasses for $19.95. You want to be sure that your shopping cart reports the sale to your inventory database, so you know to stock more sunglasses, or to tell the customer you're out of them and will ship them within two weeks. Be sure that whatever shopping cart you buy, it can communicate seamlessly with your inventory database in real or near real time. Second, make sure that your shopping cart system works well with your billing database. Third, you want to be sure that if you are going to check credit cards in real time rather than batch processing at day's end, your shopping cart should communicate well with the credit card clearinghouse.

Whether you're using a catalog template or a shopping cart engine, you've got some very interesting possibilities in front of you to amortize the investment you've made in the site, software, and advertising it took to get shoppers to your site. If someone buys the Elvis gold lamé jumpsuit, you may want to do a bit of cross-merchandising. For example, if a customer buys the jumpsuit, he or she can save 20 percent on the blue suede shoes. You can cross-sell items from your company or from other companies. American Airlines offers tie-ins with Marriot Caribbean Resorts, so you can buy a complete package deal. A recent trip to the Speedo store here in New York City serves as a good parallel to real-world cross-selling. I went in to buy a bathing suit. The second one was half price, so I bought two. That allowed me to save additionally on swim goggles, so I bought a pair of them. At this point, the dollar amount of my purchase "entitled" me to buy anything else in the store for 40 percent off, so I bought a day pack. By the time I got out of there, I had spent over $150! I went in looking to spend around $30. They got me.

Merging Online and Offline Catalogs

Some of you reading this will already have catalogs in print and/or on CD-ROM. If you start an online catalog, you're looking at a third assembly line. However, if you house all the information in just one database and tweak the information appropriately for each channel, you can trim those three assembly lines down to perhaps one and a half. This practice is called *diversified publishing*.

If you look at Digital's Direct Catalog at http://www.pc.digital.com/products/ products.asp, you'll see the catalog for Digital Equipment Corporation's PC Division (see Figure 6.6). On the face of it, the appearance isn't fancy. The cool thing really is how that catalog was put together behind the scenes. Managed by Convergent Media Systems, the entire database is used to produce the catalog you see online, the CD-ROM version, and the print edition as well, but each version is still customized to be most practical for the medium in which it appears.

For the online version, there's more emphasis on online products, while the graphics are reduced in file size so they load faster at the customer's computer. It is also updated much more often than its other two counterparts. The CD-ROM version has higher-resolution graphics and can support video and sound, while the print version has high-resolution graphics with more succinct specifications to cut down on the cost of printing and distribution.

Figure 6.6 This catalog appears online, in print, and on CD-ROM.

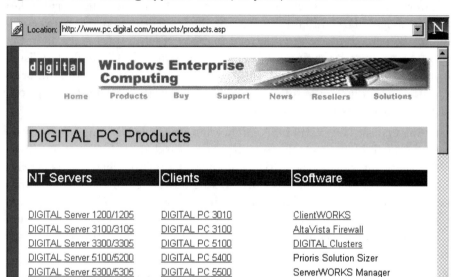

Other companies are addressing this niche as well. Adobe has been pushing its Acrobat software as a single-application template (http://www.adobe.com). If you produce a catalog in Adobe Acrobat (which allows for multiple editing functions while in production, as well as translation back and forth directly to PostScript), you can migrate that format online, to CD-ROM, or to print. Update one document, and they're all updated or ready to be updated at the next scheduled time.

Stretching Your Online Ad Dollars

If you want to stay in it for the long haul, you're going to have to promote your site on an ongoing basis. I just went over several ways for you to gussy up your site so that it adds value for the customer. I often advise my clients to spend less money on their site and more on the marketing of their site, as mentioned in Chapter 9, "Public Relations the Internet Way." You may have the best Elvis gold lamé jumpsuits in the world, but who will know if they can't find you or never heard of you? You also don't want to have an over-promised site that's a letdown when surfers come visiting. It's a tricky balancing act you must manage in order to succeed and make a profit.

One way to strike a balance is to look for cooperative ad dollars. In the physical world, it works like this. Let's say you're a Chevrolet dealer. Chevrolet Corp. makes co-op advertising dollars available to you, the dealer. Chevy may pay between 50 percent and 80 percent of the retail advertising. The result is a full-page ad in the newspaper that touts a Washington's Birthday sale, with eight Chevy dealers listed at the bottom, yours being one of them. Chevy gets some extra branding impressions, while you retailers get a full-page ad in the newspaper, each attracting your local customers. It's a win/win situation.

Retailing and the Net is still in its infancy, but I'm already seeing co-op dollars being made available in exactly the same way. Intel is making $100 million available specifically for co-op advertising on the Net as of fall 1997. Just as in print and TV ads, the retailer or manufacturer taking advantage of these co-op funds will have to display the Intel Inside logo prominently on the site. If you're handling the merchandise of a national manufacturer, vendor, or service provider, you would do well to inquire about such a program. If they don't have one in place, perhaps they should start with you.

Most of the top 20 visited sites have either transaction components to them or key relationships with retailers. Expect many of these cross-merchandised and co-branding relationships to come together and fly apart when it becomes apparent that the configuration isn't working as planned. In short, the Internet marketplace is a real-time focus group.

Team Selling on the Net

There was a time when the manufacturers told the retailers what to do. For the most part, these tables have turned, both online and offline. Whomever has the customer wields the power. This is why a company would pay AOL tens of millions of dollars to be the exclusive book or flower store on its service. Most of the major search engines are cutting deals with a wide range of retailers for a percentage of the sales revenue. It's why Amazon started its Associates program, where you receive a percentage of a sale when a customer buys a recommended book from your site.

While the major players are now cutting deals that provide for the life-time revenue share of that customer, the smaller sites have only gotten a percentage of the specific sale made on the CD or book that was referred to from your site. So if you recommend *Bob Dylan's Greatest Hits* and I click on the link, I go from your site to CDNow. If I buy that CD, you get a percentage of the sale. However, if I buy additional CDs, or come back another time to buy something else, you don't receive any additional revenues.

At the time of writing, there is a new model emerging for referred sales online, whereby the referrer receives a percentage of the revenues derived over the lifetime of that referred customer. This model closely reflects the way cellular phones and cellular phone services are sold. The store that sells you the phone also sells you the phone service with at least a one-year contract. That store then gets a percentage of revenue from each call over that next year. In fact, that store may even use the actual phone itself as a loss leader, just to get the revenue stream from the calls you make. As they say in the advertising business, give the razor handle away for free and you'll sell the customer razor blades for life.

LinkShare is an online company that will actually keep track of all the revenues over the online lifetime of a customer and then distribute the appropriate percentage of that customer to the site that originally referred him or her. You can either initiate the offer to other Web sites via LinkShare or see what other deals and percentages other Web sites are offering you for referring business (see Figure 6.7). In either event, LinkShare offers a good index as to who's offering what team-selling programs on the Net (http://www.linkshare.net).

Figure 6.7 LinkShare technology lets a referring site share in the lifetime value of that referred customer.

Unintended Consequences

One of the things I have noticed about setting up shop on the Internet is that often what you expect to happen doesn't, while other things you never dreamed of happening, do. One of my first clients was Hotel Discount. Client Dave Ray and I guesstimated that 20 percent of the traffic to this site would come from Europe. It did, but what we didn't expect was that Europeans would account for about 50 percent of the room-nights booked. Using retro-logic, we deduced that someone coming from Amsterdam to Chicago will book more room-nights than someone from New York, since the European is coming from a greater distance.

This is the exciting part of the Internet, where unexpected things happen with regularity. It's the sign of a medium rife with possibility, success, and yes, even failure; in fact, there will be many more failures than there will be successes. Predicting what will fail and what will work is very difficult because there are so many variables and forces at work simultaneously. That's the nature of any medium. Intellivision Dumont TVs went out of business, while TV dinners became a hallmark piece of Americana. I suggest that you attempt a few different angles that are all somehow related to each other, so that if one or two fail, you've got the remaining components that survive. Remember not to spread yourself too thin, as then no one retail endeavor will enjoy enough of your resources, attention, and focus in order to succeed. Although the Elvis site that sells gold lamé jumpsuits may not survive, the "Elvis Sighting of the Day" list, used to remind subscribers about the site, might turn into a mini-media property of its own.

Resource Center

Book Stacks Unlimited   **http://www.books.com**

Some smart incentive programs, more than 500,000 titles, and well-populated forums combine to make this site a fresh alternative to Amazon Books. Purchasers are rewarded with bonus points, called *bookmarks*, each time they purchase specially marked books. They can then use the bookmarks to receive additional cash discounts on purchases.

NetBuyer   **http://www.netbuyer.com**

Ziff-Davis' huge, one-stop source for computer hardware and software. Browse the categories, read the reviews, compare the products, then click to order from over 180 featured vendors and manufacturers. It's so simple that you may never brave the computer mall crowds or interact with decidedly unhelpful sales staff again.

Always Open for Business, A Merchant's   http://www.mercantec.com/
Guide to Opening a Store on the Web   support/aob2.html

Although authored by Mercantec to sell its online commerce products, this 19-page guide contains some solid advice and provides a good starting point for learning about online commerce. An "Are You Ready?" quiz for merchants and additional tips on how to successfully market and operate a store in cyberspace. Target is small- to medium-sized businesses.

Server Check   http://www.netmechanic.com

Server Check is a new, free tool (from the providers of the handy Check Links and Check HTML services) designed to test the reliability and performance of your Web server. Simply enter the URL of the page you want to test, and the Server Check robot will monitor your server for the next 8 hours, accessing the page every 15 minutes and measuring the amount of time required for each step in the retrieval process. After 8 hours, an emailed assessment is returned to you, which includes a comparison to the Server Check average. If desired, a flash email message can be sent each time your server fails to respond to one of the tests, which can help pinpoint critical outages. A handy tool and a nice demo of the Server Check Pro commercial product.

The Meta Medic   http://www.northernwebs.com/set/

This Web-based freeware application (from the makers of SET SIM PRO) will aid Webmasters in fine-tuning their META tags for the best possible results in the search engines. The mediBot will spider your URL and give you a report on your METAtags, tailored to what the search engines are going to need. In your haste to access this free service, do not neglect to study the extensive search engine tutorial for Web designers, which explains how to design your pages with search engine performance in mind.

Buyer's Index   http://www.buyersindex.com

This specialized search engine has turned the catalog industry on its ear by providing free listings to 3500 retail and wholesale mail order catalogs and Web sites. Shoppers can search the database for their desired item and are rewarded with a brief contact list of those companies that wish to sell that item to them. Buyer's Index hopes that users looking to buy will bypass traditional search engines in favor of a more specialized search and that catalogs will pay for advertising and "enhanced" listings to lure a captive audience into its marketspace. Buyer's Index can carry up to 9000 word-searchable product names and keywords from each listed company.

LinkShare Corporation　　　　　　　　**http://www.linkshare.net**

The LinkShare Network hopes to revolutionize online commerce by matching member merchants with Web site owners who want to create an online storefront for their target audience, minus the hassles of product inventory or costly merchant servers. Participating merchants and site owners utilize LinkShare's proprietary software to establish a co-branded, commission-based business relationship. RTP (Referral Tracking and Payment) technology allows participants to review traffic and sales reports on a daily basis and generates commission statements each month. Currently in public beta test mode (the software is available free of charge for trial use), this is a transaction-based distribution solution whose time has come.

ONLINE EVENTS, PROMOTIONS, AND ATTRACTIONS

How to Make a "Scene"
and Draw Them In

If you have a Web site, any kind of Web site, it automatically puts you into two businesses you may not have been in before: publishing and promotions. Running a Web site feels like running a catalog, newspaper, or magazine, as it needs periodic updates. In this environment of many-to-many, you need to promote your site in order to draw in your target constituencies. This way, they can see exactly what you've updated, be it content or merchandise. The attraction that you design needs to relate to your wares.

The delicious irony I wish to share with you here is that this notion of promotion reaches back much further than most of us realize. In the introduction of this book, you probably noticed a picture of a letter from Thomas Alva Edison to my great-grandfather, Edmond Gerson. My great-grandfather was a showman and promoter in the 1870s and Edison, "The Wizard of Menlo Park," wanted him to take his version of the telephone out "on the circuit." Just as Barnum & Bailey put the Ringling Brother's Circus on tour, there were those like my great-grandfather who would bring around the wonders of the world, like Gertrude the Headless Woman.

My point here is that nothing much has changed, with or without the technology. If you want to get people's attention, sometimes it's a good idea to put on a show, especially in a many-to-many environment like the World Wide Web, where so many sites are howling for your attention. Online, that show may or may not be in real time. For example, the Rogue Market (http://www.roguemarket.com) gives away T-shirts to winners of its "Celebrity Stock Exchange" on an ongoing basis. Obviously, the price of a T-shirt isn't that big a deal, but when you add it to the fun of playing a game where you can buy shares of Elvis while selling Madonna short, you have the makings of an ongoing, rolling event. This event or attraction draws over 5 million impressions a month.

In this chapter, we'll explore different kinds of promotions you can hold and discuss some of their respective trade-offs. Should you have one big annual blow-out, shooting your wad all at once, or should you parsimoniously dole your budget out on a monthly, or even weekly, time table? Well, this is your lucky day, because in this chapter, you'll find the answer to these questions and many more . . . step right this way! We'll cover:

- One big event versus many smaller ones
- Periodic promotions
- The Riddler solves some riddles
- Networking promotions
- Email as a promotional tool
- Promotions for professional services
- Talk talk talk
- Now showing at a Web site near you
- Financial incentives
- Creative promotions

One Big Event versus Many Small Ones

So, what kind of promotion, event, or attraction is right for you? One big attention-getter, or ongoing "smallies"? This conundrum can be thrown into high contrast by comparing it to the lottery. Some argue it is better for a great number of people to win $10,000 and let word of mouth propagate from the ground up, rather than having fewer people winning a million dollars. If you go with many people getting smaller amounts, you lose the news value and thus some of the awareness from the top down. Clearly, the people running lotteries have made the decision that a very few get a lot of money, while the runners-up win a #2 pencil.

In the case of the Internet, you first need to figure out what kind of people you want to attract. If they're the kind of people who are drawn to the lottery, then go for the "blow-out" type of event. But let's say you're trying to attract the type of person who may be wary of the "one in a zillion" chance of winning. If you were Music Boulevard, you could have an ongoing promotion, whereby you had a 1-in-20 chance of winning a CD every time a purchase was made.

If you were going to buy CDs anyway, it's a good chance that an ongoing online promotion would be just enough to lure you into buying from Music Boulevard instead of CDNow. In fact, it may be enough of an incentive for you to buy from

Music Boulevard online rather than the CD store down the street. In this case, you have to appeal to the practical side of people's natures. After all, that's why so many people are on the Internet in the first place: for the value they can extract from it.

> **TIP** Have two promotions that you alternate from one month to the next. For instance, one month you could offer 10 percent off all CDs in stock. The next month, you could offer a 1-in-10 chance of winning a CD every time a purchase is made. Each time you toggle from one to the other, be sure you herald the "new" attraction in paid advertising and in press releases.

You also have to ask yourself what you are trying to accomplish. Since I derive a significant amount of my income from public speaking, I set very specific objectives that call for establishing more relationships with meeting planners. So I, along with Laurie Meyer, who owns the Programs Plus Speakers Bureau, started MeetingPlannerTips.com (see Figure 7.1). Since it was the first of its kind, we got very good exposure in the trade press that covers that industry.

Meeting planners who sign up for the service get two tips every week in one email. One is an online tip about a site that can help them in their work, provided by me, while the other is an "offline tip" that gives pointers on planning a successful meeting, or negotiating. The email is short and sweet, which is how the reader wants it and keeps the cost of running the service down. Less content means less time, and less time means less money, as both Laurie and myself can spend our respective hours against billable time or other paying activities. Both of our names are in front of meeting planners every week. Who do you think those meeting planners are going to call when they need a speakers bureau or an Internet expert to address their meeting?

These weekly soft touches keep us top of mind with our target audience inexpensively. I refer to this highly targeted tactical approach as "micromarketing," the boundaries of which are very specific. Deborah Lilly, who runs another speakers bureau called Speakers Bureau Unlimited, observed that there will be a secondary audience as well. She pointed out that other speakers bureaus will sign up for the service so that they can keep their name in front of their own clients, who happen to be meeting planners, of course. This passing along of information is called *propagation* by techies. I call it spreading the gospel.

Executing a micromarketing plan with very limited objectives keeps costs down and return on investment high, but your particular situation may call for a campaign that is larger in scope. Getting news value out of your promotion is becoming a higher and higher stakes game, as the noise level of Web sites shouting for attention increases. The early starters in each category grabbed headlines in the trade and general press for being first. As the competition for attention increases, I think it'll be the deeper-pocketed players who will ante up larger and larger sums to garner media attention.

Jerry Sharasuki, vice president of marketing and development at Yoyodyne, a games and promotions company (http://www.yoyodyne.com), coordinated the $100,000 American Express Shopping Spree, which required online shoppers to buy from 1 of 10 American Express sites they visited. This promotion served many marketing aspects on many different levels. It probably got a lot of people over that "first-time hump" of buying online. It also showed that American Express provides good sales support to the merchants who accept the American Express credit card. Even if the amounts of those sales do not equal the profits garnered from the aggregated sales, the promotion served an important part in building good relations with its sales channels. The promotion also served as a sales and traffic builder and acted as a branding device between provider and sales channel. This will let American Express say to its merchants, "Look at how we support you. It's

Figure 7.1 Chase created MeetingPlannerTips.com to get the attention of and to stay in touch with meeting planners.

Interface designed by Conor Sheridan.

another reason you should accept the American Express card." Finally, when this promotion started, it brought about a great deal of publicity in the press, thus making the general public more aware of American Express.

Periodic Promotions

Assuming you are running periodic promotions, you should be building a database of the audience you're attracting. I talked to David Rae, CEO and chairman of Attitude Network, which owns numerous extremely well-trafficked sites, including Happy Puppy (http://www.happypuppy.com) (see Figure 7.2) and Games Domain (http://www .gamesdomain.com). These two sites represent the two most popular places on the Net for people to download game demos.

Rae feels that "It's not enough to go to a prospective sponsor with a simple advertising or promotional idea. We find there are normally five elements we have to present in a campaign: database creation, advertising, promotion, event coordination, and public relations."

He employed all five elements for author Tom Clancy. His company designed a series of advertisements for the Politica game. The product was introduced with Tom Clancy in an exclusive online chat. That led into a promotion, which involved

Figure 7.2 The most popular site for downloading games holds many promotions.

being able to play the online game for free the entire year. In order to be eligible, the person had to first review a demo of the game online and then register in a newly created database. In two weeks, 40,000 people were registered, which was double their expectations.

Now they have a database of 40,000 Tom Clancy fans who are prospects for Clancy's company, Red Storm Entertainment. Since the database is jointly owned by Rae and Clancy's companies, both can mine it for different purposes. They do not aggressively attack or spam the email addresses residing in this database. "After all, we don't want to alienate those people, since they're our bread and butter," says Rae. For the initial event, all of their publicity was due to a broad PR blitz that covered the waterfront, from all of the game magazines to *AdWeek* and *USA Today*.

Who, How, Where, What, and When to Promote

David Rae observes a move from advertising to promotions. It's more fun for both the sponsor and audience alike. Rae explained,

> In the past, we've given away Ford Explorers, dungeon crawls through the most ghastly dungeons in Europe, and one grand prize that sent a winner to combat flight training school in a Mig over the Arizona desert. I don't know that the size of the prize is as relevant as how tightly it fits with the topic matter and the target audience's predilections. The promotions that work best are narrow and deep, highly tuned and highly targeted. If the prize attracts too wide of an audience, you'll get people you don't necessarily want. Sometimes, even if you do want them, there are other media that will deliver those numbers at a lower cost, like television.

Rae sees a shift from simply running ad banners to running ad banners with some kind of promotion on them. He also notices that many promotions are dreamt up just two weeks prior to their actual launch. These instant attractions aren't easily promoted in print because it takes too long to coordinate the creation and purchase of that medium to run in time. Rae feels that radio works better for his type of promotions, since the medium is more immediate and gives you the ability to target a very densely concentrated audience, like using a San Francisco rock & roll radio station. By its nature, radio immediately draws people toward promotions and events.

Rae wonders why *reach*, or how deeply you hit a given niche, is usually neglected. These are my sentiments exactly, as I've always thought it's better to continuously hit a tightly defined core group rather than a diffuse audience every so often. If you do in fact focus on a tightly defined audience, the viewer will more likely perceive you as being interesting, instead of getting fed up with your campaign. We've all experienced the phenomenon of being turned off by a repetitive ad. At first, those little talking Budweiser frogs may have seemed innovative, but after seeing them eight times during the Superbowl, a viewer can get annoyed, due to what the advertising industry refers to as "wear out." If you're going to cater to a tightly defined niche many times, be especially aware when a campaign turns from positive reinforcement into constant annoyance.

However, Rae emphasizes that this phenomenon can easily be avoided on the Internet. For example, his company uses software that automatically changes the ad banner if the surfer doesn't click on it after three or four times.

The Riddler Solves Some Riddles

Riddler (see Figure 7.3) is one of the oldest sites on the Net where you can actually play its games in real time (http://www.riddler.com). Geoffrey Judge, senior vice president of technology and operations development of 24/7Media, the parent company to Riddler, corroborates with David Rae's observation that, overall, prizes are getting smaller. Judge recalls the promotional launching of Microsoft's Internet Explorer 3.0, in which Riddler participated by giving away a two-year

Figure 7.3 One of the first and most innovative online gamer sites keeps drawing them in.

lease on a Ford Explorer. He told me, "If that promotion was held again today, it wouldn't be as big of a news story, since bigger prizes are pervasive." He prefers those prizes to be cash, instead of physical goods since, often, winners want the cash value instead anyway.

I asked him how he authenticates the people who are winning these prizes and their information. Judge explained to me that a person gets a user identification name, plus real name, address, and so forth, when he or she first registers. When I signed up, I found myself being more truthful about the information I provided, knowing that I might win something later. Sweepstakes and contests tend to increase the truthfulness of the information people enter into online forms when they register. If the users think they may win something, they'll want to be sure they fill out the registration form correctly, so they can receive prizes. If I were to win one of their games, Riddler would then email me with a confirmation of the information I provided when first signing up. If everything matches, Riddler will send me the check. However, if the prize value is substantial, Riddler goes to far greater efforts to authenticate your information, like getting your Social Security number and notifying the government with a 1099 form.

At the end of the registration form, I noticed a free trial offer for a magazine that can now be sent to me, since I've presumably given my correct mailing address. Judge told me that 7–10 percent of people say "yes" to general interest magazines, such as *Time*, *Worth*, and *Money*, while about 10–15 percent of people say "yes" to magazines that are more "Net-centric."

One of the more interesting anecdotes Judge shared with me is that people do in fact play games for no prizes at all. The game has to be intriguing enough, have some competitive challenge, or both. Judge has also learned that people like fast-loading games with no user downloads. For example, one of its games is called "Scrambler Squared." You don't have to register to play; therefore, there are no prizes involved. It is really a branding game. You compete against other people to see who's the first to put together a logo that is scrambled into 25 pieces. Another one of Riddler's hottest areas is a multiplayer crossword puzzle called "Checkered Flag." If you don't fill in those words fast enough, your opponents can really humble you.

Judge told me that the original harvest of players was amassed from a scavenger hunt Riddler held on the entire World Wide Web. He told me, "We hid hints on thousands of sites that agreed to participate. They had to feature a Riddler logo and host the hidden hint somewhere on their site." This contest brought in hordes of surfers to their site.

That scavenger hunt also gave birth to the Commonwealth Advertising Network. Judge explained to me, "On that network, we sell ads that run all over the Internet to our sponsors, in addition to using some of the unsold space for our own purposes in driving traffic to the Riddler site. We've found that running print ads hasn't been a successful endeavor, so we're not continuing with them. Even game publications haven't been successful; I feel their audience is more of the 'twitch-gamer' variety, rather than the intellectual and puzzle gamers we normally attract."

Networking Promotions

Other companies in this online promotion space see the importance of working with a network of sites, as Riddler has by creating the Commonwealth Advertising Network. Cofounder of NetStakes, Dan Feldman, buys a lot of advertising avails across a wide array of Web sites, including the DoubleClick and Petry networks. He likes these and other large advertising networks because they can consistently deliver the volume of impressions needed to drive enough traffic to the promotion site in order to make it successful. Whether you, the reader, have this kind of budget or not, take your cue from the experiences of David Rae, Geoffrey Judge, and Dan Feldman. That cue calls for you to prepare a significant, outbound, highly targeted campaign that heralds your promotion. Otherwise, you'll have the best darn promotion no one ever heard of.

Sweepstakes

NetStakes runs sweepstakes. The difference between a sweepstakes and a contest is that sweepstakes require no skill, while a contest does; therefore, sweepstakes are entirely random. Feldman told me that NetStakes prefers doing sweepstakes because "we get our best retention rates and 'through-put.'" NetStakes only makes a participant register only once; if you participate in future sweepstakes, you just have to provide your email address. NetStakes really wants to keep the barrier of participation low. Many people don't have the time to commit to playing a game of skill or answering lengthy questionnaires. They don't want the amount of involvement a contest demands.

Feldman goes on to explain why it's also important for his company to structure promotions with its own respective channel, or network, which itself succinctly defines its target audience. Sports-minded surfers visiting http://webstakes.com (the actual site where NetStakes houses its promotions, shown in Figure 7.4) will naturally want to travel through the sports channels. Likewise, sports marketers will be interested only in the sports-minded surfer. They have the ability to find each other within this channel.

Figure 7.4 NetStakes provides highly targeted audiences for different kinds of promotions.

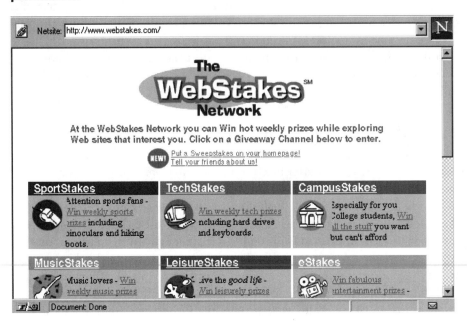

There is a well-rounded mix of different industries, or channels, that is represented at NetStakes: sports, technology, business, entertainment, music, family, travel, and leisure. It offers different prizes, depending on what area a visitor is in. For instance, the family channel might be giving away educational software or a home entertainment system, while the business channel would give away Zip drives or Palm Pilots. Each channel has multiple sponsors. They each, in turn, pay NetStakes to send them traffic. NetStakes runs online ads both on the Web and in the 600,000+ email list that people requested to be on.

NetStakes also develops customized promotions and software for its clients. If a company wants to host an online sweepstakes but doesn't want to be involved in the actual conception, development, management, execution, and fulfillment of the project, this company will design it for them.

Feldman also agrees that one of the most effective methods for building traffic is by the email database they've accrued over the past two years. He says, "It works like a 'push/pull' model. We can push messages out to those who have specifically requested them, and then we can pull them into the sweepstakes loop." Notice the distinct pattern emerging, whereby the promoters of Happy Puppy, Riddler, and NetStakes all place a great emphasis on an email database, which preferably contains more than just email addresses.

Email as a Promotional Tool

I can't stress enough how important it is for you to develop an email database when planning an Internet promotion. Virtually all Net marketers, myself included, speak of its importance. Perhaps the biggest mistake marketers make is to go to the effort and expense of planning a campaign, only to let those people get away, quite possibly never to return. One company, Insight Computer, markets promotions to its user database of 115,000 people. It tests different subject headers, as well as different body copy. Insight found that by using whimsical ploys such as "Is our product manager losing his mind?" it will receive a better response than a more serious subject header such as "Bargain Blow-Out Sale." Insight gets dozens of orders it can track directly back to its outbound campaign.

While I have always touted the simplicity and ubiquity of simple email delivery, even those times are a-changing. Chris Knight, founder of SparkNet, a major player in email distribution services, informs me that *enhanced email* is becoming more and more popular as a greater number of people use Netscape Mail Direct and Internet Explorer Mail Reader, both of which support enhanced mail. This means you can send banners, graphics, even entire Web pages through the email system. It delivers more sizzle, since its colorful graphics can allow for a brighter display of what you have to offer. It also lets you click over directly to a site from your email program.

Many large email service providers such as Chris' offer the user both simple and enhanced email. If you choose to make your outbound messages available to your subscribers in the enhanced format, try to keep the file size down by going easy on the graphics. If they are too heavy, the email document will be the size of a Web page, 30K or more, and will take as long to come in as it would to download on the Net. You know how people hate to wait, so don't import the whole World Wide Wait into people's emailboxes.

Promotions for Professional Services

Sounds like an oxymoron? Not really. I do it myself. Every year, I have two events that market me and my business. In the spring, I promote "The Best of Larry Chase's *Web Digest For Marketers*." In the fall, I promote limited free access (one month) to the archives of *Web Digest For Marketers*. Over the years, I've harvested numerous clients whom I can directly track back to those promotions. Similarly, when Morgan Stanley puts up a whitepaper on Internet commerce or Internet advertising, that too can be considered a promotion, or *an event*. It's usually referred to as a loss-leader instead, but it has the same fundamental approaches in place. All loss-leaders, at heart, are really just promotions.

This idea of offering free access to one's database is used often on the Net. Hoover's Company Database (http://www.hoovers.com/subscribe/subscrib.html) usually costs $12.95 a month. It has run "free month" promotions in *Web Digest For Marketers*, and other places, in order to raise its profile and get more people to subscribe. In fact, it's a common practice for a database to go live for free at first, with a clear understanding it will become a subscription service thereafter.

Just the idea that something you currently get for free will eventually become a paid service often serves as a strong incentive for people to go and see what value is being offered. For instance, people accessed the *Wall Street Journal*'s free service for many months before the pricing plan kicked in. As a result, the *Wall Street Journal* had 400,000 subscribers when it was free. A fraction of those people stayed on when it went to a subscription-based model. Over time, however, the *Journal* has built a subscription base approaching nearly half the original number of free subscribers. Its brilliant move was to keep the pricing extremely low, discounting for print subscribers. Had it charged too much, it would've destroyed its advertising rate card, since a much smaller group would have subscribed; therefore, the *Journal*'s advertising revenues would have been substantially less than they are now.

Talk Talk Talk

They say talk is cheap. It isn't necessarily so. If you want to have live chat sessions online, it's not usually an expensive endeavor. The software and setup can range from free to $30,000 or more. You can even dodge the whole hosting aspect and hold the chat at a place like TalkCity at http://www.talkcity.com, which can set up a section for your company's events and put you on its master schedule. The expensive and/or time-consuming part is promoting the event. You might consider having a weekly or monthly schedule of chats, featuring different speakers. In this way, you can maintain an ongoing promotion that publicizes the schedule as a whole, while also featuring the upcoming events.

On the other hand, you could spontaneously promote an event, as Merrill Lynch has been known to do. During a particularly bumpy period in the stock market, it featured its co-chairman in a chat room, advising nervous stockholders. Again, it depends on your constituency and what you want from the program. You may hold a chat to simply build goodwill and not even push the product right then and there. There are no hard and fast rules.

I was once a guest on Jill Ellsworth's AOL Marketing Chat, which is held every week. It was a fun thing to take part in, held in one of the AOL auditoriums with other guest speakers on the "stage." The AOL Audience Hall held 300 people. I, as a guest speaker, could talk with other guest speakers and watch the audience members log in and out. I kept wondering, "Was it something I said?"

| TIP | When holding a chat event, you need to check out the options available to you in regard to audience/speaker interactions. In an "auditorium" setting on AOL (for AOL members only) or Excite Chat! (for anyone on the Web), speakers are segregated from the audience, and each "row" of the audience is not only free to speak among themselves, but you will neither hear nor see them. Questions are filtered via moderators. This can work in your favor, but you need to decide on the level of interaction you are looking for with your attendees for these promotional events. Other types of chat do not segregate the speakers from the audience at all, but make it all one big, happy (sometimes rowdy) family, giving it a more intimate feeling, but harder to control at times. |

I noticed the traffic to my site spiked considerably a few days after the chat event. Believe it or not, people actually do pull the archives of these chats and read them. Some people actually prefer to read chats in archive form, since they can then control the read rate, rather than it being dictated by the guest speaker's typing speed, or lack thereof. For a schedule of what's happening in which chat rooms around the Web, check out http://www.quarterdeck.com. OnNow's listings (www.onnow.com) are very comprehensive as well, with links to all the software you'd need for any given event it has on the master schedule from all over the Net. Also take a look at Yack Inc. (http://www.yack.com), whose chat listings are so popular, they've been syndicated to 15 newspapers through United Media.

Community Events

Some say a community constitutes calling a bunch of people together. They're right. As discussed in Chapter 5, "Your Brand Image and the Internet," community is a component of marketing, specifically event marketing. However, it isn't everything by a long shot. It's not a good idea to simply assume you've got a guarantee people will buy from you because you hold a community-type event for your constituents. There are those who say the community concept is overrated and overhyped. "I think the community concept is a myth," challenges David Rae. Real-world communities offer certain protocols of behavior that aren't necessarily in place online, such as mutual obligations. "The online community is more like a crowd at a basketball game or a rock concert than Mayberry," Rae concludes. Match that bit of sobering information with Matt Lederman's reply (co-founder of the Rogue Market, Figure 7.5). He wryly muses that "We're building a community one lunatic at a time."

My advice to you is that if you want to try and build a community, by all means, do so. However, be very clear as to what you expect out of it. More likely than not, you'll be putting up a lot of time, money or both, into building that community. Perhaps you'll amass a database that will become the asset that you can go back to time and time again when you have your specials or promotions. You'll

Figure 7.5 The Rogue Market is a celebrity stock exchange that causes millions of fans to participate monthly.

need to calculate the maintenance, growth, and upgrades for that database. What return will it give you over what period of time? More than likely, it's impossible to say. Try to put in some projected numbers and contrast your figures to the more real cost of maintaining the database. Is it all worth it to you?

Live People as Attractions on the Web

Egghead Software (http:www.egghead.com) features a novel attraction at its Web site: live people to help you (see Figure 7.6). Using Palace software (http://www .thepalace.com), you can go up to the customer service window, 24 hours a day, 7 days a week, and get a real live human to help you! Ask if that latest upgrade or patch for Adobe Photoshop is in yet, and the person at the other end will ask you to wait a minute while he or she goes and checks. What will they think of next?

Additionally, Lucent Technologies (http://www.lucent.com) has a system whereby a live telemarketer contacts you and then pushes Web pages to your machine, based on what you tell that person on the other end of the phone. This marriage of people and technology seems like a winner to me. Think about it: Even a self-service gas station has attendants to help you out.

Figure 7.6 Egghead Online uses real live people as an attraction.

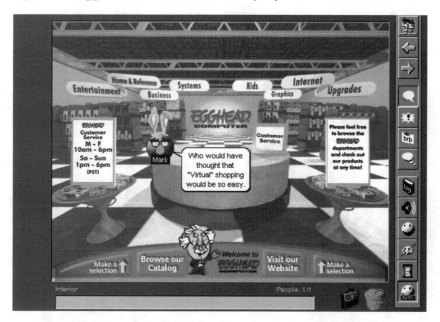

Now Showing at a Web Site Near You

New and innovative ways to lure you into one site over another are always being developed and tested. Netcentives (http://www.netcentives.com) has an interesting added-value approach that rewards surfers with frequent flyer miles (see Figure 7.7). Participants get a certain number of miles just for filling out a registration form, and can build up their stash by buying something at a participating site, like the ProShop at Golf Web (http://proshop.golfweb.com). This is a way for Golf Web to add value without cutting its prices, which would only serve to commoditize its merchandise, something a pro shop wants to avoid.

Another ingenious value-add is the Kodak Picture Network (KPN) at http://www.kodak.com/go/kodakpn. For $4.95 per month, Kodak will post your developed pictures on its Web site. This allows far-flung family members to view your pictures from anywhere around the world. A user simply takes her pictures with any type of camera, even those $10 disposable kinds, and then brings the roll of film to a retail developer. When she has to specify what size she wants their prints and the quantity, she can also choose to have her pictures on the Kodak Picture Network. When the user gets the developed pictures back, she'll find a PIN number printed on the envelope that gives her access to her photos online. All she has to do is simply enter

Figure 7.7 Online retailers now offer frequent flier miles through Netcentives.

the PIN number when prompted to do so on the KPN site, and she can then view all of her pictures on the Web. By the time you read this, you'll even be able to set up different albums of pictures, whereby you can share different albums with different people. A college student may want to show his mom pictures of studying in the library, which can be separated from all the pictures of his drinking buddies. The two shall never meet! Whomever sees these photos can also order duplicates, which can be mailed or, for an even faster option, printed at a kiosk located in retail outlets. At the time of writing, about 30,000 photo retail counters offer the ability to have your pictures posted on the Web. By the end of 1998, there will be about 5000 photo retailers offering the kiosk service.

Mark Cook, marketing manager of the Kodak Picture Network, told me, "Kodak is currently using banner ads to attract people to our Kodak Picture Network. We are also moving to in-store promotions. Since the store selling the processing services gets a transaction markup, it's in its best interest to see the size of the sale increase." He also pointed out to me that many stores are even starting to consider the photo processing traffic as a loss-leader to build overall store traffic. If one store offers the KPN service and another does not, the one that does will attract that Internet user into his store. That Internet user, as you know, is more than likely a very attractive customer for that retailer.

Audio and Video in Promotions

RealAudio and AudioNet seem to be the two dominant audio formats currently used on the Net. Lots of broadcast networks, radio stations, governments, and companies are putting audio components on their sites. It makes sense. Should you do it? If the content is being used for other purposes, such as promotions, I would say "yes." If transmission on the Web is its only purpose or usage, I'd think very hard about it. While RealAudio and AudioNet play pretty well on a 28.8k modem, audio streams do take up a significant amount of the provider's bandwidth. Yes, many users do have and use the audio plug-ins out there. But keep in mind that in addition to the server software you need to push the audio stream to them, you may also need to invest in additional bandwidth if your audio stream becomes a hit.

However, I am much less optimistic about streaming video. Visuals require significantly more bandwidth than audio. As a consequence, you get only a few frames per second of video. Compare that to full-video motion, which is 30 frames per second. While it's true that many people have the ability to play JPEG videos, they take a considerable amount of time to download. One fast food chain offered its television commercials for download this way. It made no sense to me whatsoever. The proposition was you would spend 10 minutes downloading a commercial you would otherwise fast forward over if you saw it on television. What were they thinking?

Streaming video flies into the surfer's machine much faster, allowing him or her to view images on the fly. But these images are only a few frames a second, compared to the 24 frames of film and 30 of television. I once saw a video banner of a guy hitting a golf ball. While it was a first, I nearly fell off my chair laughing. What value do I, as a surfer, derive from this? Over time, the technology will get better, when more surfers have and use those plug-ins. Until then, I recommend using a more practical venue.

Financial Incentives

People love a bargain, no question. Bargain hunters can develop some serious online shopping habits. There are Web sites that cater to such value-seekers, such as H.O.T! Coupons (http://www.hotcoupons.com), which will notify you when there are coupons available in the category you like. CoolSavings (http://www.cool-savings.com) is another such site, and many more are piling on the bandwagon (see Figure 7.8).

Figure 7.8 Financial incentives are a big attraction on the Web.

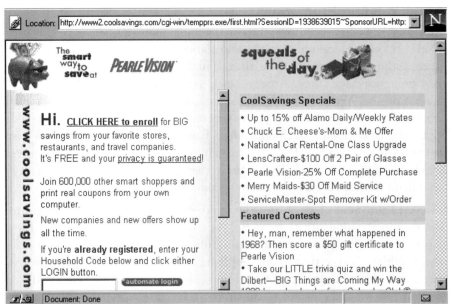

Using information from purchases, such as credit card numbers or their shipping or billing addresses, track the geographic location of the people who are buying from your site. Then run support print ads for your promotions in those regions in which you have the most buyers.

Since you're printing the coupons yourself, you're saving the manufacturer a lot of money by not having to print them, mail them to you, and hope that some small percentage of recipients of that direct marketing campaign actually respond. Someone once asked me, "What would happen if a person printed dozens of '$50 off your new printer' coupons?" I replied that if that were my site, I might even pay you to do so! It would truly be a win/win situation.

Auctions

Another high-value online delivery system is auction sites. I know people who are literally addicted to them. One well-educated person said to me over lunch the other day, "I've got a real online shopping jones." I mention auction sites in other chapters, but one of my favorites is the original, Wehkamp, in Holland. Go to http://www.wehkamp.nl. and click on the auction hammer. Wehkamp is Holland's largest cataloger (see Figure 7.9). It uses this site to "blow out" older inventory. What's interesting is that the prices go down, not up. In a Dutch auction, the auctioneer sets a price for the merchandise and keeps reducing it until somebody commits to buying at that price. When an auction is in session, the one who puts in the first bid gets the product. The auction sites in the United States usually work in reverse, whereby the price is run up by competing bids. For some other interesting auction sites, see the resource center on the companion Web site for Chapter 8, "Direct Marketing and Sales Support."

Whether you want your auction to go up or down in price, you still have to consider whether it is more cost effective for you to have your own auction site or farm out your merchandise to an existing site that already has an audience and profile. Remember, if you do start your own, you've got the substantial cost of promoting it. If you don't promote the event well, you won't have a big audience. Those few visitors will also end up getting your merchandise at incredible bargain prices, since there won't be enough demand in place to drive or keep the price up.

Gambling on the Net

Just as gambling exists in the "real world," it's also springing up online. It has become a major cultural, legal, and moral issue. Ironically, the initial response

Figure 7.9 The original online auction site was put up by a Dutch direct marketer.

from the general Internet population has been far from overwhelming. Many are reluctant to trust that online gaming sites will be completely honest.

One of the more popular sites is US Lottery, at http://www.uslottery.com. It is owned and operated by the Coeur d'Alene Tribe in Worley, Idaho. To be eligible to play, you need to be at least 18 years old and live in state where lottery tickets are sold. Here's how it works: The tribe sends you a CD-ROM with a 10-megabyte program. When you download this program to your hard drive, you are now able to purchase the lottery tickets. You can do so either through the Internet or by phone or fax. It costs a minimum of $25 to open an account. Now you're ready to play the games. On the Web, go to the online ticket window and select from BlackJack, Bingo, 21, slot machines, and others. Each of these games work like scratch-off tickets, where you immediately find out whether you've won or lost. Now, if only we could get those slot machines to pay off by spitting out coins from the floppy disk drives . . .

Creative Promotions

You position yourself as a smart player if you make technology do the bidding for you. Your promotions should always flow naturally out of your products or service.

Lycos, the search engine, promotes itself through its "Search for Missing Children" campaign. It makes sense that a search engine would sponsor a search for missing kids.

Introducing a new idea usually garners a great deal of attention, both online and offline. For instance, "The Trip from Hell" contest was an idea I conjured up with David Rae, who owned Hotel Discounts at the time. It was the first use of the "hell" genre I am aware of. Since then, it has been copied many times, but doesn't have that same initial impact anymore. A similar take on this idea is the "Worst Experience with a Salesperson" at http://www.techsell.com, which is used to promote its book, *The Buyer's Guide to Handling Salespeople.* This book trains people how to handle pushy or irritating salespeople. By submitting your own torrid examples, you can win $500. Why do these two contests work so well? They are both things everyone can relate to, and they automatically bring about a myriad of examples with which we can all commiserate.

On another note, there is the "Guess the Wreck" monthly contest, hosted by the Hudson Valley Auto Appraisers (HVAA) at http://www.hvaa.com/guessthe.htm. You can win a $50 U.S. Savings Bond by estimating the cost of damage to a pictured car on its site (see Figure 7.10). To help you out, HVAA gives hints and a list of parts that were needed to fix the actual car.

Or, for those editing fanatics out there, you can win small-dollar prizes, cigars, magnetic poetry kits, and other small items for proofreading Chris Conti's Web page (http://www.americaninternet.com/conti/al.html). His site features a "virtual book," but with school, papers, and other time constraints, he doesn't have enough time to spellcheck the pages himself. Simply email him his mistakes and the URL of the page on which it appears, and he'll send you a prize. Shrewd or slothful? You be the judge.

All of these examples point out that whether you're big or small, you don't have to spend a fortune on your promotions, but you do have to spend some time making sure they match your product's attributes and your audience's tastes and desires. The concept for your promotion should be so good your competition will say, "I wish I thought of that first!"

At the beginning of this chapter, I noted that things haven't changed all that much since the time of Thomas Edison's letter to my great-grandfather, discussing the promotion of his "musical telephone." It's true. Use your gut instincts. Human nature hasn't really changed all that much. The difference between then and now is that there are computers and wires serving as conduits between you and the audience, where back then it was face to face. People still spark to a bargain, inspiration, greed, fear, and the other handful of primal traits with which we're

Figure 7.10 Win a $50 U.S. Savings Bond in the "Guess the Wreck" contest from the HVAA.

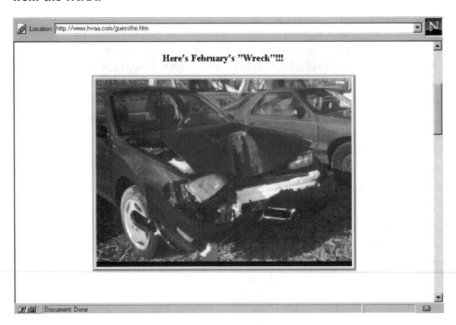

endowed. Is Tom Sawyer getting all the kids to help him whitewash the picket fence so very different from Chris Conti getting others to proofread his Web site? Not really. What both Sawyer and Conti did was make it fun for the participants.

Finally, ask yourself the following question, "Would I myself be attracted to this offer?" If the answer is "no," go back to the drawing board. If the answer is "yes," first do a "disaster check" by testing it on some other people. Then, give it your best shot. Good luck . . . your chance to hit the jackpot is coming up next!

Resource Center

CoolSavings   **http://www.coolsavings.com**

A coupon service that lets members clip and print their own coupons for free, after signing up. Just download the CoolSave coupon manager software, then search the site by product category for everything from fast food to rental cars. Coupons can be printed on inkjet and laser printers for redemption. This is an especially good idea for grocers and others to pay attention to, as it has the potential of yielding considerable savings in printing, mailing, warehousing, and handling coupons.

Web Magnet   http://www.webmagnet.com

Web Magnet is an Internet publicity provider that specializes in promoting Web sites through contests, directory listings, press releases, and advertising. Web Magnet looks at contests all day long, and it knows a good one when it sees it. Thus, Web Magnet created its value-added "Best Contests on the Web" and "Best Sweepstakes Awards" features, which both rate on a 4-star system based on criteria such as graphics, concept, prize value, and ease of entry. This site is a good first stop for inspiration and guidance when planning your own online contest. While there, be sure to check out Ideas For You, which is an excellent 25-page primer on how to promote your site.

ThreadTreader's WWW Contests Guide   http://www.4cyte.com/ThreadTreader

This site compiles current contests by theme, prize, entry deadline, and name. It also allows you to find relevant contests via the SweepSearch search engine. Simply enter keywords, and corresponding contests will be summarized for your review, which is a good way to quickly scope out what competitors are offering. This site promises the most complete, updated guide to contests worldwide, so if you're feeling lucky, surf on over.

Promo   http://www.mediacentral.com/promo

Despite the popularity and value of sales promotion, a good online magazine devoted to the topic is difficult to find. *Promo*, brought to us by Media Central, is an excellent resource for promotional marketing information. Topics include news and trends analysis surrounding alternative media, cause-related promotions, couponing, sports promotion, games, contests, sweepstakes, in-store marketing, interactive promotions, sampling, and more. Equally valuable are featured resources such as *The 1997 Annual Report of the Promotion Industry*, which literally brings facts and figures together, and the top promotional agencies highlighted in the *Promo* 100.

Ticketmaster Online's "All Access"   http://www.ticketmaster.com

This is a live forum for artists to talk to their fans and promote upcoming shows. It directly links chats with online ticket and merchandise sales.

DIRECT MARKETING
and Sales Support

8

Whether you know it or not, you're a direct marketer. Every time you ask for a sale, a job, a signed contract, or to start a new relationship, you're soliciting a response. Direct marketing (DM) or direct response always includes a call to action. Since the Internet is interactive, that call to action can be answered in seconds or minutes, rather than in weeks or months, as in traditional DM. Understanding and adopting many classic DM practices is critical to mounting a successful marketing campaign on the Net. Knowing where traditional DM stops and where the new practices begin will be your edge.

In this chapter, you'll learn how traditional DM disciplines are similar to that of the Net, as well as how they're not. Two case histories will show you online DM practices that aren't even possible in traditional direct marketing. You'll get valuable insight into the following areas:

- How Net marketing is like traditional direct marketing
- Direct marketing online-tracking techniques
- How direct-marketing copy is like online copy
- How online direct marketing differs from offline DM
- Online mailing lists versus offline mailing lists
- Direct marketing on the Web
- Online direct marketing supporting offline DM efforts

How Net Marketing Is Like Traditional DM

Some of the best Internet marketing books aren't Internet marketing books at all, but rather classic direct-marketing books. While you dig deeper into how the Net can be used for marketing, look at some of the "bibles" and key principles of direct marketing, and then figure out how you can apply some of these time-honored practices to your situation on the Net.

Loyalty and Retention Programs

These are programs that are meant to keep the existing paying customer happy. If employed correctly, the Net can be very good at keeping existing customers satisfied.

A good example of this is American Airlines (http://www.americanair.com). With your frequent flyer code, you can go into an exclusive area and find out how many frequent flyer miles you have accrued. This actually lets the customer peer into the American Airlines database, which is a complex technological feat that it should be congratulated for. Similarly, Federal Express lets you track your package pretty much in real time (http://www.fedex.com) and even schedule pickups directly from its Web pages.

You don't have to be that sophisticated. One of my first clients, 1-800-Flowers, sends, at your request, an email reminding the customer of a future birthday or anniversary, based on your previous buying patterns. Another instance is the Amazon.com bookstore. It offered to inform me, via email, when the discovered Jules Verne manuscript about Paris in the 1960s was translated into English. Amazon did inform me, and I ultimately bought the book. I didn't care that it was a *mailbot* that performed this service, rather than someone physically sitting down and writing to me. That's okay, it was the thought that counted. In this case, the thought was a piece of programming that offered good customer convenience.

> **Mailbot** comes from two words, *mail* and *bot*, where *bot* is short for *robot*. A mailbot is a piece of mail automatically sent out upon request. It may be sent right away, or scheduled to go out days, weeks, or months later, as a reminder message. Mailbots are also used as confirmation notices. Sometimes called *replybots*, these messages can tell you your order or email has been received and will be acted upon on a certain date.

FireFly (http://www.firefly.com) and other online personalization programs are dedicated to creating and maintaining customer reminders, personal information tracking, and other technology that allows companies to provide such customer retention programs. These programs can do everything from recommend to a customer what he or she would like to buy next, based on past information stored on personal preferences, to reminding a customer when a spouse's birthday is coming up and offering Web links or other information concerning gifts or cards for the day.

This use of technology is excellent DM thinking, but also says something about these companies and how they think and do business. Naturally, I bought the book from Amazon when I was notified of the English translation. Therefore, these reminder services serve double duty as a DM and branding tool, since they leave me with a good impression, as well as motivating me to give them my business in the future.

This practice is also used in the financial services category. Brokerage houses and financial firms are big on loyalty and retention programs via the Net. If you have a Smith Barney (http://www.smithbarney.com/) or Merrill Lynch account (http://www.ml.com/), you can get higher grades of information on their sites than is normally available to just anybody. On a similar note, Dean Witter Reynolds, Inc. (http://www.deanwitter.com), allows users to create a customized personal homepage based on their attitude toward investment risk, where they can check a daily "state of the market" area or can tune in for a weekly commentary on the stock market by Dean Witter's chief investment strategist, Peter Canelo. There's also plenty of news and commentary, as well as a financial guide to help users determine their financial objectives.

In times past, you would not think of a utility company offering incentives to do business with it because it was the only game in town. But with deregulation hitting that industry as this book goes to press, utility companies realize the importance of loyalty and retention programs. One of my clients, Con Edison, an electrical utility company, currently offers its customers fast and easy online payments and will be adding other valuable customer services online in the near future. This is done as a means by which to hold onto its current customer base.

Acquisition and Prospecting Programs

Fishing for new potential business is extremely cost effective on the Net if you do it right. Let's take two companies that acquire new names for their mailing lists by advertising on my *Web Digest For Marketers* newsletter: *American Demographics Magazine* and an industry newsletter called *Web Marketing Strategies*.

Every *WDFM* subscriber is a potential lead for these two publications, in this case. Many of these leads take the trial subscription offer for their print versions and are converted into prospects. When the trial subscription expires, these prospects are asked if they want to convert to a paying subscription. Of course, many don't, but some do. Those who do are considered "closes," as in closing on a sale. If a trial offer is placed in a well-targeted environment, more people will opt to pay to continue their subscription.

The publisher who runs the promotion calculates the final costs by taking the amount of money he or she has spent on the program and dividing it by the number of *closers*, or people who ultimately subscribe for money. The cost of closing each subscriber may be as much as one year's paid subscription. The publisher figures that's okay because that subscriber will be around for a few years. Online, you can bring down the cost per conversion because you don't have the costs of producing a DM mail package, postage, handling, and backend fulfillment for the initial promotion package. In DM speak, this is known as "the cost of acquisition."

American Demographics Magazine and the *Web Marketing Strategies* newsletter have had incredible success squashing the cost of these conversions to a small fraction of what they'd normally be. For two years, *American Demographics* has been running a three-month free print subscription offer on my *WDFM* homepage. Every time someone fills in the online form, he or she short-circuits all those traditional costs. The request goes directly to *American Demographics Magazine*, where it's entered into the temporary mailing list. If that request came in the mail, *American Demographics* would have additional costs keying in all the information the prospect had filled out on paper. Online, the prospect is effectively filling in his or her own subscription information for the magazine. Think of it as a type of self-service gas pump.

Since the cost of running such a promotion is so inexpensive, *Web Marketing Strategies* (which costs $199.95 a year) decided to take the money it saved and plow it into providing an even more attractive offer in *Web Digest For Marketers*. It extended the free trial period from one month to three, a $50 value. When this ran to a highly targeted audience, the response was phenomenal. That issue of *WDFM* went out late one evening, and within the first hour of the next business day, the publisher had 20 requests. The final figures showed scores of requests that came in over the next few weeks, solely from *WDFM*'s online offer.

WDFM Case History

I run acquisition programs for my *WDFM* online newsletter. For about $245, I garnered 1200 new subscribers. Here's how I did it:

Many people who read *WDFM* buy and sell advertising. The unit of measure they use to compare one ad buy over another is *cost per thousand*, or CPM. I decided to feature and promote CPM calculators (as a computer program) that the surfer could use on the *WDFM* site (see Figure 8.1). A programmer friend of mine wrote the scripts in a half hour and didn't charge me for them. In fact, Matt Lederman didn't even want his name associated with it because it was such a simple program! Therefore, there were no costs involved to create the initial attraction. I then put out a press release announcing the calculators available at the *WDFM* Web site. It was picked up by Reuters and a host of other wire services, which brought people to my site by the tens of thousands. They used the calculators, and many signed up for *WDFM* thereafter. I have since received a great deal of business from those people who joined the list back then and have later called on me to consult, speak, or provide content for them. How do I know that? Because I asked them where they heard of *WDFM* in the subscription registration form. The point is, you don't have to spend a fortune to acquire prospects that can later be converted to profits.

Figure 8.1 Using computer code that I got for free, I attracted 1200 new subscribers.

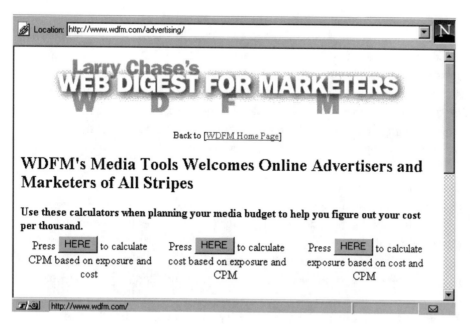

The lessons here were two-fold:

Keep it simple and focused. The CPM calculators were nothing more than simple multiplication and division functions. A $1.00 hand-held calculator can do these functions and much, much more. However, people like single-function tools. People have toasters despite the fact they can toast their bread in the oven. Also, these scripts were done in simple *CGI* language that every surfer can easily use. No fancy Java or Shockwave downloads here. That would only serve to limit the number of surfers able to use the calculators, thus defeating the purpose.

Get to Know Web-Speak!

CGI stands for Common Gateway Interface. CGI scripts enable surfers to fill out forms online, use calculators, and other basic interactive tasks. Just about every browser out there can work with a CGI script, as it is a program based on the server you're browsing to, not your computer. Often you will see a page that requires a "form-readable" or "forms-compatible" browser: This is a page that uses CGI scripts.

Java does some very slick things. The basic ability to read Java language is built into all the major browsers, such as MSIE, Netscape, and Opera. However, in order for it to work properly, your computer has to have little Java *applets*, or mini-applications. These applets often come to you on an as-needed basis, embedded on a Web page and downloaded as you access the page. This means you have to wait for them to download if you're on a slow or average connection. I recommend that Java applet usage be kept to a minimum, until the technology develops further.

Shockwave is a popular *plug-in* program (from Macromedia Products) that gives you multimedia experiences and sound. The program itself must be downloaded and installed for your browser (there are separate versions for Netscape and MSIE, as they use different platforms for plug-in technology) before you can see the Shockwaved presentation on a Web page. Again, I suggest these types of applications be used in controlled circumstances.

Those CPM calculators had an affinity with the core product of *WDFM*, which in turn has an affinity with my customer base. I call this *hypothesis marketing*. If you like the CPM calculator, then you'll like *WDFM*. If you like *WDFM*, then I want to know you.

DM Online Tracking Techniques: Tracking Results in Minutes, Not Months

I used to have a link on the *WDFM* homepage called "Other Sites to See." These were some of my favorite sites. Some of them were marketing related, some weren't. I looked in my logs and saw that only 3 percent of people were clicking on that button. So I changed it to "Don't Click Here if You Have a Life ;)". Three times as many people now click on that very same link. On a much larger scale, you can do the very same thing with your online DM campaigns. Traditional DM'ers call this *split copy testing*, a traditional practice in which you send out three or more test packages and see which copy draws more. This copy can be in the form of an offer, a sales letter, or any other direct marketing copy. Here's how to take the traditional practice and apply it online:

First, come up with two or three offers for your product or service. Then make some banner ads that tout this offer and set up advertising to place them on other Web sites that draw the types of people you're looking for. Need a free banner in a hurry? Head off to http://www.coder.com/creations/banner/ where you can create banners online in minutes: Simply type in your copy, select a font, select the finished banner size and color schemes, then submit. Voilá, you have a banner ad to place on the Web site of your choice. If you can afford to make a few banners, I urge you to do so, as graphics typically attract more attention than text-only banners. Put call-to-action words in your banners. Words like *Click Here, Enter...,* or *Click Now* usually increase clickthroughs.

Okay, now you've got three offers running, in order to see which "pulls" best. There are three ways to know which offer is doing what:

Set up a unique Web address on your site to which each banner will point (in other words, a separate Web page within your site). Then, you simply compare which address has the most traffic. You can set up a page counter, in fact, to check traffic easily (another simple CGI script available premade on most servers). It doesn't mean that this offer will result in the most conversions, however. It simply indicates which initial offer attracts more prospects. This approach is very inexpensive and easy to implement. It is literally just the cost of another Web page, which is often free once you have set up your Web site.

Referrer logs are logs your Web site has that tell you from whence all visitors came, how many hits each page received, and other statistical information on each Web page at your site. Although your server has these logs, it is not inconsequential to have them displayed in a usable format. It takes significant effort from your techies to get this information into a usable format. It can cost you a few hundred dollars, or a few thousand dollars. I had Mike Laskin, a computer science student from the University of Pennsylvania, set up my referrer logs for a few hundred dollars and have been using them for years. Commercial packages can run upward of $10,000 and deliver much more information that you may or may not need. These referrer logs (shown in Figure 8.2) are hyperlinked, so I can actually go to the page where the surfer was just before visiting my site. There is further information about referrer logs and what packages are available in Chapter 4, "http://007—Spying on Your Competitors and Yourself."

Probably the simplest way to track which offer pulled in a prospect is to simply ask the prospect himself, if you're planning on having him fill out an online form at your Web site. Simply have the copy of the banner concentrate on the selling attributes of the product or service. Then, ask the prospect where he or she heard of the offer, which will tip you off as to which banner he or she saw. However, I find many people just don't remember where they were before your site. The confusion factor out there is enormous and can easily throw off your findings using this approach. Remember: They call it *Web surfing*. A person could've been on 20 sites prior to yours and not even be aware of when he or she moved from one site to another. I remember running ads on the BigBook search engine, people often said they saw my ad on the Big Yellow search engine. If you're on a tight budget and need only an idea of which ad is pulling for you, do consider this method.

How Direct Marketing Copy Is Like Online Copy

The best traditional DM copy has every sentence supporting or leading to a sale. It's similar on the Net. Netizens like to get to the point fast. Web sites are like so many pieces of direct mail. There are plenty more where they came from—too many more, in fact. If a Web site or a direct mail piece doesn't state its case quickly, it is history fast. This isn't to say that long copy isn't appropriate. In many cases it is, both online and offline. Typically, you'll see longer DM copy for considered

Figure 8.2 Referrer logs show from whence your visiting surfers came.

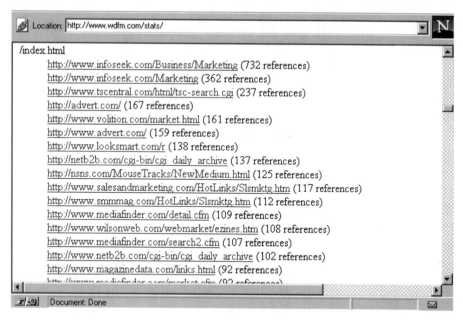

Location: http://www.wdfm.com/stats/

/index.html
    http://www.infoseek.com/Business/Marketing (732 references)
    http://www.infoseek.com/Marketing (362 references)
    http://www.tscentral.com/html/tsc-search.cgi (237 references)
    http://advert.com/ (167 references)
    http://www.volition.com/market.html (161 references)
    http://www.advert.com/ (159 references)
    http://www.looksmart.com/r (138 references)
    http://netb2b.com/cgi-bin/cgi_daily_archive (137 references)
    http://nsns.com/MouseTracks/NewMedium.html (125 references)
    http://www.salesandmarketing.com/HotLinks/Slsmktg.htm (117 references)
    http://www.smmmag.com/HotLinks/Slsmktg.htm (112 references)
    http://www.mediafinder.com/detail.cfm (109 references)
    http://www.wilsonweb.com/webmarket/ezines.htm (108 references)
    http://www.mediafinder.com/search2.cfm (107 references)
    http://www.netb2b.com/cgi-bin/cgi_daily_archive (102 references)
    http://www.magazinedata.com/links.html (92 references)
    http://www.mediafinder.com/mrkt.cfm (92 references)

Document: Done

purchase items, such as financial services, office equipment, and other business-to-business products.

Ad banners are nothing more than "outer envelopes" with a teaser piece of copy. In the same way I want you to click on my banner and come to my Web site, I want you to read my outer envelope and see what's inside. There are people who look at banner ads as a vehicle for brand advertising. I disagree with this. A banner with your logo on it is useless, the same way an envelope with nothing inside is useless. Your banner ads should have a call to action, a tease, or an out-and-out offer. I see banners as a component to a DM campaign, just like an outer envelope.

The Limited Way a Brochure Is Like a Web Site

Brochure copy and Web site copy have some things in common. This is *not* to say that your brochure should become your Web site. Far from it, for reasons I'll get into later. But the way a prospect approaches a Web site has some striking similarities to the way one looks at a brochure. These similar approaches should be reflected in the copy.

Let's say you've got a 12-panel brochure. It's not safe to say that every recipient of your brochure is going to start with the first panel. It may fall out of the envelope and reveal the back panel first. The brochure could unfold, or the reader could open it up and start in the middle. Because it's uncertain where the reader will start reading, copy points are often repeated in a brochure.

The very same is true for a Web site. Don't assume that everyone who visits your site begins with your homepage. Search engines are very apt to show your underneath layers before your homepage. Why? Your secondary layers usually have more words on them. The search engine figures those pages with more words on them are more important and rates them higher. Therefore, surfers are coming in from your side doors, which can be confirmed in your log files. This means that there should be key pieces of information about you and your product on every single Web page on your site, since probably only your competitor or your best friend looks at every single page.

Dr. Ralph Wilson, publisher of *Web Marketing Today* (http://www.wilsonweb .com), pointed out that I should offer my free subscription to *Web Digest For Marketers* on every single page of the *WDFM* site, as well as the parent company, Chase Online Marketing Strategies. This is what he does for his *Web Marketing Today* newsletter. He was absolutely right. My subscription rate increased 15 percent after doing so. Additionally, my contact and call-to-action information is automatically added in whenever we create a new page for the site.

Your copy style should be succinct, like your brochure copy. It should inevitably lead to a point. If it doesn't, you will confuse and bore the visitor and ultimately lose him or her. Your copy should ask for the sale or some call to action, which is something I notice many Web sites aren't good at. If your product or service is a *considered purchase*, then the copy should resemble that of a sales letter, which educates and informs as it sells. Keep in mind that the longer the copy is, the more apt someone is to print it out. In this case, you've just switched your medium from online to offline, which is not necessarily a bad thing, since the customer has made the switch himself without any added cost to you up front. Having said all this, I will now say there are distinct ways in which your online copy should differ from traditional DM copy.

A car or life insurance is a **considered purchase item**. As the name indicates, considered purchase items take some consideration before buying. That consideration usually means doing some homework by digging for information that can help you make an educated decision. The "deep information" is what the Net is good at serving; therefore, the Net is a good place for marketing considered purchase items.

How Online Direct Marketing Differs from Offline DM

For years, I've been pointing out that Internet marketing most similarly resembles direct marketing, as both are couched in one-to-one terms. Even with all of the similarities, there are distinct and critical ways in which Internet marketing and direct marketing differ.

Brochures

Earlier, I explained why your copy approach for a Web page can and should match that of a brochure. It's a dangerous analogy for me to make. Why? Because I run the risk of your misinterpreting that as license to simply take your print brochure and slap it up on the Web. I don't want you to do this, although if you have no money to develop specially tweaked communications for the Net, no Web site is often worse than *brochureware* Web sites. At least brochureware Web sites give some information. If you take this no/low-cost approach, at least make sure your graphics are of a *small enough file size*, so they load quickly. Nothing ticks off visitors to a Web site more than a slow-loading graphic that does nothing for them. But for the time being, let's assume you're going to do something more than simply upload your brochure to your Web site.

> **TIP** Add up the file sizes of all the graphics on your homepage. They shouldn't come to more than 30K in size. If they do, the page will take longer to load and start to make the surfer impatient. I advise my clients that all other pages on a site thereafter should be no larger than 20K. Restricting the file size of graphics gives you fewer and lighter graphics visually, but faster response times, which your visitors will always appreciate.

A print brochure is *pushed* out to the recipient through the mail, but you must *pull* or lure people into your Web site. In other words, you're asking them to take the effort to visit you. Simply putting your Web address on all your collateral pieces, sales materials, and advertising will help those who are wanting more information about you when they see the Web address. But, perhaps they're not quite yet in the buying cycle for what you have to sell. You must entice them in by offering them something of value. The first call to action is to ask them to visit the site. There are three basic lures that will pull people to your site:

1. Financial incentive

2. Valuable information

3. Utility

Hundreds of Web sites point to *Web Digest For Marketers*, while only 40 point to its parent, Chase Online Marketing Strategies. Why? Because *WDFM* offers more information through its review of marketing sites. It offers financial incentive with specials posted for Net marketers, and it offers utility with the CPM calculators or other handy products. So even if people aren't looking for my seminars, training, or consulting at that moment, they come to the site, sign up for the biweekly newsletter, and thereby enter into my "sphere of influence." When they do need the services I vend, they naturally think of me and then get in touch because I am not at all bashful about reminding them of the other services I offer in each and every issue of *WDFM*. I firmly believe the reader finds the sell copy useful not only to inform them of other things I do, but to tell them where I'm coming from. It tells them why I'm doing this newsletter in the first place. Too many times, I will go to a Web site, find useful information provided, and not know why that provider is doing it. Don't let this happen to you.

You should give thought to what your constituency will find useful. Very often, it's something you already have inhouse. In fact, *WDFM* originally was made for internal purposes, so we could stay on top of what was going on out there. When I realized we needed more attractive cyberbait, I posted the newsletter on the Web. Thereafter, I made it available for free via email. The list grows at 100 subscribers per week. Last year, 60 percent of my income came from readers of *WDFM* who requested professional services.

> **TIP** When you figure out what your loss-leader is, promote it in all online and offline materials. This is a come-on to get you into the store or Web site. Bloomingdale's may sell you a canvas bag at below cost to get you in the store, where you then buy a sweater for $120. This is where the store will make back the loss and then some.

Although the content of *WDFM* is easily converted into print (its reviews are syndicated to *Advertising Age* and *Business Marketing Magazine*), the Retirement Cash Flow Analyzer at http://www.culife.com/retire/is not. This is where the Web excels and differs from traditional DM. If you're using that analyzer, the chances are that you're a candidate for Commercial Union Life Insurance Company of America, or CULife (see Figure 8.3). In the same way, Prudential offers a wealth accumulation calculator (http://www.prusec.com/wlth_cal.htm). If you're attracted to it, Prudential wants to get to know you better. When you surf the Web for good examples of these lures, examine carefully how these companies try to convert you from a passerby into an ongoing relationship. Some do it seamlessly, while some drop the ball and don't do it at all. By offering these calculators, companies are using utilities to lure in their prospective visitors.

The critical mistake most Net marketers make is to blow their entire budget on building the site's Web pages and leave little or nothing for the promotion or the building of utility, event, or savings programs. It's important to remember not to spend all your money on the Web site itself. An example of this was when I was once doing a competitive reconnaissance in the music industry. I found a fantastic promotion in which I could win Eric Clapton's guitar. Despite my exhaustive surveying of the Net for music promotions at the time, I saw nothing that heralded this neat event. The promotion wasn't even on the top-level page of the site, but rather buried layers underneath. The Web address was as long as your arm. What's

Figure 8.3 If you are attracted to this calculator, it's a good bet you're a prospect for CULife, which provides it.

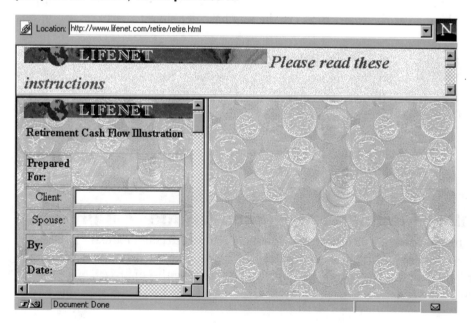

the point if your customers can't find your events, which would then draw them into your site?

Online versus Offline Tone

Advertisers call it *tonality*. Publishers call it the *voice*, while software designers call it *look and feel*. Whatever you call it, there are differences in the ways you present your wares online versus offline.

Generally, people online like quick bursts of information. Remember that the screen is glowing, whereas paper is much more restful to look at. The file size of your graphics needs to be much smaller online. Yes, you do sacrifice a great deal of aesthetics; however, this is understood by the user and is actually appreciated when the online page loads quickly. Remember, this is direct response—users want to hit your Web site and get a response directly. Can you imagine what it would be like to be forced to turn the pages of a catalog ever so slowly? You wouldn't stay with that catalog very long, nor will you with a Web site that reacts similarly.

While cyberspace is endless and costs relatively little to put up more copy, that doesn't always mean you should. People like you when you respect their time. Of course, there are products that need extensive explanation, such as cars, insurance, and travel—considered purchase items that require "deep information," as I've mentioned previously. In these cases, you want to be sure to give the prospect everything he or she wants to aid in the purchase decision.

 In deep information copy, use a David Ogilvy practice of planting an offer far into the text. If the reader responds to the buried offer, you probably have a well-qualified lead on your hands, since he or she got that far into your copy. In addition, by planting the larger pages further in, you will save surfing customers much time if they don't want to look at such detailed pages until later in their buying cycle.

Online Mailing Lists versus Offline Mailing Lists

Renting or leasing lists offline is a time-honored practice and industry in DM. You lease a list from a list broker or publisher, get the names printed on labels, and send out your mailing. However, I urge you not to take this approach online. Why? How do you feel when your mailbox is full of unsolicited email? Most people I know automatically delete them and don't think too highly of the sender. You're leaving a bad impression (bad branding and image) and getting poor responses as a result. There is much movement toward limiting or even regulating *unsolicited* (unasked-for) advertisements sent via email, which is considered *spam* mail. I don't care if you can buy 700,000 names for $75. You're going to tick a lot of people off for very few sales or none at all.

A solution is opt-in mailing lists. You can now obtain mailing lists where people actually *opt in* to receive these emails. People who are into sports will say, "Sure, send me solicitations about hockey or baseball." This is relatively new and not yet proven in the marketplace. The prices I've seen in this arena are also pretty high. At the time of writing, the going rate seems to be around 15 to 25 cents per name, which costs out to $150 to $250 per thousand. Comparatively, leasing a traditional list of a respected publication like *Ad Age* costs $125 per thousand. It's my observation that new media need to price themselves lower, to attract the skeptical buyer. It should be cheap enough so that it's a no-brainer proposition. The vendors of these opt-in lists will argue that you save money on the production, handling, and postage. That doesn't make a difference. It's new territory and I expect to pay less for that which has not been proven over time. You may use this argument when negotiating such buys.

Furthermore, I notice that people often agree to receive commercial emails, only to forget that they did indeed agree to receive them. If the user has forgotten that he or she signed up for such service, the email can appear to be spam, even though it was in fact requested. I personally have seen people specifically request to receive my *Web Digest For Marketers* newsletter only to write back, sometimes even months later, in an enraged tone, demanding that they be taken off the list and claiming they do not know how they got on in the first place. When I check my database, I can see that they did indeed sign themselves up and it would appear they merely forgot. If this happens on a branded newsletter, such as *WDFM*, you can imagine what the confusion factor would be on receiving email solicitations from a number of different resources, none of which are familiar to the user.

Another email approach is the bonus program, such as BonusMail (http://www.bonusmail.com) available through RocketMail (www.rocketmail.com), and other free Web mail services (see Figure 8.4). The user fills out a questionnaire and then sees appropriate ads. The more ads the user views, the more credits he or she gets. Those credits are ultimately exchanged for gifts. It's an interesting twist. I do wonder what sort of audience will exchange their time for ad viewing. This advertising seems to be targeted toward students and 20-somethings.

Figure 8.4 Email bonus programs are another way to get viewers to take in ads.

Make Your Own Mailing List

A far better way to obtain an online mailing list is to simply create one. Again, I point to *Web Digest For Marketers*, which has over 12,000 subscribers at the time of writing. The offers and ads are placed within the content, clearly delineated. Anyone can stumble into a Web site by accident. When people subscribe to my newsletter, I have a good idea of who they are, since they filled out a form in order to receive the email, proving that an ad in *WDFM*'s emailed newsletter is actually worth more than a banner ad on the Web site: We know who these people are and what they want in the way of products, events, and promotions.

TIP — The higher the quality of the content offered, the more information you can ask for from your potential customer/subscriber. That additional information will come in handy when you sell ads that will be distributed to that list, narrowing the target audience substantially.

At least twice a week I'm offered opportunities to trade the *WDFM* list for another email list. I never do this. It would only serve to dilute my relationship with my subscribers. Additionally, it makes more sense from the advertisers' point of view to have their offer within the requested content, rather than some seemingly unrelated standalone offer that pops up one day in someone's mailbox, only to be summarily deleted. Furthermore, my subscribers would not be happy with me if I did sell the list out to other firms. It is considered poor Netiquette, just as it is poor etiquette in DM, to sell mailing lists without informing your subscribers that their names may be used for other promotional items.

Add Some Ads to Your Mailing List

If you start or have a mailing list with unsold ad spaces on it, check out List Exchange at http://www.listex.com. There you can swap ad avails with other lists of similar ilk. In this way, you can help each other build your respective audiences. This bootstrapping method simultaneously builds audience and the appearance of having a larger advertising base. That's important when the next advertiser comes around with money.

Make sure your sponsor's ad gets results so she or he returns to advertise in your online newsletter or mailing list again. Give the ad away at first, if you have to, until it does work, and be sure to agree that your sponsor will write a testimonial about how effective the ad was on your list. This and other testimonials will help convince future prospective advertisers that your newsletter or mailing list is worthy of their budgets. What if the offers within these ads don't get a satisfying response? Like any good direct marketer, you must test, test, test, and never stop testing. You may find that certain types of products or services pull better on your list than others. This will help you direct your sales focus when attempting to sell space. There's no reason to go after advertisers who will only wind up frustrated and not advertise with you again.

How Much for Mailing List Maintenance?

If your list is just beginning, you can run a one-way mailing list right out of your mail program, bringing the cost of distribution down to nearly zero. I did that with *WDFM* until it grew past 1500, and that was really pushing it. At that point, I also wanted more information from the subscriber in exchange for the subscription. I then needed to store that in a database, not in my email program. Making a mailing list that goes out to dozens or hundreds of people isn't hard at all and varies from one email program to the next.

Here's how it works for basic email programs: Have a file that holds all the email addresses of the people who have requested to receive your mailings. Put a comma and a space after each address. When you are ready to send your mail out, simply copy all of the email addresses from the document where you keep them and paste them into the "Bcc:" field and then Send. More sophisticated programs that rarely cost over $60 allow you to keep all of those email addresses parked in a special place within the program itself. You give that list a name, such as "MailList," and when you're ready to send your newsletter, just put "maillist" in the "Bcc:" field and the program will know to grab all the addresses you've previously set up and send your newsletter to each and every one of them. I do suggest buying an email program that does this, such as Eudora from Qualcom. This feature alone is a time-saver for you. Another time-saving feature worth its weight in gold, found in sophisticated email programs, is the power to filter your incoming mail. So, for example, if you're tired of getting spams that read "free offer" or "make BIG $$$," they will automatically be siphoned off to a mailbox you can call "spam," where you can simply delete them en masse, rather than plucking them out one by one from your "In" box.

Short of running the list from your email program, the least-expensive way to go is use a *majordomo* or *listserv*. MD is list-serving software that's free. You can either have a techie install it and maintain it on your server (usually it is now included as part of your Web server software), or simply pay a local provider that already has it installed. At the time of writing, you can run a list of 1000 people for just $9.95 from a Net provider in Portland, Oregon. Your local prices shouldn't be too different from this. Even if it was 100-percent more, you're still only talking about $20 a month. For a complete reference of other majordomo lists, you can check out E-Mail Marketing Resources' list of list-hosting services at http://www.exposure-usa.com/email/listhosts.html. By the way, it isn't necessary to use a local provider. My *WDFM* newsletter is sent out of Green Bay, Wisconsin, while I'm in New York City. If you're on the phone with your list provider a lot, you will have long-distance charges, of course, unless they have an 800 or 888 number.

For $500, SenseNet's Sean Allen wrote a script for me that extracted the new subscription information that people filled out on the site and parked it in the database on my computer where I could get a better look at what I had. When I figure in the ongoing support labor needed to keep that system going, it cost me about $175 per issue (not including editorial costs). There are pitfalls to this, however. Over time, I wound up getting hundreds of dead emails from accounts that had been closed out. Worse, I would get scores of "I'm on vacation" messages, from what are called auto-responders, sort of like email answering machines. This is a real pain in the aggregate. Manually unsubscribing and changing addresses kept increasing labor bills. The larger the list grew, the more hours it took to keep it up.

I stayed with this system until the list grew to 7000. Now *WDFM* sits on a server where new subscribers are automatically entered into a database. The service I use now is called SparkList (http://www.sparklist.com). What is unique about this service is that it marries the housekeeping tasks of list management to the *WDFM* database, so that when someone unsubscribes or ceases to use his or her email account, that person is taken off the mailing list and simultaneously deleted from the mailing list. I had not seen this double-barreled approach anywhere else previously. This service costs $250 a month because it single-handedly updates the database with new subscribers, deletes email accounts no longer in use, and distributes the newsletter to all or part of that list. No other place that I know of (and I have looked very hard) offers this duality, at the time of writing, but other services will undoubtedly come along to offer similar functionality (see Figure 8.5).

Figure 8.5 SparkList is an industrial-strength mailing list service that marries list management with database functionality.

Another alternative to SparkList is Revnet Systems (http://www.revnet.com), which offers you two options:

1. For about $50 a month, you can run up to 10 of your lists using Revnet's GroupMaster Express software, which it will run for you on its own server at its Web site. This is the base rate, which will suffice for most mailing lists. If your list grows into the thousands, there are incremental additional charges. Another nice feature of Revnet's GroupMaster Express is that it will automatically delete email accounts that are no longer active.

2. You can also buy the GroupMaster software outright for $495 and manage the lists yourself on your own server. In the long run, this will be cheaper, but you do have to maintain the software and the upgrades. If you have the technical capabilities inhouse, this is a good way to go.

The following is a real-world example of why this ability to have the mailing list talk to the database is so very important. I recently got an inbound lead from someone who wanted me to do some consulting for his company. The person who contacted me mentioned that someone else in his company had forwarded my *WDFM* to him. He declined to answer who that was. I wanted to know how strong the referral was. While on the phone with him, I looked in the *WDFM* database under his company's name. There was only one person from that company subscribed: the president. That told me that the referral was a decidedly strong one, and that knowledge strengthened my negotiating position. This was not the first time that having more information on my subscribers (which they voluntarily offer) came in handy. It won't be the last time, either.

If you don't need your list so personalized, you have other cheaper options open to you. You can have a list management company handle sending out mail to your list. If you don't have a burning need to have those different pieces of information on your subscribers in a database, such as name, company, and title, this is a very good solution for you.

L-Soft (http://www.l-soft.com) runs the most well-known list management software called LISTSERV. You are charged based on *throughput*, or how many bits of information you send through its pipe. So, if your messages are many and long, you'll pay more. Someone I know recently was quoted $900 to run a very active discussion list of 4500 people. This product is called EASE. They will also sell you LSMPT software (the standard "list serve" software) that will run on your server, which, in fact, may already have the program preinstalled.

List Management

Clean your lists! People's email addresses tend to be much more transient than physical addresses. It is easier to move from one provider to another than from one home to another. Also, people's email addresses change when their jobs change. Cleaning your list will help you in three ways:

1. You'll receive far fewer "bounce-backs" from email addresses that no longer exist.

2. If you are selling ad space on an email list that boasts 10,000 people, but only has 6500, it will negatively skew the ad response results that your advertiser is looking for. Traditional direct marketers look for a 2-percent response (plus or minus, based on the list and the product category). Online responses often tend to be lower, but there is no cost of production or distribution, which more than compensates for lower response rates on online mailing lists. If you quote your audience at 10,000, when actually it is 6500, it will further depress the response rate. You want to be sure you're selling a quality product in this case that delivers exactly what you are promising. Both you and the advertiser will come out stronger in the long run. The cleanliness of your list is also a good selling point.

3. You will be seen as being a good Netizen for not taking up bandwidth by sending email to nonexistent addresses, which will only bounce back from their old accounts to your mailbox—more clutter.

Piggybacking on Someone Else's Mailing List

One of the least-expensive ways to reach a highly segmented audience is to simply sponsor a mailing or discussion list that's already out there. There are two basic kinds of lists: *One-way* lists just go in one direction; for example, *WDFM* goes from me to 12,000+ people. Therefore, each subscriber can only receive from me and can't add comments to my newsletter.

Two-way lists are discussion lists. Discussion lists themselves come in two varieties: *moderated* and *unmoderated*. On a moderated list, the postings are moderated by a list manager (for content), and the group is often limited by "voting in" new members, rather than an open subscription (where anybody could join). An unmoderated list is an anything-goes proposition. I think of mailing list discussion groups as extremely segmented talk radio, where many only listen (online, it's called *lurking*) while a smaller percentage of people speak. Since you want the environment to be somewhat controlled, you'll more than likely want to advertise and run your discussion group as a moderated list.

If you're interested in seeing a moderated discussion list specifically for the marketing niche, I recommend Online Advertising Discussion List at http://www .o-a.com (see Figure 8.6).

If you are an online list manager who wants to promote your list, or are thinking of starting a list, I suggest you subscribe to SparkNET's SparkList (http://listpromotion.sparklist.com). This is a mailing list of list owners who are interested in promoting their lists.

Advertising on one-way or two-way lists is what I often recommend to clients because it's one of the most cost-effective uses of an ad budget. You reach a no-waste audience with practically no production costs since the message is all in *ASCII*. Since this medium is such a bargain, you can afford to make a really enticing offer to this crowd. Try it, you'll like it. For very little money, you can win the hearts and minds of these list devotees for what must seem like nickels compared to what brand budgets normally run.

Figure 8.6 Online Advertising Discussion List is one of the most popular and active online discussion lists about online marketing.

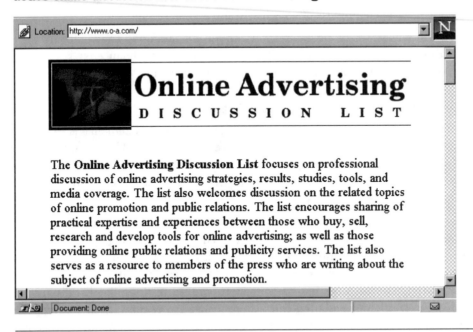

All materials ©1997, 1998 The Tenagra Corporation http://www.tenagra.com.

ASCII stands for American Standard Code for Information Interchange. ASCII is simple, unformatted text (nothing but "hard returns" show up) that can be read on any computer platform. Most email is in ASCII text. It's ugly, but ubiquitous. It has led to some interesting Net habits for writing, such as equal signs or underscores surrounding a word to be emphasized (such as =this=), the rise of what is now called *ASCII art*: pictures drawn using only characters from a normal keyboard, spaced to make a picture, and *emoticons*, or little pictures using ASCII characters to portray a smile, a frown, or another emotion (a smile is :-) for instance—turn your head sideways and you'll see the smile).

| TIP | Use someone else's list to run promotions (assuming that list accepts advertising). Set up one of the pages on your Web site to receive visitors who see your offer in one of these mailing or discussion lists. By lurking in the list, you'll gain a pretty good idea of what will make this group move to action. Then, buy some ad space and make the offer that is available on your Web site. When they come in, make sure you attempt to convert them to an ongoing relationship somehow. Offer to update them on points of interest you can provide them via email. You won't get nearly all of them, but that's okay. About 20–25 percent of the people who visit *WDFM* enter the sign-up process, but only 15–20 percent complete that process. Why? They don't want to give me all the information I ask for, such as name, title, company, email address, and where they heard of *WDFM*. That's a trade-off I can live with, since many of the ones who complete the process are extraordinary people that I'm happy to know about.

The following thought may occur to you: "Hey, why should I pay for an advertisement, when I can simply post to the list for free, with my ad copy or offer being the focus of the message?" *Do not do this!* This will be seen by the other members of the discussion list as being entirely self-serving and an abuse of the forum. What you can do is have a *signature file* that gives your URL and other information, as a sort of an addendum to your message (see Chapter 4, "http://007 Spying on Your Competitors and Yourself," for more on sig files). This is another good reason to use a sophisticated email package, as it allows you to automatically tack on your signature information, without having to key it in each and every time. My sig file always includes the free offer to *WDFM* and points to a Web site featuring my most recent article.

The message you post should provide information, observation, a response to someone else's posting, or an honest question. Having said that, it is not entirely inappropriate to "inform" that discussion list about a timely posting of something truly valuable to that list that is found on your Web site. This is especially true when someone else on your list asks where he or she might find such information. I know what you're thinking: "Hey, I'll get a friend to ask, 'Where can I find this information?' Then I'll be the hero by saying, 'Low and behold, it's on my Web site!!'" Yes, people do this from time to time, but you'll find that discussion list members will pick up on this pattern if you repeat it and not think too highly of you. Don't risk your long-term reputation for such fleeting games.

If an existing newsletter or discussion list matches your topic or audience, join it. See how much, or if any, advertising is on it. See who's advertising and what they're saying. Note how many ads there are in an issue and if that number remains constant over a few issues. Just like any other medium, this will give you an idea as to the strength of the advertising *rate card*, or the price list a media outlet uses to charge for advertising exposure. If there aren't many ads, you might be able to strike a better deal. You might also see if the list owner is amenable to barter. If he or she is loaded with paying advertisers, the answer will probably be "no."

Direct Marketing on the Web

The most effective Web sites are ones that successfully fill a highly defined niche. Sounds just like direct marketing, right? Your mission is to find "affinity sites" that relate to your DM efforts. These are Web sites that you, your product, or your service have some affinity with. American Airlines, Avis, and Hilton Hotels are considered affinity Web sites since they all have something in common; namely, people who travel.

There are three basic ways that these affinity links work:

1. Engage in an equal barter with another site. This is when no money changes hands. You point to each other's sites, delivering about equal value.

2. You pay for links. You need them a lot more than they need you, and you are willing to pay for it. This is paid advertising.

3. They include you in a resource center of links containing sites like yours. No reciprocal link is necessary.

How do you find these sites? For starters, you can do a search to see what turns up. Remember to do this from a few different search engines, as no two cover the exact same territory on the Web.

Web Targeting Services

Instead of buying banners on just one site, you might want to buy across many different sites in order to capture a particular audience. Ad networks are set up to help you make these buys. The first and most well-known of these networks is DoubleClick (http://doubleclick.com), which will sell you a batch of *impressions* targeted to meet your specific needs (see Figure 8.7). The more highly targeted the audience, the higher the cost per thousand, just like in any other medium. Individual sites, rich with demographic data gathered with the cooperation of the user, are doing this segmentation as well. For example, the *New York Times* can specifically expose your ad to only women aged 18–34 who read books and make more than $50,000 annually. Most individual sites don't have this depth of information from their users because, as mentioned earlier, they didn't ask for it up

---

Figure 8.7 DoubleClick is the original and largest online ad network that will sell you ad space across scores of Web sites, instead of your buying that space on a site-by-site basis.

front, or didn't feel the user would part with that information in exchange for access to the site. Asking for this sort of marketing information is a barrier for the user and often gives him or her pause to consider if he or she really wants to give that information away.

> An **impression** represents the viewing of an ad by the surfer. Impressions are a much more realistic measurement to use rather than hits. One person visiting a single Web page can account for 10 hits, but only one impression. Beware of any site that attempts to sell you on the inflated number of hits it gets.

Online DM Database Mining

There are four basic ways I mine the *WDFM* database, and I think of new ways all the time. That's part of the fun and creativity of online database marketing:

By country code. This is one of the most obvious ways to segment subscribers. Each year, when I go to Holland for my seminars, I locate all the .nl (Netherlands) subscribers and then write them a note.

> *Dear Dutch WDFM Subscriber,*
>
> *I'm coming back to Holland again and wanted to let you know I'll be there between the dates of October 11 and 17th. If you want me to speak to your organization or consult with your firm, please let me know now so I can put the time aside for you.*

By company. There are times when we want to find out who we know in a company we're interested in doing business with. More often than not, there's at least one person or more inside the company we're targeting who subscribes to *WDFM*. In fact, *WDFM* has dozens of people in many Fortune 500 firms. I also might look for words like *Times, Journal, Tribune,* or *News* to see what press outlets are reading the newsletter. In fact, I contacted a number of the firms that contributed valuable research to this book through the *WDFM* database.

By job title. When selling ads on *WDFM*, it helps to know we've got scores of EVPs and SVPs and hundreds of VPs. When looking to promote this very book, I was delighted to find over 280 editors who subscribe to *WDFM*.

The list at large. My opening comments in each issue of *WDFM* always mention something about my speaking, consulting, or writing activities.

Invariably, this generates inbound leads from those who are interested in having me do something similar for them. I don't go on endlessly about these activities, however, and I do make a point of enriching that copy with valuable information. If I didn't, I'd lose the readers. Even if they don't buy my services right then and there, at least they walk away more informed about something that I referred to. After all, email is ugly. You constantly have to reward the reader with good prose, financial incentive, or quality content. In other words, you can't wow them in ASCII, the way you do on TV. That is perhaps a good thing.

Selling ads on *WDFM* is due largely to the strength of knowing who's in the database. If you run a list where you only have email addresses, you can take a pretty good guess based on the list's topic and the subscribers' domain names. But it is a powerful sales tool to be able to tell a prospective advertiser how many VPs, SVPs, and EVPs you have. However, if you're not planning to sell ads on your list, the additional effort and expense of collecting all that information may not be worth your while, unless you yourself need this information for your own purposes. If the topic of the list is self-targeting enough, you may circumvent the databasing aspects and save yourself some real money up front and down the road.

 If your logs show that a number of people from mmm.com have visited you, this means that one or more people from 3M were on your site. The same thing goes for ibm.com, digital.com, and so on. Someone hitting your site from panix.com or interport.net means that he or she is probably from New York City metro, as these access providers are local to New York. Many locales have indigenous access providers.

Search Engines from a DM Perspective

As you can imagine, it's important to know what search terms people are going to use when looking for a company like yours. You can actually buy a word from just about any search engine—a word that will bring up your ad each time the word is searched for in the engine. I was one of the first ones to do this a few years ago, so I got terrific deals for my clients until media buyers caught on. Here's how it worked for one of my first clients, Hotel Discount:

Along with the volume of impressions we bought at InfoSeek, I asked to have some keywords thrown in for added value. Back then, they didn't charge because no one understood the value. We got hold of some very valuable category words like airline, travel, hotel, and reservation. When people searched on those words, they got a Hotel Discount banner at the top, along with their search results. In retrospect, I wish I had obtained the word *weather*, which is normally one of the top 100 words searched for. Travelers often search on the word *weather* to see what conditions are like at their destination. The clickthrough rate went from an average of 2 percent to 15 percent and higher.

Today, InfoSeek does charge a premium for these words at $55 per thousand. In other words, for every 1000 times the word *weather* is used and your ad appears, you pay $55. Some words are less popular than others and you may be able to get a break. The major words in the major categories are worth more than words in less-frequented categories. You'll probably get the word *lobster* or *scuba* for less than you'd pay for *mutual fund*. I suggest you pick a few words you're interested in buying and enter them into a search engine again and again to see how many times your competition's ad comes up and how many times a randomly selected ad comes up.

The randomly selected ad runs in what's called *general rotation*. This arrangement is similar to what traditional media charge for premium placements. You spend less money on ad space if you allow the newspaper or TV/radio station to stick the ad in where it fits most easily. This is called *run of station* or *run of paper*. The online equivalent is *general rotation*, where someone who is looking up *pterodactyl* might get the Hotel Discount banner on the search engine.

If you find these general rotation ads running more often than not on the words you're interested in, it may mean the search engine has a large inventory of exposures available for this word, and not many people have bought it yet. That's important information to have when negotiating the price.

Find out where you stand with the search engines by using PositionAgent (http://www.positionagent.com). You give it a search word and it enters it in a few

Observing Search Engine Habits

Sit with other people in front of a search engine and ask them individually to look for something in your category. It's a good idea to do this with people both inside and outside your industry. Note which words they use most. This will not only tell you what words you might want to buy from the search engine, it will also tell you how to write the copy on your site so your firm comes up higher in the search results (see Chapter 4, "http://007—Spying on Your Competitors and Yourself," for more information on how to do this). While you're watching people do searches in your category, you may see

Continues

Figure 8.8 Stay on top of where your site comes up with did-it.com.

different search engines and comes back and tells you where your ranking is in each. It offers a subscription service for improving your search rankings as well.

Another good tool to help you figure out where your site stands in the search engine listings is did-it.com (http://www.did-it.com). It's a free service (see Figure 8.8). If you want to radically move up in the search engine results, you may want to pay for did-it's enhanced service that will optimize your rankings in each of the search engines. At the time of writing, this costs $300 for a startup fee, plus 25 cents per clickthrough. It's in did-it!'s and your best interest to get as many clickthroughs as

them tiring after 20, 30, or 40 sites found by that search engine. So what good is it if you're 432 in the listings? Not much.

Often the search engine visits your site and dumps a certain percentage of your site into its own memory or database. Since it only has so much room, it may take only the first 150 words of your site and actually show those words when showing the surfer the results of what it's found. Make sure those 150 words telegraph a message to the reader of that search why they should visit you. Make it compelling from the user's point of view. In other words, make it so compelling that even *you* would click on it.

possible. I suggest you have a plan in place to recuperate some of those quarters you're paying did-it, either by selling something on your site, capturing the profiles of your visitors for your database, or having them subscribe to something. Having paid advertisers' display banners on your site will also help defray that 25-cent cost per clickthrough.

Compare the results you get with did-it's checker to Position Agent. Not only will it tell you where you come up in search results, but it will inform you when you are no longer in a search engine database, or have dropped in ranking from where you were. Pricing and subscription information is available at its site.

Online Direct Marketing Supporting Offline DM Efforts

One of the richest areas for you to explore is how to have one medium assist the other. Because the Net is such a quick and cheap test bed for what pulls and what doesn't, you should consider using it not only for online campaigns, but for offline efforts as well. Testing print offers takes months of preparation and handling, not to mention expenses. In certain categories, you can get a quick response on what offers may or may not work for print mail pieces. This will not be as scientific as an offline mailing list you can buy, because you won't be sure of the authenticity of the respondents online, unless you prescreen them via telemarketing or some other channel. But it can give you an indication of which test packages to peruse and commit to when putting print offers together. The package that tests best will become your *control package*. I caution you here. Your mileage will vary depending upon your category, audience, and quality of sample on the Net. Proceed with open eyes. Then be sure to write an article about it so you can get additional mileage out of the experience.

A **control package** is a classic direct-marketing practice. You create multiple offers for the same product. You run them separately and track which offer *pulls* better. Whichever one wins then becomes the control package. This control package is the one you use in the field and try to beat in the future by creating an even better control package for your next gambit.

As you can imagine, there are a whole range of ways the Net can be used to help traditional direct marketers work smarter, faster, and cheaper. For one, you can get your traditional mailing lists cleaned up online. MAILnet (http://www.list-cleanup.com) is one such example. MAILnet offers a wide range of list-processing services directly through its Web site using an online upload of *ASCII-delimited text* database files. List owners can merge/purge, update addresses, and have files CASS certified to take advantage of postal discounts through bar coding. MAILnet will return updated files in as little as three hours.

> **ASCII-delimited text.** Since ASCII doesn't allow you to make fancy tables or other formatting, commas are often used to "break," or separate, one piece of information from another. In such a file, a person's name would have a comma after it, so the address would "know" to appear on the next line. Most database programs allow you to save your files as *generic* ASCII- or comma-deliminated text files.

List broker and manager Edith Roman (http://www.edithroman.com) offers a search engine with access to over 30,000 traditional mailing lists worldwide. Direct marketers won't want to miss Edith Roman's set of freebie calculators: one figures the ROI on a mailing, one helps determine how many pieces to send out, and another computes the benefits of an NCOA (National Change of Address) update on your list.

Type in a ZIP code and get a profile of the residents living there. This fun "Lifestyles" game is only one of the resources available to marketers looking for specific audiences. National Decision Systems (http://www.ends.com) has a large selection of market research products and services available for sale at its site, including such geographic profile information. Free information, like the "Top 10 Growth MSAs," can be found behind its Fast-Facts button.

There are two sites that present the best and the brightest of direct marketing packages (in the traditional sense):

Cyber Caples at http://www.caples.org. John Caples wrote *Tested Advertising Methods*, the bible of the direct response biz. That industry honors him by naming the coveted DM Awards after him. Those awards can now be seen on the Web, a medium that is so very suited to those who have mastered the principles of direct marketing.

National Mail Order Association at http://www.nmoa.org (see Figure 8.9). This site is key for those who recognize that even in the age of email, direct mail (or *snail mail*) remains a viable and necessary marketing tool. You can explore examples of vintage campaigns, such as a 1941 mail order journal by Paul Muchnick. Who knows? You might get some good ideas for your offline as well as online direct marketing efforts.

Figure 8.9 Check this archive for classic direct mail campaigns that will inspire you when you're creating your own new ones.

Other links that can be used as resources are as follows:

- Direct Magazine—http://www.mediacentral.com/Direct
- DM News—http://www.dmnews.com
- Catalog Age—http://www.mediacentral.com/CatalogAge

Catalogs and the Net

For presenting a wide array of products, there's nothing quite like the Internet, for better and for worse. You can't put enticing, high-resolution pictures in front of visitors without having them wait, but you can do other things that print doesn't do as well, providing yet another way online direct marketing can support offline direct marketing efforts.

You can have a dynamic catalog, which deletes an item when you run out of it. This way, no one calls your 800 number (at your expense), only to be told that the item is out of stock. If you have a product that consists of a number of components or peripherals, you can use what's known as a *configurator*, which adjusts the price of a configuration based on the different components you assemble. Dell Computer uses this tool on its site (http://www.dell.com). (Dell makes well over $1.3 million a day in direct sales on its site.) A prospective buyer puts in the monitor size, amount of RAM, speed of the processor, and so forth that he or she wants, and the configurator spits out the price of that configuration. If it's too much money for the user, he or she simply tries a smaller monitor, a slower CPU (central processing unit; i.e., the computer's engine), or a less-expensive soundcard, and the configurator gives the prospect the slimmed-down price for the slimmed-down computer system. That's much cheaper than having a telephone representative take the time on the 800 number to figure out all of the variables. For an even more complex example of this, take a look at 3Com's Network Designer, where you can design a whole network for your office this way.

Even if the user doesn't buy the product online, the cataloger has saved a bundle by not having to send the paper catalog to that person. You may have to ship loads of catalogs to potential customers before they even buy, if they ever do at all! When you stop to calculate the savings of sending multiple catalogs to someone who may or may not buy something, you've got incredible savings. Remember, the person who visits your online catalog is already near or in the buying cycle for your product. Why else would he or she be there?

AMP Connect is a catalog site where functionality reigns supreme (http://connect.amp.com). Available in eight different languages, the AMP Connect catalog boasts a database of 70,000 AMP parts for use in the electrical and electronics industries (see Figure 8.10). Users can search by part number, family, alphabetically, or by picture. Can you imagine how much it would cost to print, distribute, and warehouse a catalog of this size?

> **TIP**
>
> If you're going to put your catalog online, do your homework first. Go to http://www.buyersindex.com, where you'll find over 7500 catalog links and a search engine to help you locate the ones relevant to you. Learn from those who came before you. What are they doing right? What are they doing wrong? What can you do better? I urge you to also look at a few catalogs that aren't in your category. You can probably learn from them and be the first to migrate some of those practices into your business. This can give you an edge over your competitor, at least for a while.

Figure 8.10 The AMP Connect catalog is one of the largest and most sophisticated sites on the Net.

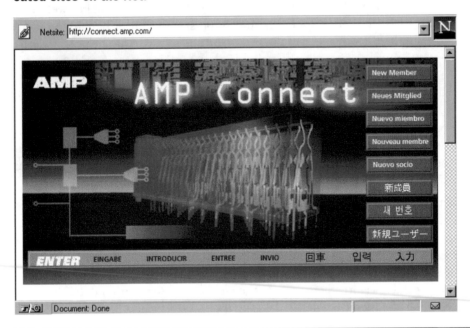

If you're interested in deeper information on catalog engines and options, please read Chapter 7, "Online Events, Promotions, and Attractions."

Online Direct Marketing: A Threat or an Opportunity?

It's both. Over time, some percentage of the business that's being handled by traditional DM will migrate to the online world. Historically, new media do partially cannibalize their predecessors. A good example is how computers found a new sales outlet by offering to sell the consumer right from the magazine or newspaper page. This ultimately took sales away from computer stores. If you feel threatened by this, I suggest you consider the options you have: You can either cannibalize your own marketshare, or have a competitor do it for you. When this cannibalization will occur depends on the industry you're in. Computers, business-to-business, travel, telephony, books, and financial services will be affected sooner than soft goods or packaged goods.

To a direct marketer, in my estimation, the opportunities far outweigh the drawbacks. You can open up new markets, some of which you aren't even aware of yet. You can better serve your existing customer base with loyalty and customer retention programs. You can better serve yourself by reducing costs of DM programs, increasing speed to market of materials and products, and lowering your overhead.

In short, if you're a direct marketer, you're going to be doing business online sooner or later, so it might as well be sooner. Embrace this medium. Marvel at its potential, and know it's limited only by your keen imagination as a direct marketer.

Resource Center

American Airlines   http://www.americanair.com

This site is a prime example of how classic direct marketing practices can be migrated and employed on the Net. AA lures you in (call this an *acquisition program*) with its NetSaver discount program that emails you every Wednesday with last-minute cheap seats. The incentive for you to buy tickets online is the offer of an additional 1000 frequent flyer miles. Then AA offers to show you how many fly miles you've accrued thus far by giving you a PIN that lets you see your account information. Cross-merchandising tie-ins with Avis are featured as well, just like they are in the monthly hardcopy statements received by snail mail. The more you drill into this site, the more you learn about how to market smartly on the Net.

Direct Marketers On-Call   http://www.dmoc-inc.com

Direct marketing professionals, and those who are in search of direct marketing professionals, will want to stop by the DMOC site. The site basically offers matchmaking services for DM pros and the rest of us who need them.

Cahners Direct Marketing Services   http://www.cahnerslists.com

Cahners is the nation's largest provider of business-to-business subscriber lists and databases. However, do not be fooled by the ineptly named WebXpress service—although users can search for and price targeted mailing lists online, ordering is still handled via telephone or good old-fashioned snail mail.

Direct Value to You   http://www.DV2U.com

Visitors to this Metromail site can register to receive free catalogs and offers from direct marketers, catalogers, and publishers. Offers include catalogs, discount coupons for name-brand appliances, and trial offers for books. DV2U collects customer information in a variety of ways. General demographic information is collected when users register at the site. Offers are then served based on these criteria. Visitors are also asked to complete a questionnaire designed to find out what they would like to see as future offers. This survey taps deeper into the customers' buying habits and demographics. In return for supplying information, visitors are registered in a $25,000 sweepstakes. They will also start to receive targeted offers via USPS-delivered direct mail.

Inside 1:1   http://www.marketing1to1.com/1:1/wt.cgi/articles/inside-1to1.html

This weekly newsletter is written by Don Peppers and Martha Rogers, the same people who authored *The One to One Future: Building Relationships One Customer at a Time* (Currency/Doubleday, 1997). Delivered direct to your emailbox, the newsletter usually contains one article about 1:1 marketing techniques and information about marketing 1:1 site updates.

National Mail Order Association   http://www.nmoa.org

This site is key for those who recognize that even in the age of email, direct mail (or *snail mail*) remains a viable and necessary marketing tool. Make sure to visit the Mail Order Museum (still under construction) to explore examples of vintage campaigns, such as a 1941 mail order journal by Paul Muchnick.

DM Plaza   http://www.dmplaza.com

This is your one-stop shop for direct-marketing information. The site houses everything from supplier directories to tools, job listings, and advice. DM Plaza is also running an interesting promotional campaign: If users add a link to DM Plaza's sister site, TelePlaza, to their site, they get listed in DM Plaza for free. The site appears to be fairly new, so directory listings are still growing, which means those listed get marquee presence.

Edith Roman Online   http://www.edithroman.com

List broker and manager Edith Roman offers a search engine with access to over 30,000 mailing lists worldwide, more than any other service anywhere, according to Steve Roberts, president of the company. And direct marketers won't want to miss Edith Roman's set of freebie calculators: one figures the ROI on a mailing, one helps determine how many pieces to send out, and another computes the benefits of an NCOA (National Change of Address) update on your list.

Rover Search Service
http://www.roverbot.com

Attention online direct marketers. Finally, Net marketers are attempting to come up with more innovative and effective ways to get their message across than the dreaded email spam. Rover claims to generate custom mailing lists by "exploring Web pages that meet your criteria," using indexes and search engines as starting points. Is it any better than simply flooding the email airwaves? Take this bloodhound for a test drive and find out. The first 250 results of your search are free.

MediaCentral
http://www.mediacentral.com

Recently redesigned, Cowles New Media's MediaCentral Web site is an exhaustive guide to direct marketing, advertising and promotion, broadcast, cable, print and interactive media, and media technology. In addition to providing news and commentary, MediaCentral's links to media, agencies, e-zines, critical URLs, and money-making picks bring the best of the Web's media-related sites to your fingertips. A free weekly emailed digest and upcoming forums for discussion and information sharing are welcome interactive features.

American List Counsel List Connection
http://www.amlist.com

ALC surrounds its mail list services with incredibly useful and thorough guides to direct mail success. Did you know that September is the best month for a direct mailing? Start planning now with the "Countdown to Mail Date Checklist." Save time and save money by discovering the ultimate secrets to direct mail success (just how many motivational words can you spot in that sentence?). But that's not all . . . you can also browse 10,000+ mail lists by category and get a Quick Quote from the ALC specialists. A must-see reference for any direct mail marketer.

Cyber Caples
http://www.caples.org

As you probably know, John Caples wrote *Tested Advertising Methods*, the bible of the direct response biz. That industry honors him by naming the coveted DM Awards after him. Those awards can now be seen in the Web, a medium that is so very suited to those who have mastered the principle of direct marketing. In true direct fashion, this site is a no-nonsense site. FCB Direct in New York clearly did migrate DM concepts to this site, since the graphics do load directly; that is, fast. The minimalist and loose interface is appreciated greatly for this reason. The art directors thought of what it's like to wait for screens to load at 14.4k instead of how the page would appear in their print portfolios. Nice writing, too, right down to the "Let us have it" page encouraging the visitor to let 'em have your thoughts, musings, and recommendations on how this site can reach perfection.

DMA: Best Practices in Interactive Marketing http://www.the-dma.org

This recently released report focuses exclusively on best practices in interactive marketing as they relate to direct marketing. The Direct Marketing Association commissioned consultants from Price Waterhouse to perform the study, which profiles the solid, innovative tactics companies are using to gain strategic advantage from the Internet. It examines close to 40 companies in business-to-business and business-to-consumer marketing in a wide variety of industries and contains good news: Integrating a Web site into the marketing mix helps companies save money, streamline operations, and gain new customers. The report is available for a modest fee, or check out the site for the key facts contained in the online Executive Summary.

MAILnet Services http://www.listcleanup.com

Send your list to the cleaners! MAILnet offers a wide range of list-processing services directly through this Web site via an online upload of ASCII-delimited text database files. List owners can merge/purge, update addresses, and have files CASS certified to take advantage of postal discounts through bar coding. MAILnet will return updated files in as little as three hours.

PUBLIC RELATIONS,
the Internet Way

"The Internet is the Golden Age of Public Relations," says veteran public relations man Dan Janal, author of *The Online Marketing Handbook* (John Wiley & Sons, 1997). PR and the Net have a very basic core value in common: information, both its creation and transmission. Public relations can handle more detail than a typical corporate image or branding ad campaign in traditional media. For that reason, it is playing a more pivotal role in the online marketing mix.

Public relations is so central to marketing on the Net, I've found I will stage an event on the Internet just to get coverage in traditional and online media. In this chapter, I'll show you how to take advantage of the parallels between traditional public relations and the Internet. You'll find out about:

- How to get noticed in a cluttered environment
- Protocols for interaction with online journalists
- News hooks, cyberbait, and outrageousness
- Writing for the Net
- PR in a many-to-many medium
- Point-to-point PR
- Event public relations
- Where and how to post your PR
- Using PR circuits
- Trolling the Net for information about your own company
- Anti-PR sites

How to Get Noticed in a Cluttered Environment

The launch of my online marketing firm in 1993 drew incredible press attention, both on- and offline. The sheer novelty of such a firm was enough, back then. Today, marketing firms come online every hour. Announcing a new Web site is akin to announcing you have a new fax machine in the office. The noise level of Web sites screaming for your attention is getting louder by the minute.

How do you get above this cacophony? Be the first at something. It may be the first at giving a rhinoceros away online, assuming you are promoting African safaris. The lure to your Web site should be something germane to the product or service you are vending.

Focus

As the publisher of *Web Digest For Marketers*, I get scores of press releases that simply say in the header: "New Web Site." It looks comical against the blizzard of other similarly positioned pitches I get daily. Getting above this din is key to reaching your audience. The second emphasis should be getting that audience to your site. How do you do this? *Focus*. Focus on your core audience and the core message to deliver to that audience. I want to see a reason to care about your Web site right in the header of the mail message or press release. Your Web site, as well as your PR campaign to *promote* it, has to be focused and deep.

Don't Be a Mile Wide and a Half-Inch Deep

Instead of blasting releases, both online and offline, across the globe, I advise clients to spend their money more adroitly. It's better to identify one audience, thus being a mile deep and a half-inch wide, than the other way around. A tightly targeted program that hits your constituencies again and again over a series of weeks and months will be a better use of your budget, whether you're a small business or a multinational firm. Consider not only your audience, but also the valuable time of those receiving your message. Why should you bother an editor at *Vanity Fair* about a software upgrade? This editor will employ the minimal amount of energy to dispose of your efforts. I've often seen trash cans right below a fax machine for easiest access to dispose of untargeted messages. Put yourself in your receiver's shoes; you'd do the same.

You may say, "It's so effortless to send email to everyone. Why not just let those discard the messages that are 'off-topic' for them, and hit the rest who might be interested?" It's a fair question. Some people do just that. If you're on a shoestring budget, that may be all you can do, as targeting does take time and money. However, if you aim well-thought-out messages to the right people, who happen to need such information now or in the near future, you've got a better chance at getting press. In short, give them news they can use.

Protocols for Interaction with Journalists Online

Be careful. I know many journalists who still prefer faxes and actual snail-mail press releases to email. Why? If you go to the trouble of sending your press release via offline means, it conveys extra effort on your part to the journalist. Email is too easy. Even if the trash can is positioned just below the fax machine, it's still just as effortless for a journalist or editor to simply press Delete on his or her computer's keyboard when the subject header reads: "BlimpWare Revolutionizes the Financial World with Its Web Site." Instead, tell them the end benefit of your site without all the hyperbole. Make them want to go there by getting to the point quickly and with a minimum of fuss.

> **TIP**
>
> *Never* attach a press release to an email, unless you have prior consent from the recipient. It is tantamount to shoving a press release down someone's throat, as it not only ties up his or her computer, but his or her time as well. As the file comes in ever so slowly, the journalist or publisher is seething, cursing you out, and vowing never to give you any publicity ever.

This is not to say email shouldn't be used as a public relations vehicle. Send your press releases to only those people who previously agree to accept them via email. If the journalist knows you personally or by reputation, he or she usually agrees. Some add a caveat by saying, "Don't inundate me with your emailed press releases." Some journalists jealously guard their email addresses, to prevent people from gaining easy access. When a journalist's stealth email address is found by a PR spammer and then exploited . . . well, let's just say it doesn't help the sender's brand image in the mind of that journalist. For every one person who reads your unsolicited emailed press release, you might be alienating a hundred, or even a thousand, other people who otherwise may have given your site a good review or favorable press coverage.

When calling journalist to get permission to send a press release via email, listen closely to their voices. If they sound like they're stressed and on a deadline, offer to call them back at a more convenient time. When you have a *brief* dialog with them, simply say, "I have an event or Web site launch coming up. With your permission, I'd like to email you the press release." Give them the major point of the release. If they're not comfortable accepting the press release via email, ask what medium they prefer. Speak quickly and succinctly. This telegraphs to them that you respect their time.

Become a resource for journalists. Email them information relevant to their beat. Don't overdo it by sending them these snippets too often. Respect your own time as well, and don't spend hours trolling the Net for "gifts" for them.

News Hooks, Cyberbait, and Outrageousness

News hooks make your press release newsworthy. Assuming you've got your highly targeted audience in mind, get to work on designing something that appeals to them. Previously, the mere introduction of a new site was a news hook in itself. In the early days of the Web, when the GE Plastics catalog went online, it made the *NBC Evening News* on television.

These days, you need something more dynamic to get the attention of increasingly skeptical journalists and their audiences. You also need to consider all the people out there who aren't connected to the Internet and whether or not they'll see your message. As of this writing, only 40 percent of all households in the United States have computers, and not all of them are hooked up to the Net.

Make your message something newsworthy. IBM's Deep Blue chess match was a fantastic news hook. The Web site was a huge success. Some chess fanatics probably got online for the first time just to get to that page. The fact that IBM put up real-time reporting on the match said a great deal to people who never actually saw the site, but certainly heard about it in traditional media venues offline. This spin-off effect is often greater than the online event itself.

Cyberbait consists of many different characteristics, depending on what you have to offer the public on your Web site. A good example is Awalt Group (http://www.awaltgroup.com), which also happens to be a public relations agency. Awalt Group specializes in financial communications and investor relations. It has taken a cue from the auto industry, where visitors to its company's Web site can now try a "test drive" program before they actually buy anything. Visitors simply submit a description of their public relations needs to an Awalt Group representative. Within 48 hours, the company will send back suggestions, samples, and related bibliographic notes, thus luring you in with free input on your PR plan. You're considered a somewhat qualified lead for them because you're attracted to their offer. Naturally, they'll try to convert you to a sale at some point: the convergence of public relations and direct marketing.

An outrageous PR campaign was one I did with Hotel Discount (http://www .hoteldiscount.com). We ran ads and a press blitz for "The Trip from Hell" contest. To my knowledge, it was the first contest of the "from Hell" genre. In addition to the online advertising we bought, it drew a great deal of offline press coverage. Curious visitors came by the thousands to read about other people's horror stories on business trips. Many, of course, added their own. People bookmarked that part of the Hotel Discount Web site and kept returning, months after the event had finished. Since then, there have been oodles of imitations of this PR campaign, such as "Jobs from Hell," "Salespeople from Hell," and so on. As I've said before, the important point is to try to be the first in a category to do something innovative on or with your Web site. With Hotel Discount, we certainly succeeded in that.

Whatever you conceive of should flow naturally out of your product or service. "If you're going to show a man upside down in an ad to get someone's attention, you'd better make sure you're selling zipper pockets," said Bill Bernbach, the creative genius behind the ad agency Doyle Dane Bernbach. DDB was famous for breaking the rigid rules of advertising in the 1950s, 1960s, and 1970s. When I worked there, I learned to make a left turn, when everyone else in the marketplace was making a right turn. In short, you have to be different to get above the clutter, especially if you're a small company. Even if it is a mediocre public relations campaign, big companies with big budgets will get attention by sheer repetition. When you're a small company with a small budget, you may only have one exposure, so it had better be good.

Another good example of "breaking the mold" was the first underwater Web site. It was put up (or down, depending on your point of view) just off the coast of Florida, by NOAH, with the help of Electronic Data Systems (EDS). A habitat, mounted inside and outside with cameras, was tethered to a barge at sea level. From the barge, a transmission was beamed to shore, where the signal was picked up and fed into the Internet. Bill Mapp, my client with EDS, personally scuba-dived to the habitat and then helped configure the Web server. It was my privilege to propagate announcements of this premier across the Net. The press coverage of this event was understandably enormous; both NOAH and EDS were big news for the event's nine-day duration. Millions came to the Web site to see pictures and videos of sharks, along with other fish, flora, and fauna, eerily gazing at the camera. I actually received thanks from many sites and discussion groups for notifying them of the event.

> **TIP** Being first may well get you some news attention. Even if it's not in the general press, it may get in the business press, or your trade industry press. As for coming in second? Well, who was the second guy to cross the Atlantic? Don't know? That's the point. Be the first in order to gain recognition and coverage.

In Chapter 8, "Direct Marketing and Sales Support," I mentioned Con Edison as a good example of practicing retention marketing by offering an online payment option. There is a PR angle as well. The New York press outlets picked up on the story of Con Ed's new online payment system. It had an Internet angle, which usually makes for good copy, as well as a local angle. Con Ed was reported as offering the latest and greatest in customer service. It cast Con Ed in a very positive light. In my experience, it's rare that utilities get played that well in the press. Proof for the formula of being first in a niche market!

Writing for the Net

Good Net copy comes from the same mold as any good interface design. You always want to help the individual get what he or she wants in the fastest manner possible. Forcing a person to read through self-aggrandizing statements and bombast in a press release is tantamount to enticing visitors to your site, only to make them suffer through too many clicks to reach the main attraction. It feels manipulative. So, get to the point.

Newswire services and journalists use the "inverted pyramid" style of writing, which puts the most important facts first. All that follows is supporting copy to fill in the details. News stories are written in this way because it is never known where exactly the story will be cut off by an editor, or by a page turn. Advertising copy is written the same way: few words, big ideas.

Online, your variable is the attention span of your readers. If you don't dish up the core information right away, you're not apt to keep them. If you do get their attention, they'll stay with you only as long as it suits them. They are in the driver's seat. Therefore, every line of copy you write *must* either inform, entertain, intrigue, or give some financial or emotional incentive, if you're to keep their attention.

When I was a wee sprout, I remember reading *Life Magazine* . . . the whole magazine, including the ads and the copy to those ads. You really got your money's worth back then. There weren't six gazillion Web sites, 9000 cable channels, teeming hordes of magazines on the newsstand, email, videogames, and other sundry media to compete for our attention. Today you're not just competing with other Web sites, you're competing with every form of media out there and vice versa. We live in the Media/Information Age.

Put in this perspective, it's not too hard to understand why people aren't bowled over by a Web site when the first thing they see is a 30-second soundbyte of a CEO that takes two minutes to download. That sounds like a short amount of time, but realize that in two minutes, you can make a pot of coffee, read the front section of a newspaper, or boil an egg. They would probably be pleased, however, if that same CEO's speech is in quick-loading text format, giving them a clue for a contest to win an Ethernet network with all the trimmings for their office, or directly addressing a flaw in that company's product and how it can be remedied.

A Sample Press Release

The following is the actual press release I wrote that drew tens of thousands of people to my site. Note that I poked fun at my own Web site, while delivering useful information. Also, note the keywords at the top, which I will explain later in this chapter.

KEYWORDS: ADVERTISING, INTERNET, MARKETING, MEDIA, WEB, NEWS, ONLINE, ADVERTISER, NET

Contact information:

Larry Chase/President Chase Online Marketing Strategies
847A Second Avenue, Suite 332
New York, NY 10017
email: larry@chaseonline.com
http://www.chaseonline.com
VOICE +01 (212) 876-1096
FAX: +01 (212) 876-1098
Head: Mind-Numbingly Simple Web Site Helps Marketers Calculate Media Buys.

New York: Larry Chase, Publisher of Web Digest For Marketers *at http://www .wdfm.com, introduces* WDFM's Online Media Tools. *The new area debuts by featuring three calculators that help advertisers figure out their cost per thousand, that common denominator that sets the tone for media negotiations. These "CPM" calculators are specifically at http://www.wdfm.com/advertising.*

"While these tools deliver high value utility, the technology behind them is not at all break-through; in fact, it's rather elementary," Chase observed. "That scripting was so basic the programmer, Matt Lederman, pleaded with me not to credit him publicly," Chase concluded.

Larry Chase's Web Digest For Marketers *is the original Net marketing publication that is currently read by over 70,000 readers. Since subscriptions were made free six months ago, WDFM's readership grew by thousands virtually overnight. In addition, over 50,000 people now read highlights of WDFM in* Net Marketing, *a monthly publication sent to all subscribers of* Business Marketing Magazine, *as well as the high-tech crowd reading* Ad Age. *Chase is fond of saying " . . . more people read* Web Digest For Marketers *offline than online."*

WDFM is a biweekly summary of the latest marketing-oriented Web sites, from Chase Online Marketing Strategies. The analogy that Chase insists on using is that of a three-legged stool, whereby one leg represents Publishing (as in WDFM), the second leg is Consulting in Online Marketing, and the third leg is Seminars. In fact, Mr. Chase will be giving seminars in New York and Holland this Fall on six different aspects of Net Marketing. Chase's favorite seminar of the week is, "How to Sell Your Net Project to Upper Management." Others include examinations of the Net from financial, retail, and sales perspectives.

Chase says, "Employing technology that is easily accessible to millions for practical purposes is the thread that runs through good Web marketing sites, each in their respective niche." Chase neatly refers back to his plain vanilla CPM calculators when he says, "These calculators are very handy for people who buy media. Those are the sort of people who would want a free subscription to WDFM. And anyone who subscribes to WDFM is someone we want to know ourselves."

The point is that text itself is a graphic. If only a certain number of words are typically used in most press releases, it literally all starts to look the same, merely because it *is* all the same! Of course, the meaning of the word needs to say more than what it's replacing, or else it comes across as hyperbole. We see plenty of that already. When I see a good word used well, I want to thank the writer for reminding me of that word and its usage. These details have everything to do with your relationship with the public.

Writing Press Releases for the New Ways People Consume Information

Notice the keywords at the top of the press release just shown. They are there more for automatic filtering agents than for humans. Many people prefer to adjust their

Use unusual words in the header or body of the text that make your copy stand out. Don't be obvious about it, nor should you assume a "go-to-the-dictionary-and-look-it-up attitude," either. I was told later by some reporters and editors that they picked up the story because the whimsical header popped out at them amid all the other self-serving headlines.

When putting your URL in the message, always start it with "http://" rather than just "www.xyz.com." Your press release is apt to be read in someone's email program. That program is likely to make that URL (one that begins http://) a "live link." This means that the user can actually click on the address within the mail message and be transported into his or her Web browser and over to the site. Whatever you do, do not simply use "yourname.com," without an email or Web prefix. Remember: People are easily confused about Internet addressing conventions. Many don't know the difference between an email address and a Web address. I know this because I had to explain the difference to an extremely successful entrepreneur who's worth millions. He's no dummy. He's just unfamiliar with this new territory called *cyberspace*. We have all needed to learn this new language. Help your customers by not confusing them as they learn their way around.

Formula: In all your press releases and PR info sent to the public, for Web addresses, use "http://www.xyz.com." For email addresses, use "myname@xyz.com."

own thresholds for information these days, rather than having a magazine or news-paper editor do it for them. Be aware of automated filtering and how to cater to it.

Filtering agents scan the Web and press releases for keywords that the user selected. The higher up in the document that these words appear, the more important they are to the filtering agents; hence, the greater the likelihood of their getting to the people who are looking for content based on those keywords.

PR in a Many-to-Many Medium

Email update services, such as NewsHound for $4.95 a month (http://www.newshound.com), deliver news stories to you according to your preferences. You give the filtering service keywords in which you're interested, and the stories are sent to you by email each day. Many services also let you rate the importance of each keyword on a scale of 1 to 10. The more often these keywords are used in a press release or news story, the more likely the recipient is to see that story. Additionally, some services rate the importance of these keywords based on how soon they appear in a story or press release. It's for this reason that I put the keywords at the top of a press release and not at the bottom.

In addition to services that send you news stories via email, there are numerous Web sites you can visit that provide a similar service. The original site that started this free concept was CRAYON (see Figure 9.1), which stands for Create Your Own Newspaper (http://crayon.net). It's the online version of Nicholas Negroponte's "Daily Me."

Another example is Excite's NewsTracker (http://nt.excite.com), which is also a free service that will comb wire services such as the *Advocate*, *Business Week*, *Scientific American*, and even the *Boston Phoenix* and create a personalized "newspaper" for you

Figure 9.1 Choose only the stories in which you're interested with CRAYON.

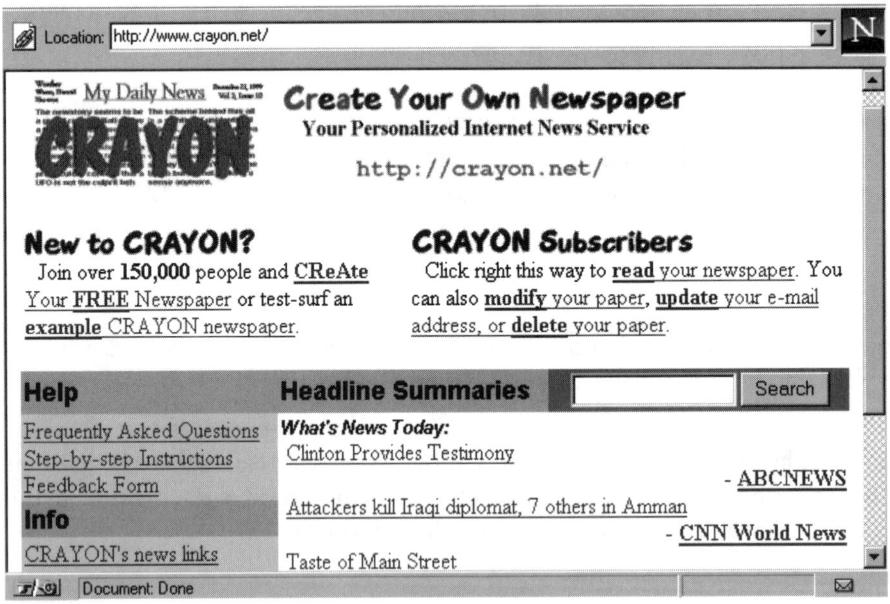

each day. For a complete listing of its sources, check out http://nt.excite.com/sources.html.

Another free site is My Yahoo! (http://my.yahoo.com). It offers some of the same resources as CRAYON, but also gets its information from such news services as Reuters, CNN, *Wired* News, and PR Newswire (see Figure 9.2).

Individual Inc.'s NewsPage (http://www.individual.com/services/services.htm) is a paid-for, basic Web-delivered news service (see Figure 9.3). Because you pay for it, you get a richer mix of news services in addition to what the aforementioned offer. NewsPage is broken down into industry groups. You can retrieve archived articles and draw from even fancier databases on an à la carte basis.

Another example of how people are consuming information differently is The Mining Company (http://miningco.com). The Mining Company features 500 areas, such as publishing, travel, gardening, and so on, that each have an actual human who trolls the Net, specifically looking for pertinent information and sites on the given subject (see Figure 9.4). These Web pages are often contained in *frames* on The Mining Company's site. A problem arising with the use of frames is that a person might like what he or she sees on your site and wants to visit it

Figure 9.2 My Yahoo! scans Reuters, CNN, and other news services for stories of interest to you.

Figure 9.3 NewsPage separates stories into industry categories.

directly, instead of through someone else's frame. A good way to deal with this conundrum is to put your URL on every page so that visitors, even if they are really "located"at another site, can tell where you are and how to get there directly. If you don't want to put your URL on every page, at least have your email address along with the rest of your contact information. Many Web sites do this, discreetly, at the bottom of the pages.

 TIP If you're in a framed site and you wish to go directly to a site seen within that frame, use your mouse button (hold it down on a Mac; use your right mouse button on a PC) until a popup menu appears and offers to open up the link in a new browser window. However, don't count on many users knowing this trick. This is why I suggest you have your URL, or at least your email address, on every page. This way, those looking at you through someone else's frame can get a clue as how to visit your site directly.

Figure 9.4 The Mining Company uses humans, instead of software, to filter through the Internet in order to see what is of interest to you.

Using Frames

One way to create a Web page is to code a *frame* to actually link to another site and pull its content onto your own page. Think of it as a way to pour milk from someone else's refrigerator into a glass on your table. There is quite a bit of controversy about this particular use of frames, specifically in the realm of copyright and fair use laws, which have not, unfortunately, caught up to the Net yet. Is it fair, or even right, to pull someone else's material into your site? Or is it the same as creating a link to them? The debate continues. In the meantime, actually going to someone else's site can be far more interesting as well as fulfilling, since you are no longer "stuck" in someone's frame while you cruise around.

Push Services

To help further splinter the market, there are now *push* services that heave information of your choice to your desktop, in a unique graphical format, without your having to go actively out on the Web yourself. There are already a plethora of push services, but I'll just highlight the original service: PointCast.

PointCast (http://www.pointcast.com) has over 1 million users who use its software, which retrieves information based on chosen preferences. Every day there are new "channels" to choose from. In fact, you might want to set up a channel for your firm, since it costs nothing! Why? Because there are so many competing push services, they each want to attract you to use theirs. The only cost is the preparation of information in a format that is needed to push your information out to those who request it.

Setting up a channel that has nothing but a stream of press releases may not attract a significant audience other than financial analysts (if you're a public company), competitors, and trade journalists. On the other hand, that may be just fine for your purposes. If you want more users to select your channel, you'll have to provide information that is newsworthy, informative, or entertaining. If it isn't available by the time you read this book, *Web Digest For Marketers* will soon be one of those channels that you can select. Instead of getting *WDFM* fortnightly, you will have the option of getting a review a day delivered to your desktop via one or more of these push services.

Point-to-Point PR

If the content of your PR effort is of sufficient value to your target audience, you'll find them requesting it via a channel on a push service, such as PointCast. You may also find them revisiting your site regularly (hopefully, prompted by an email reminder from you) to pick up the information, or they may request that you send it to them directly via email, in a method called *point-to-point PR*.

> **TIP**
>
> If you put an offer on your site to send information, or update visitors via email, tell them exactly what to expect. Be honest! I recently signed up for an update service that does indeed send me information and updates to its site, but the information is almost always self-serving press releases. I did notice that buried in *some* of the press releases are useful bits of information. However, I seriously doubt people are going to take the time to ferret out the useful from the useless. This practice doesn't leave the user with a positive feeling toward the firm doing this.

I work with a company called Cushman Wakefield, which is one of the largest commercial real estate firms in the United States. In fact, it is so large, it has a department that solely produces quarterly information and trends on commercial real estate values in major markets. An abstract of this information is first released to *The Wall Street Journal*, where it is then published. This is a good example of getting more mileage out of information you already have. Cushman Wakefield further repurposes this data by making charts and trends available on its Web site. This information was previously sold, but CW decided to offer it for free, in order to extend its public relations' efforts. In Chapter 6, "Retail: Setting Up Shop on the Net," you saw how this PR tactic, often referred to as *loss-leaders*, can have an impact on building inbound leads.

John Kremer, consultant and author of *1001 Ways to Market Your Book*, offers a weekly email tip sheet of ideas. Within that newsletter, he mentions his other services and products. Hundreds of people, myself included, request the newsletter. Kremer is very savvy about the amount of information he puts into each newsletter. He doesn't overdo it. Unfortunately, many senders of such newsletters often go on forever, pontificating and expounding extensively on whatever is in their minds that week. People don't necessarily want that. Less is usually more in the medium of plain email text.

I was faced with the same choice when I started my newsletter. A number of people advised I do a "Larry Speaks" type publication. I felt a greater number of people would pay more and immediate attention to the coverage of Web sites, which is something that is timely and newsworthy. This is especially true of the many journalists, always on deadline, who want a quick scan of what's going on out there with new business-oriented Web sites. As a consequence, nearly every national magazine, newspaper, and network has someone in its operation who subscribes to *WDFM*. Those journalists, editors, producers, and other media professionals wind up needing quotes on Internet stories at one time or another. When they do, my name will be on the top of their minds, since they see my name and service fortnightly. I'm providing them with a commodity they can well appreciate: well-edited information that might help them do their jobs. This process has to build good relations.

> **TIP** Less is more. If you're going to send out an email newsletter, keep it short, or at least keep each module short. Remember: You can always point them to the Web site for the complete story. In fact, it's a good idea to remind your readers to visit your Web site for one good reason or another.

For the first year and a half of publishing *WDFM*, I was very leery of putting commercial messages in the newsletter. I then started working soft-sell copy into the introduction. Nobody said anything, nor did I receive unsubscribe requests because of it. After that, I put in a special offers section. Again, no one minded. In fact, it proved to be successful at drawing qualified leads to those who advertised offers aimed directly at the audience. After a while, I put a few *email banners* in as well. Instead of balking, people responded to the ads themselves. As a consequence, *WDFM*, originally geared as a PR tool, has converted from a cost center to a profit center for me.

> **Email banners** are ads in email newsletters. They have the approximate shape of an ad banner found on the Web. Since most email doesn't support graphics, the space is taken up with a few lines of selling text copy. They are often set off from the surrounding content by having equal signs or asterisks above and below their border.

> **TIP** If you advertise in your press relations efforts, clearly differentiate between editorial and advertising.

It's important to keep in mind that I built the franchise up to a certain point before I introduced commercial content. In Chapter 8, "Direct Marketing and Sales Support," I spoke about the ratio of quality content to the amount of information you can ask for. If you're going to ask for more than an email address, the prospect needs to know that he or she is getting worthwhile value in exchange. The same is true here. Whether you're going to promote yourself or another firm, readers are going to have to feel strongly enough about the content not to mind, and even to embrace, the commercial messages. If they do mind, they'll unsubscribe and *flame* you, because they will feel you pulled a *bait-and-switch* on them. Bait-and-switch is a sneaky and self-defeating promotional tool whereby you lure someone in by offering them something of value, then switch them off to another offer that they didn't bargain for, of lesser or no value. If you accept money from advertisers and they don't get sufficient results, then you've lost credibility on that side of the quotient as well. Having said all that: If you are providing quality content to a sizable audience, it may be worth your while to test advertising. Take a segment of the mailing list and run a different introduction that's slightly more commercial and see what reaction you get.

Flames are nasty emails sent by someone who really doesn't like what you did. When this happens on email discussion lists or Usenet groups in great numbers, it's referred to as "Flame Wars." Provoking or participating in these is a pure waste of time, though they can be entertaining to observe at times.

If you moderate a two-way discussion list, it's often understood by those who participate that the *moderator* (that's you) needs to subsidize the running of the list with sponsors. As moderator, you might filter out unnecessary messages, edit messages, create or help create a FAQ, and help nudge topics back on track as well. Of course, it's important to make that clear when you start the list, or to indicate if you already have a list going that isn't currently accepting advertisers. I go so far as to ask my readers to make the effort to read and respond to the ads and offers; I tell them that by doing so, it helps *WDFM*, which in turn helps them.

If you're successful in getting advertisers to underwrite your content, you've effectively gotten out from under the costs of your own email public relations program. In fact, it may very well turn out to be a profit center for you.

TIP

When providing point-to-point email information service, don't overdo it. The point is that there's more than 1 or even 100 ways to get your PR efforts to your target audience. Traditional news outlets used to be the only game in town. Now they're only one of many. With so many people getting their news from so many different sources, public relations opportunities are nearly endless.

Event Public Relations

Of course, not all your PR efforts need to be information based. You can hold an online event and publicize that fact. One of the most effective events I've seen is when eShare (makers of ChatWare) donated peripherals and copies of its software to the survivors and families of TWA Flight 800. Grieving families were brought together and able to support one another through the use of the core product of this company. The deed literally spoke for itself. This is an example of "good usage"of the Net for communication purposes, not to mention superb PR for eShare itself.

Very often, Web chats and other events are staged so that statements can be made and then reported on in press releases. A few dozen or hundred people may have seen or heard the actual event, yet millions may wind up reading about it in a newspaper, hearing about it on a TV news broadcast, or seeing it in some online venue. This is a very clever tactic.

> **TIP**
> When staging an online event for press relations purposes, you'll want to notify search engines. Most search engines will pay more attention to your event if the Web address is configured in a certain way. For instance, search engines will pay less attention to a Web site whose address is http://www.webgrrls.com/events/jan/index .html, and pay more attention to http://www.event.webgrrls.com/. This extra addition to the left of the Webgrrls domain name is called a *subdomain* name. Setting up a subdomain name requires techie skills, but may well be worth it in the long run. You may consider setting up one subdomain name and holding different timely events there, rather than setting up a new name for every event.

Kodak has implemented a unique way of using Web-based chat. It doesn't use a chat room for big public impressions. Instead, the press itself is the target audience. Kodak has actually held press briefings and conferences on its site, without the presence of the general public. This is similar to what you would see on television and is cost effective for both the company and the publisher alike. Of course, it contains some costs, but this practice of online press conferences will become more widespread as chat software becomes more ubiquitous in our society and more available for easy use on the Web.

Time and cost savings will be the main force to propel this practice into more common usage. Think about it: Journalists are always on deadline. It's a pretty attractive proposition to get instant, first-hand information without having to travel across the country or across town. They won't even have to leave their own desks! In addition, the journalist will also have the transcript available in text format, which makes it much easier to cut and paste quotes, rather than transcribing them. This efficient use of time and resources will be a boon to trade journalists, who are already overwhelmed with press releases and conferences, as well as researching various products for their respective industries.

Chrysler uses the Net in an interesting way for press relations as well. It has a secured, restricted area to distribute high-resolution photographs of its upcoming models. Again, this saves the trade journalist and his or her publication much time in not having to send the pictures via overnight carrier, as well as being able to put those digital images directly into the publishing production line. Chrysler presumably doesn't want to make these pictures available to the general public because it has the potential of having too many people pulling the images down and clogging up both the server and its pipeline. Those photos also might be *embargoed* and not available to the public at the time they're made available to the trade press. *Embargoed* is a news term that tells the media outlet not to release a story until the specified time. This is often used with the release of government statistics, such as inflation and unemployment figures. The wire services deliver these stories early so local news operations can incorporate the story into newscasts, which are then broadcast shortly after or at the release time.

Where and How to Post Your PR

It seems that lately, everyone has their own ideas about how and where to post your public relations announcements and press releases. Though some of it may be hype, there are always a few gems of information you can put to use.

What's New and Search Engines

You have some options as to how to go about it. One is posting to "What's New" sites. For my money, there are about 10 that are worth your time and a few hundred more that are going to have less of a payoff. You can also use a "one size fits all" posting engine that will do it for you automatically. In this category, I recommend Submit It! at http://www.submit-it.com, which is as good as any and better than most. It's great if you're on a limited budget. The downside is that each search engine you post to is a little different. Some ask for 25-word descriptions, while others let you go up to 50 words and beyond. You have to use the lowest common denominator approach on the keywords and categories chosen. Some search engines have 6 categories, while others have 8 or 10. Plus, the search engines are always changing their submission requirements. In other words, it's a moving target. Still, the price is right (free) and it doesn't take much time. Other than Submit It!, you can look at other services that do similar things (some free, some not) at Yahoo!'s list of posting engines at http://www .yahoo.com/Business_and_Economy/Companies/Internet_Services/Web_Services/ Promotion/.

Human Posting

Another option is using human posters. If you have the budget, nothing beats a human, because humans can make intuitive decisions. A robot can't. It's as simple as that. Eric Ward's NetPOST (http://www.netpost.com) is the most established and respected in this field, in my opinion (see Figure 9.5). You might also train someone inhouse at your business to do this on a regular basis, if you have the manpower to do so. Time-Warner found it more cost effective to have me train

Figure 9.5 NetPOST is manned by a human, not a robot.

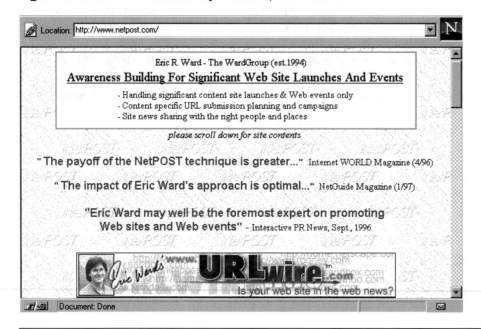

its people to submit updates to the search engines than to pay me month by month to do it for them.

 TIP Visit NetPOST's Web site and you'll find detailed articles on when to use robots for posting and when to use humans.

Usenet Newsgroups

Posting your new URL to Usenet newsgroups is yet another option. This type of posting must be done by a human. The appropriate discussion groups must be located, monitored, and judged whether it is sensible to post an announcement there. Things to look for in a Usenet newsgroup:

1. Do other firms post useful messages to the group?

2. How long are those messages?

3. Are they purely informational, or is there some commercial flavor to them?

4. Look for the Frequently Asked Questions (FAQ) file associated with the newsgroup; this will often answer questions you have on the subject. Do not post blind questions to the group before you read its FAQ first.

5. Who moderates the group, and what is their email address (in case you want to ask questions after reviewing the FAQ)?

6. How often can you reasonably post without being intrusive?

Mailing Lists

Finally, you can post to mailing lists. Mailing lists come in two varieties: one-way and two-way lists. Both show up in your email box. A one-way mailing list goes from one to many. Two-way lists are discussion lists of members who reply to each other in a rolling discussion over time. If the topic is consistently close to your information, I suggest you join and participate in the list. However, do not just post your entire press release! Just like newsgroups, many mailing lists have FAQs; inquire about this and see how the conversation is flowing before barging into a discussion right off. Make an effort to contribute valuable information to the discussion once you have introduced yourself, and your PR information, as well. There's more than one reason to join a discussion list. You'll probably learn something from other constituents of this list. It's also an excellent place to network. Who knows, your next job or client may come from a contact on that list! Visit eZines' database at http://www.dominis.com/Zines/. Find those 'zines that are suited to your topics, then contact the manager/editor/publisher to see what you need to do in order to submit your press release (see Figure 9.6).

Using PR Circuits

There are two paths to travel here. I suggest you take them both: online circuits and offline circuits.

Offline circuits to distribute your press releases are the traditional PR circuits, such as PR Newswire and Business Wire. It is just as important (and sometimes more so) to use these circuits, especially with all the media attention the Net now garners, in order to be seen and noticed.

 Instead of buying a national circuit for $400 or so, save money by buying a city circuit, which costs around $145 for New York City at the time of writing. Smaller cities usually cost less. With that you get distribution in two industries from PR Newswire, such as manufacturing or travel. I usually take marketing and hi-tech. Sometimes I'll buy distribution in another industry, such as publishing, if it's appropriate. This is a nifty technique to stretch your budget.

Figure 9.6 Look at eZine for online publications germane to your industry.

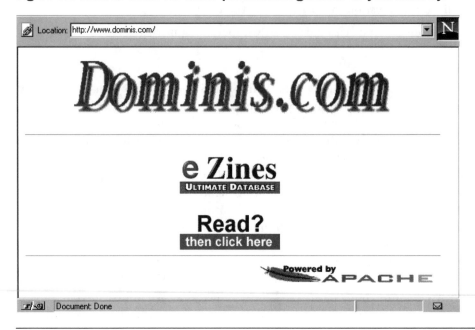

The other option is online circuits. For $225 at the time of writing, NewsBureau (http://www.newsbureau.com) will distribute your press release to over 1200 sources (see Figure 9.7). It limits the number of press releases it sends out, so that the journalists and editors aren't inundated with releases from the same source, thus diluting the impact of each release. I use three approaches: Eric Ward's company for certain high-end placements, NewsBureau to cover the lion's share of online news efforts, and the offline PR Newswire to make sure I'm getting the traditional press as well.

Trolling the Net for Information about Your Own Company

A good PR effort requires that you not only send out information, but also take in information about your company. After all, people may be talking about you out there. The old adage of "I don't care what they say as long as they spell my name right" isn't at all true on the Net. Remember the Intel debacle surrounding the computational errors of its then newly released Pentium processor? If Intel had been monitoring the Net more closely, it could have contained the problem and

Figure 9.7 NewsBureau is an efficient and inexpensive way to distribute press releases online.

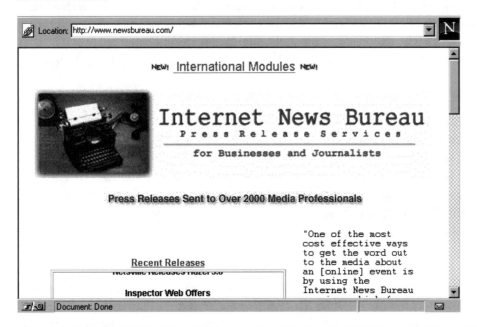

controlled it. However, the longer Intel stayed quiet about it, the more people talked. This made the situation increasingly worse, until it made headline news, even though the original "problem" was a small one that would have affected few people.

Where should you start looking? The Usenet newsgroups are a good place to start, and for that purpose I recommend Deja News and AltaVista.

Deja News (http://www.dejanews.com) has a more comprehensive collection of Usenet groups than most search engines, which seems to be infinite. Each city has numerous groups devoted to jobs, real estate, local issues, and so forth. It's hard to track local Usenet groups in Phoenix from a New York ISP's *news server*. Deja News doesn't have nearly all groups, but it has an incredible collection. Deja News also has a comprehensive program called eMarketing, which is an individualized objective analysis of your marketing needs, which you can then use to decide which of its for-sale programs is best suited for your company.

I also recommend AltaVista (http://www.altavista.digital.com) because it has the most sophisticated search engine. With it you can get a fine grind of exactly what you're trying to locate, whether it's your company name, product, or category.

AltaVista can be configured to not only look for Web pages matching your search words, but also Usenet discussion groups—you will get the postings of all mentions of your words, so be careful to narrow your search! There could be literally thousands of mentions in all those newsgroups over the last few years (and some newsgroups have been archived for more than a decade). Look for and be aware of the Usenet option when you do your search, as AltaVista's default is to search the Web only.

All About Usenet

Most ISPs (Internet Service Providers) have a news server that picks up the Usenet Internet Discussion Groups (IDGs) they decide to carry, like a newspaper carrying some wire services but not others. With thousands upon thousands of newsgroups available on Usenet alone, most ISPs limit the "regional"discussion groups to their own specific locale, figuring the users in New York City won't be terribly interested in the daily real estate listings for Phoenix, for example.

By using AltaVista, I once found out that Larry Chase was the name of an evil character on Dark Shadows! I also found seven other real Larry Chases on the Net. I immediately went to the InterNIC, where I registered the domain larrychase.com. You also want to use either AltaVista or HotBot (the *Wired* search engine at http://www.hotbot.com) to scan the Web for mentions of your firm.

| TIP | Use the little-known Advanced feature in AltaVista for your searches. Instead of getting 4 million finds, you can narrow it down to a few dozen right from the get-go. From there, use the Refine feature to filter out all the other unwanted results. Also included in the Advanced feature is a way to search for all links pointing to your pages. Use the link: search to see who's pointing to you! |

Be sure to check out WhoIs.Net, where you can survey, and even ask for, free monitoring of who is registering what domains that may use your name or company name. Tell it to track any name or keywords, and it will email you on a regular basis to let you know if any domain names have been registered using those words.

There are also services that will troll for you on a monthly retainer. You can think of these services as electronic clipping services. They're very effective, since it's their core business.

One such service is eWatch (http://www.ewatch.com/). It will monitor Usenet discussion groups, Internet newsgroups, Web sites, and even online services such as CompuServe or America Online's forums to let you know when the grapevine is buzzing. All you do is provide keywords and, in the case of Web watching, the URLs you want monitored. Each day, eWatch will send you a summary report via email or fax of the day's gossip, news, and site changes. The nice thing about the eWatch service is that, unlike other Web alerts, it allows you to specify items, words, or sections of a site to monitor for change, so you don't waste your time rushing back to a site to see that the only change is the background color. Pricing starts at $295 per month, at the time of writing.

Anti-PR Sites

Disgruntled consumer groups have formed anti-PR sites to complain about particular firms with whom they have issues. Wal-Mart, Ford, and a number of the regional Bell operating companies have been targeted by such sites. History is repeating itself here. Back in the 1960s, hippies and yippies learned how to manipulate the media in order to get press attention for their cause by staging events that the cameras would record and later broadcast. This is the 1990s version of that, Internet style.

Here again, the press picks up on the mouse that roared by way of covering such sites and fanning the flames, which turns some poor corporate PR person's job into a nightmare. What do you do? Sometimes nothing. Maybe it will go away, if the complaints are unwarranted. But if their claims have validity, you should consider approaching the people responsible for the complaint site and opening up a dialog. This has worked in a number of situations, and has actually turned into good PR for some firms, showing that they will indeed listen.

Conclusion

In this many-to-many medium, companies large and small need to devise a PR program that is unique, informative, frequent, and focused, as well as responsive, if they are to cut through the clutter in order to leave a positive, lasting impression upon the highly defined target audience. Public relations professionals are having a field day on the Internet because PR campaigns share something vital in common with the Internet: information. In this respect, the disciplines of public relations have more in common with the Net than with the superficial impressions left by 15-second glib television commercials, which impart little, if any, information.

Resource Center

EditPros   **http://www.editpros.com**

How well are you communicating? Take the Great Grammar Quiz to find out. If you fail, EditPros may be your answer. EditPros will prepare effective written communications for you to supplement your editorial and communications efforts. Browse the online newsletter and tutorial for writing tips and techniques, or simply access the business news email directory of over 250 magazines and newspapers to do some communicating of your own.

Publicity.com   **http://www.publicity.com**

Publicity in all its forms is the focus of this online magazine, which doubles as a showcase for Media Relations, Inc., a Minneapolis-based public relations firm. You'll find plenty here on how to get publicity and how to use it, plus success stories, insider tips, industry news, special Internet information, and how to avoid (or handle) public relations disasters. There's something to be said for learning from professionals who are willing to share their unique insights.

Public Relations Society of America (PRSA)   **http://www.prsa.org**

PRSA does a nice job of serving its members and informing the public at this site. Publicly accessible resources such as PRSA's *Tactics* newsletter provide visitors with good information about developing and managing media campaigns. A searchable member résumé database allows visitors to mine the organization for potential employees. Those on the other side of the employment equation may want to take a look at *Tactics'* classified advertising section for career opportunities. Drilling further into the site yields a wealth of information in specific areas of practice, such as technology, environment, association work, and others. And, knowing that all this fabulous information has motivated you to join, PRSA has conveniently provided an online membership application form.

eWatch   **http://www.ewatch.com**

eWatch will monitor Internet newsgroups and Web sites to let you know when the grapevine is buzzing. All you do is provide keywords and, in the case of Web watching, the URLs you want monitored. Each day, eWatch will send you a summary report via email or fax of the day's gossip, news, and site changes. The nice thing about the eWatch service is that, unlike other Web alerts, eWatch allows you to specify items, words, or sections of a site to monitor for change, so you don't waste your time rushing back to a site to see that the only change is the background color. Pricing starts at $295 per month at the time of writing.

A Manager's Guide to Newsletters   **http://www.managersguide.com**

If you publish a newsletter for marketing, employee or member communications, then this site is for you. Each week, a free chapter of the soon-to-be published *Manager's Guide* by the Newsletter Company is available for download. In exchange, readers are asked to complete a brief questionnaire designed to provide editorial feedback and marketing information. The book focuses on newsletters from a management perspective; in other words, the strategy, tactics, and administration needed to achieve corporate objectives and produce a successful and effective newsletter.

CLOSING TIPS

Presumably, you are about to close this book. What have you learned? What will you remember a week from now and a year from now? What follows are 12 tips to keep in mind at all times. They will serve you well. You may even want to rip this page out and tape it to the wall as a constant reminder of how to stay buoyant in these choppy, exciting waters known as the Internet.

Exponential Effect. Try to do everything for at least two reasons. *WDFM* is a branding tool, is syndicated, generates revenue from advertising, and provides information to its audience.

Contiguous Cannibalism. One man's core business is another's loss-leader. Don't let it happen to you. See if you should employ something yourself.

Don't Be a Mile Wide and a Half-Inch Deep. Focus on a few complementary areas. Spread your risk, but not too far; otherwise, your efforts become too diffused.

Be a Category Creeper. Look for interesting practices from categories next to and far afield of your industry. Be the first to migrate them into your category.

Borrow Your Customer's Shoes. Live in them all of the time, not just in front of the screen when surfing your site. Would you click on your own banners? Your buttons? Your link in the search engines? Why, or why not?

Complementary Lines of Business. Have a few lines of business that complement each other. For example, I have my publishing by way of this book and *WDFM* that brings business to my consulting and seminar lines of business. It also works the other way around.

Be Your Own Worst Critic. Not only with your interface, but with your Net marketing plans, as well as everything else. Try to punch holes in your own arguments, suspicions, and strategies. If they don't spring leaks, you've got a better chance at making it.

Creative Cognition. The challenge today is in making the new technology do your bidding, or twisting it in an unintended way to suit your own purposes. Instead of rigidly saying, "Here's the product, where is the marketing and selling channel?" stay open to, "Here's an interesting channel that already exists. What do I have that can easily be configured for this valuable channel already in place?" You will be seen as Net savvy, which will only add to the luster of your brand, be it personal or company-wide.

Market to Yourself. Be aware of your own thoughts and feelings while surfing the Net. Apply those first-hand impressions when marketing to others. If you don't like homepages that take 30 seconds to come in, it's a good bet that your target audience won't either. The term for this is "Pulse Universe." Take your own pulse and imagine that the rest of humanity might not be that terribly different.

Don't Market to Yourself. Know when to stop talking to yourself. Most Web sites make perfect sense to those inside the goldfish bowl known as your company, while outsiders look in and wonder exactly what it is you are trying to communicate. Watch closely the reactions of your target audience as they surf your site. See if they get what you are trying to say. If not, it's time to redesign. Note what search phrases they use when using search engines. They just might be different from what you use.

Redefine Problems as Opportunities. Look for solutions to problems you didn't know you had.

Keep Your Crap Detectors Set on High. My father used to say, "Believe nothing of what you hear and about half of what you see and you should be okay." That's about right when it comes to filtering through all of the smoke and mirrors in the PR wars of the Internet. We've all seen deals come together and fly apart literally overnight.

AFTERWORD

"The dance instructor saves the best steps for himself." My mother, grand-daughter to Edmond Gerson, to whom Thomas Edison wrote the letter pictured in the front of this book, told me this when I was but a mere tyke. I did not take her advice with regard to the content of this book. I held nothing back when sharing the best of what I know. But then, why should I? When it comes to the Internet, there are new dance steps to be learned and mastered every day. All the early adopters, myself included, gravitated to the Internet early on, using the awe of learning as the driving force.

My advice to you is to approach and embrace the Net with that keen sense of awe, knowing that at every turn, you'll learn more about your relationship to the Internet. To me, that is one exciting prospect. I sincerely hope you share and harness that enthusiasm. Each person's relationship to the Internet, each company's relationship to the Internet, is special and different from that of any other individual or enterprise. It is the ultimate in mass customization. That is why small and large companies alike ask me to help them define their relationship to the Internet. There is no one finite definition of that relationship for any company, but rather a series of options. Fleshing out those options, along with their trade-offs, is what I do for a living when not writing books, columns, or conducting seminars. I invite you to visit my site (http://chaseonline.com) to learn more about what my firm does. If you have questions thereafter, get in touch by either email or phone.

Larry Chase

Email: Me@LarryChase.com
Phone: (212) 824-5010

INDEX

NetPOST, 267, 268
Net.Proceed, 240
NetSaver discount program, 245
Net-savvy recruiter, 41
Netscape, 35, 102, 164
    4.0, 98, 165
    In-Box Direct, 106
    Mail Direct, 197
NetStakes, 195–197
Net-wide search, 107
Network Designer, 24
Network proxy, 99
Networking. *See* Promotions.
Networks. *See* Advertising.
New business, investigating, 107–113
News, 84–85
    hooks, 252–254
NewsBureau, 270
News-clipping service, 106
Newsgroups, 269. *See also* Internet;
    Usenet.
    archives, 58
NewsHound, 64, 106
Newsletter, manager's guide, 275
Newslinks, 84
NewsPage, 106. *See* Individual Inc.
    NewsPage.
NewsTracker (Excite), 258
NOAH, 253, 254
Noise, 58

O

OBI. *See* Open Buying on the Internet.
OCC. *See* Online Career Center.
Offline data gathering, comparison. *See*
    Online data gathering.
Offline DM
    comparison. *See* Online DM.
    efforts, online DM marketing support,
        240–244
Offline mailing lists, comparison. *See*
    Online mailing lists.
Offline tone, comparison. *See* Online tone.
Off-the-shelf referral log software, 150
OLA. *See* Oracle Learning Architecture.
One-to-one email, 126
One-way lists, 231, 232, 269
One-way mailing list, 227

Online ad discussion lists, 123
On-line advertisement dollars, stretching,
    157, 181–183
On-line advertising, 111
Online Advertising Discussion, 232
Online Career Center (OCC), 35
Online catalogs/offline catalogs,
    merging, 180–181
Online chat environments, 74
Online communities, brand
    building, 140–142
Online copy, 218–220
Online data gathering, offline data
    gathering comparison, 73–74
Online database marketing, 236
Online delivery system, 205
Online discussion forums, 69
Online DM
    database mining, 236–237
    marketing support. *See* Offline DM.
    offline DM comparison, 221–224
    threat/opportunity, 244–245
Online events, 187–209
Online focus groups, 114
Online image, migration. *See* Company.
Online intermediary brands, 137–138
Online journalists, interaction protocols,
    251–252
Online list manager, 232
Online mailing lists, offline mailing lists
    comparison, 224–234
Online merchant account, getting,
    169–173
Online methods, 74–75
Online notice, 250–251
Online qualitative/quantitative
    methods, 73
Online retail transactions, 169
Online search capabilities, 71
Online software, 171
Online Telecommuting Resources (Smart
    Valley Inc.), 46
Online tone, offline tone comparison, 224
Online tracking techniques. *See* Direct
    marketing.
Online transactions, 169–175, 175
Online-Ads Discussion List, 39
OnNow, 199